IMAGES
of America

HUBBARD

(*cover*) The Hubbard High School's football team of 1923–1924 is seen is this photograph taken facing east from in front of the present Roosevelt Elementary School (former Hubbard High School) on Orchard Avenue. The original football field was behind the school facing School Street and around 1922 the field moved to Fifth Avenue. (Photograph courtesy of Vince Pompili.)

IMAGES
of America

HUBBARD

Barbara Emch

ARCADIA
PUBLISHING

ISBN 978-0-7385-3289-9

Published by Arcadia Publishing
Charleston, South Carolina

Printed in the United States of America

Library of Congress Catalog Card Number: 2005922433

For all general information contact Arcadia Publishing at:
Telephone 843-853-2070
Fax 843-853-0044
E-mail sales@arcadiapublishing.com
For customer service and orders:
Toll-Free 1-888-313-2665

Visit us on the Internet at www.arcadiapublishing.com

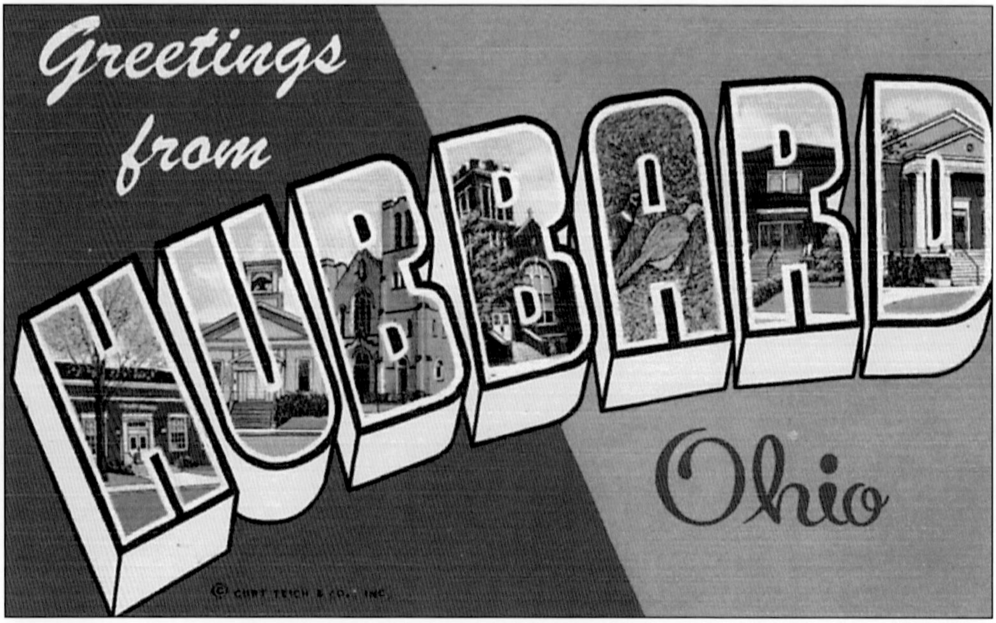

Between 1933 and 1956, Curt Teich & Company sold "Large Letter" linen postcards. This postcard was printed in 1953. Familiar buildings and symbols of Hubbard including the Hubbard Post Office, First Presbyterian Church on Hager Street and West Liberty Street, the old St. Patrick's Church on East Water Street and North Main Street, the old Grace Lutheran Church built in 1921 on Church Street, a pheasant and quail (hunting), the First Baptist Church built in 1925, and the First Methodist Church can be seen from left to right. (Postcard courtesy of Linda Clark.)

Contents

Acknowledgments

There would be no book without the Hubbard Historical Society, and I especially appreciated the help of Jim and Betsy Thompson, Jack and Lucille Wilson, Ron Wright, Bob and Nina Notman, Don and Dolly Hardin, Theresa Trucksis Hickey, Mary Jane Harbison, Emanuel Mageros, and Ralph and Cecilia Cooper. Thanks to all the people who donated pictures. Robin Zambrini helped with pictures, editing, and captions. Thanks to my husband, Ron, and sons, Todd, Kurt, and Derek for all their help. Henry Pettitt gave me so much information, especially about the old red brick school and it was very much appreciated. Thanks to Don Petrusko, Tom Gast, and John Senich for the train information, to Pat Hernandez and Doris Evans for the tornado information, to John Durkos for tornado and Interstate 80 information, to Barbara Kindler and Evelyn Schafer for help with Chestnut Ridge School. Emily Varner, archivist at the Trumbull County Recorders Archives Office, was invaluable in my research determining ages of historic homes. Wendell Lauth helped with Trumbull County history. Others I want to thank include Donna DeBlasio, Linda Clark, Eli Moga, Ed Palestro, Vince Pompili, Cathy Corll Nickleson, Lewis Corll, Harry and Betty McFall, Art and Violet Weiser, Nick and Jackie Miller, Mary Margaret Buchenic, Betty Nehls, Karen Simmons, and Cheryl Robinson, human resources manager of Ellwood Engineered Castings. Thanks to Char Lehto, chair of Steering Committee of the Hubbard House Underground RR Terminus in Ashtabula, who allowed me to take a picture of the oil painting of Nehemiah Hubbard Jr., which is on loan to the museum. A special thanks to Philip Davies from Surrey, England, for e-mailing me a picture of Tommy Davies and the first frame house in Hubbard. I was helped with the captions through a variety of newspapers, and publications including the *Youngstown Vindicator*, the *Warren Daily Tribune*, the *Review*, the *Sharon Herald*, *The Hubbard Press*, the *Hubbard News*, the February 1990 *Eagle Echoes* Newsletter, and Lawrence Stewart's Map of Early Homes in 1900. Books including *History of Trumbull and Mahoning Counties Vol. I & II*, *Hubbard, Ohio National Bicentennial Commemorative Book*, *Father Drohan's History of Hubbard, Ohio*, *1874 Combination Map Atlas of Trumbull County*, *Small Houses of the Twenties*, *The Sears, Roebuck 1926 House Catalog*, (The Athenaeum of Philadelphia and Dover Publications, Inc., New York: 1991), *Western Reserve Draft Book* (January 23, 1798: 200) and *Deed Volume B* (pp. 405–406), *180th Anniversary Book, History of First Presbyterian Church, Hubbard* (1984), *Historical Story of East Hubbard Township and Parts of Hubbard and Pennsylvania*, written by Elmer Fiedler 1976, and *The Old Church—Its Pastors and People* written by Lawrence M. Stewart on October 27, 1983. Information was also received from scrapbooks of Hubbard and Coalburg compiled by Mildred DeCoda, the Ryser family scrapbook compiled by Joan E. Hamilton, and oral history tapes of Marvel Hibler Walker dated September 12, 1985, and Bessie Barnes dated July 1, 1976.

INTRODUCTION

Many people have asked me why I wanted to write a book about Hubbard. I told them I didn't want to lose all the stories that might be lost if they were not documented in some way. Also, I wanted to cover some of the more recent history such as the 1985 Tornado and the Flood of 2003. I tried to cover as much as possible about the people of Hubbard and their stories.

This book is organized geographically. I start in the center of town, go to North Main Street, and from there to northeast Hubbard Township. I then cover the southeast, northwest and lastly, southwest.

To gain an appreciation of Hubbard's history, it's important to know how it all began. Hubbard is part of the historic Connecticut Western Reserve. In 1662, Charles II of England signed Connecticut's Charter that confirmed the original grant given by James I, King of England, to the Plymouth Colony on November 1630. Connecticut's lands extended from Connecticut through Pennsylvania, Ohio, and west to the Pacific Ocean. After the Revolutionary War, Connecticut, in 1786, ceded to the United States all its western lands except for a strip of land in the northeastern part of Ohio with the northern border being at the 42 degree 2 minutes latitude, the southern border at the 42 degree latitude (slightly north of the present Western Reserve Road), its eastern border at the Pennsylvania line and 120 miles west to the current western border of Huron County. These lands, except for a small section of land in the west called "The Firelands," and the Salt Springs tract, were sold to the Connecticut Land Company on September 2, 1795, for $1,200,000, in order to hasten settlement.

The survey of the reserve began on July 4, 1796, by a company of 52 men led by Moses Cleaveland. Originally, each township was to be 16,000 acres, however due to the inaccuracies of the measuring instruments, some were more and some were less. Hubbard Township consisted of 15,274 acres. The survey began in the southeast corner of the reserve, and parallel lines were run north (the townships) from the baseline and west from the Pennsylvania border (the ranges). Poland Township is Township 1, Range 1, as it was the closest to the baseline. Hubbard Township is Township 3, Range 1, as it is the third township from the southern border.

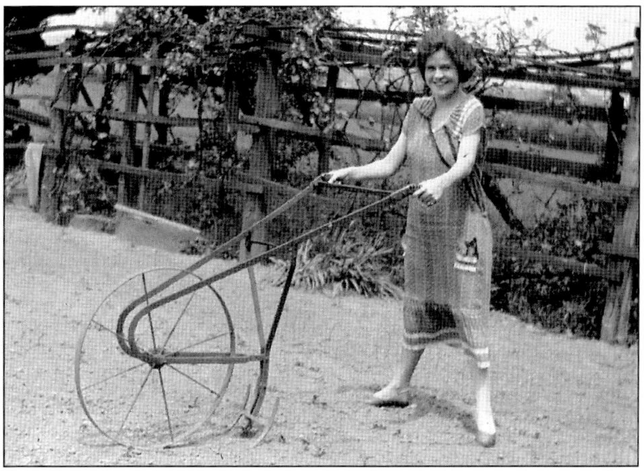

Irene Kashner is shown with a cultivator at the grape arbor behind her family home at 335 Drummond Avenue. The grapes were used in making grape jelly. The cultivator had an attachment that could be used for plowing and Irene's nephew, Jack Wilson, still uses it to plant his garden. (Photograph courtesy of Jack Wilson.)

On January 23, 1798, Joseph Barrell and William Edwards invested $25,806.46, which entitled them not only to ownership of Hubbard Township (Township 3, Range 1), and 928 acres of a lot in the 12th range, but also, Plymouth Township (Township 12, Range 3) in Ashtabula County. They sold it all to Nehemiah Hubbard Jr. on November 3, 1798, for $14,135, and he hired Samuel Tylee as his land agent to survey and sell the lots in Hubbard Township. By 1801, the 80 lots of Hubbard Township had been surveyed and were ready to sell. On September 1, 1801, Samuel brought his wife, Anna Sanford Tylee, his children, and two of his brothers, Sylvester and Alfred, from Middletown, Connecticut to settle in Hubbard Township. He and his first wife, Anna, had 10 children, Anna, Laura, Samuel, Mary, Sanford, Eliza, William, Julia, Hannah, and Maria A. By his second wife, Elizabeth Ayres Tylee, he had one child, Olivia. Samuel was the first justice of the peace, the first postmaster, and he built the first gristmill and sawmill on Yankee Run.

In the beginning, people from Connecticut, New Jersey, Pennsylvania, and other eastern states settled Hubbard. They were farmers, blacksmiths, carpenters, merchants, clerks, stonemasons, and plasterers. When coal deposits were discovered in the early 1860s, it paved the way for new immigrants from Wales, Ireland, and Germany to work in the mines. Later industries attracted workers from Yugoslavia, Hungary, Romania, Italy, and Greece. A one-mile square section of Hubbard Township was incorporated in 1868, and the first mayor was Nathaniel Mitchell. According to the Federal Census of 1960, the municipality of Hubbard, with a population of 7,137, gained the necessary population to be designated as a city. The official date of incorporation was January of 1961. In the Federal Census of 2000, Hubbard City's population was 8,284, and Hubbard Township's population was 6,020.

The years may have brought many changes, but Hubbard has retained its small town atmosphere and remains to this day a nice place to call home.

TRUMBULL COUNTY

RANGE 5	RANGE 4	RANGE 3	RANGE 2	RANGE 1	
MESOPOTAMIA	BLOOMFIELD	GREENE	GUSTAVUS	KINSMAN	TWP 7
FARMINGTON	BRISTOL	MECCA	JOHNSTON	VERNON	TWP 6
SOUTHINGTON	CHAMPION	BAZETTA	FOWLER	HARTFORD	TWP 5
BRACEVILLE	WARREN	HOWLAND	VIENNA	BROOKFIELD	TWP 4
NEWTON	LORDSTOWN	WEATHERSFIELD	LIBERTY	HUBBARD	TWP 3
MAHONING COUNTY LINE (SEPARATED 1846)					
MILTON	JACKSON	AUSTINTOWN	YOUNGSTOWN	COITSVILLE	TWP 2
BERLIN	ELLSWORTH	CANFIELD	BOARDMAN	POLAND	TWP1

COLUMBIANA COUNTY LINE UNTIL 1846

Trumbull County was measured into five-mile square townships. Originally, all of the Connecticut Western Reserve was called Trumbull County, named for the governor of Connecticut, Jonathan Trumbull Jr. In 1846, Trumbull County became its present size after the formation of Mahoning County. Before 1846, Trumbull County included the northern part of Mahoning County. After 1846, Mahoning County was formed from the townships of Milton, Berlin, Jackson, Ellsworth, Austintown, Canfield, Youngstown, Coitsville, Poland, and five townships from Columbiana County. The ranges ran east to west, and the townships ran south to north. For example, Poland Township is Range 1, Township 1, Coitsville Township is Range 1, Township 2, and Hubbard Township is Range 1, Township 3. (Table courtesy of Trumbull County Recorders Archives Office.)

One

City of Hubbard

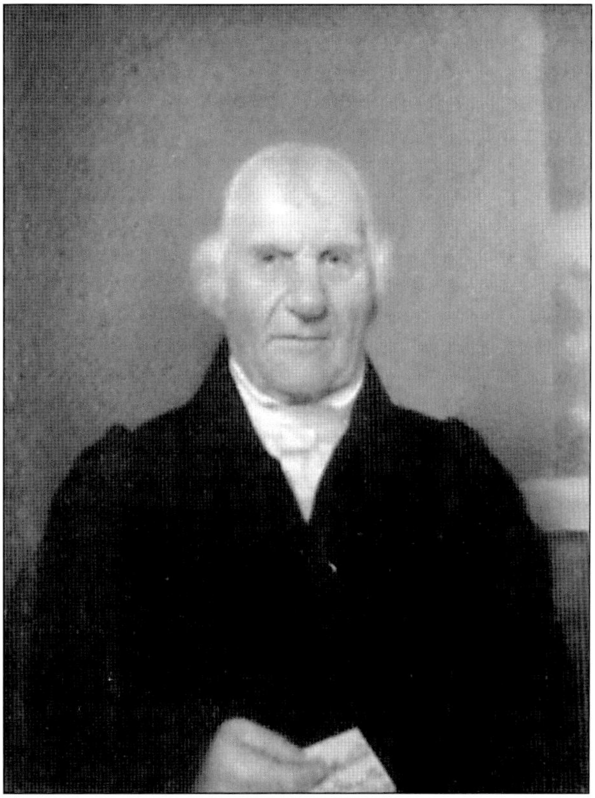

Nehemiah Hubbard Jr. purchased Hubbard Township and other lots in the Connecticut Western Reserve for $14,135 from Joseph Barrell and William Edwards on November 3, 1798. He was born on April 10, 1752, in Middletown, Connecticut and died on February 6, 1837, at the age of 84 years. He hired Samuel Tylee to survey and act as his land agent in selling the 80 lots in Hubbard Township. (Photograph courtesy of original oil painting from collection of Mary Hubbard.)

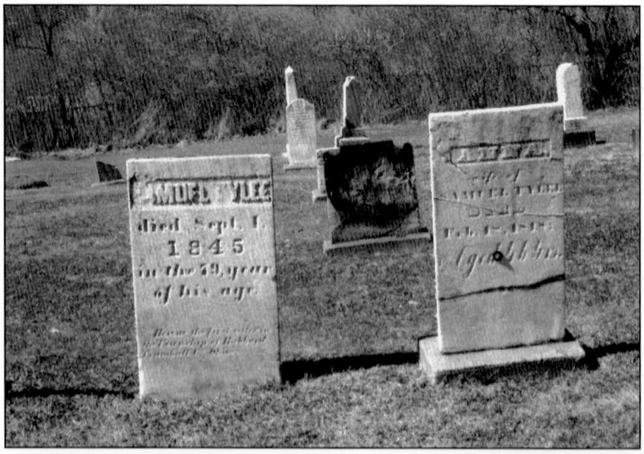

Samuel and Anna Tylee, first settlers of Hubbard Township, were buried in the Old North Cemetery. Samuel died on September 1, 1845, at 79 years and Anna died on February 18, 1818, at 46 years. A plaque with the exact wording of their tombstones was placed below the stones and dedicated on July 12, 2003.

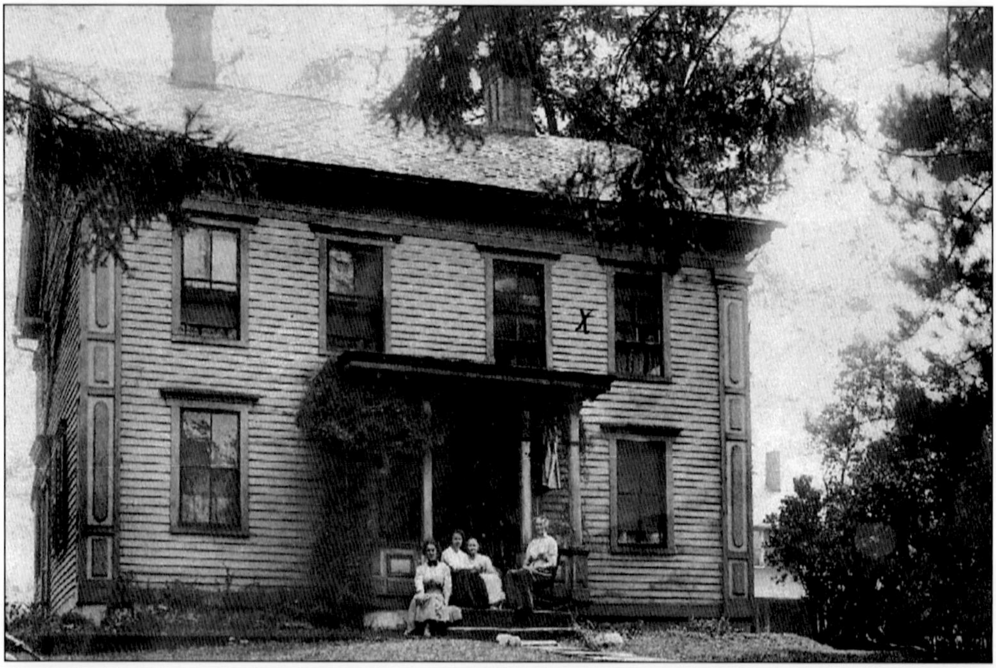

Samuel Tylee built the first frame house in Hubbard in 1808. Originally the house was located on the south side of West Liberty Street. Dr. W.S. Bond moved it to the east side of Bentley Avenue (23 Bentley Avenue) and the house is now used as a duplex. Maria Tylee Clingan and Eliza Tylee Hager, both daughters of Samuel Tylee, lived in the house. Chauncey Jewell was the next owner of the house. The Thomas Davies family lived in the house later and is shown sitting on the porch in this picture of the house from 1908. On the back of the original picture it says, "The room marked with an X is the bedroom that Martha and I share, it has a fireplace. We have 4 fireplaces in the house, which is the oldest in Hubbard, over a hundred years old. We have 2 large halls and 8 large rooms with an attic. This is not the style of house being built here now. Mama is sitting in the rocker, Aunt Grace and I are on the porch and Helen the youngest, but the largest of us is sitting on the step. A man came around and we just went out and had our picture taken just as we were." Pictured on the porch, from left to right, are Helen Davies, Jean Davies, Aunt Grace, and Mrs. Thomas Davies. I was e-mailed a copy of this picture with the X on it by Philip Davies, who lives in Surrey, England, and Tommy Davies was his great grandfather's brother. (Photograph courtesy of Eirwen De Vries.)

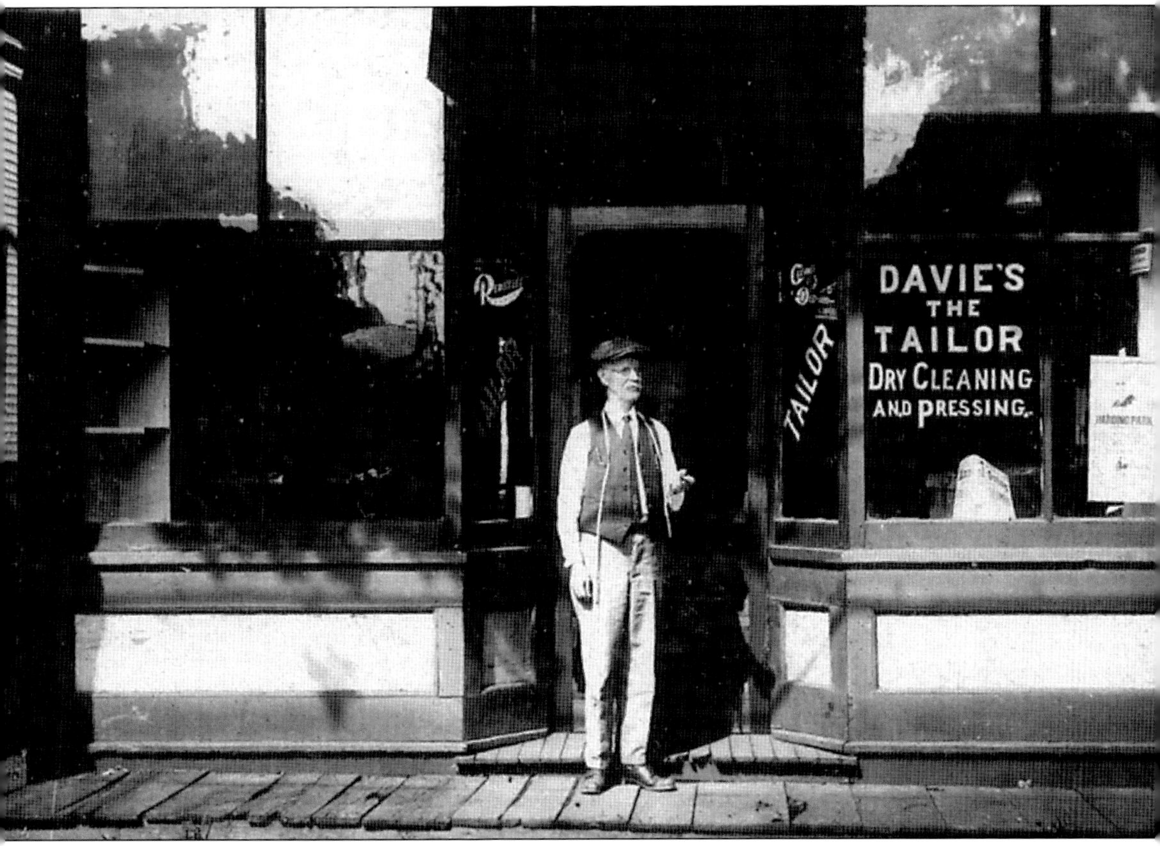

Tommy Davies was born in 1856 in a village in the County of Glamorgan, South Wales. It is not known when he came to America, but he learned the tailoring trade in his native country. His tailor shop in Hubbard was located on North Main Street, two buildings north of Orchard Street on the west side of the street. The shop faced east and there are some apartments in this location presently. He and his family lived in the first frame house in Hubbard on West Liberty Street that was built by Samuel Tylee in 1808. Henry Pettitt, whose family has lived in Hubbard since the 1840s, said that Tailor Davies made his first long pants suit in 1924 for his high school graduation and it cost him $24.95. Tommy was a Socialist and admired Eugene Debs who was a presidential candidate on the Socialist ticket in the early 1920s. Henry Pettitt remembers when Tommy ran in an unsuccessful bid for mayor of Hubbard; he would stand on the street corners and speak. The townspeople would "boo" him, probably because he wasn't a Democrat or a Republican. (Photograph courtesy of Eirwen De Vries.)

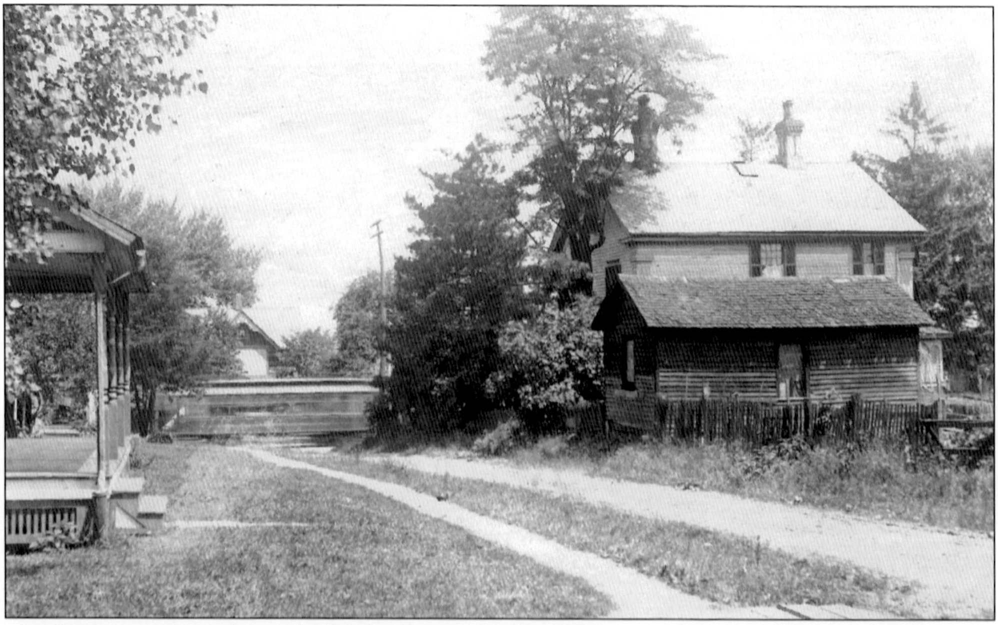

The house on the right is the back of the first frame house in Hubbard that originally faced north on West Liberty Street. Dr. W.S. Bond moved it to 23 Bentley Avenue in 1922. The dirt lane is Bentley Avenue facing north. A streetcar can be seen traveling on West Liberty Street. On its first run in 1901 it was reported to have overturned because of the sharp angle onto North Main Street. (Photograph courtesy of Nancy Gray Silvashy.)

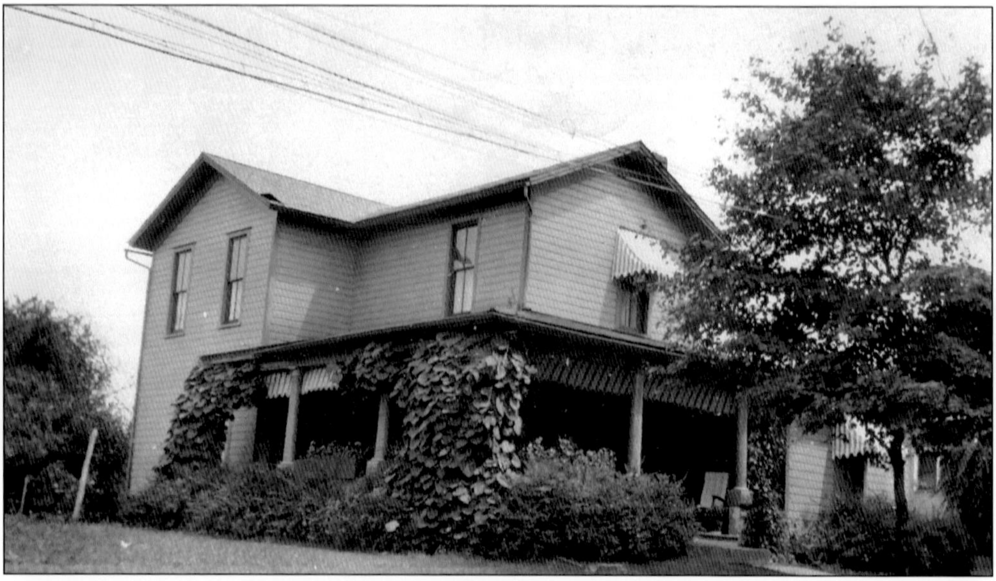

The McBride House at 27 Hager Street, Hubbard, was originally part of Lot No. 56, which was owned by Samuel Tylee, first settler of Hubbard. After his death in 1845, part of the lot was deeded to his daughter, Eliza Hager. Lorenzo Clingan bought the property in 1879 and built the house in 1883. John and Amelia McBride bought the house in 1910 from Delilah Blackburn and they sold it to their son, Charles G. McBride and his wife, Florence Ethel, in 1912 for "One Dollar & Love and affection ($1.00)." (Photograph courtesy of Hubbard Historical Society.)

Charles Gilmore McBride, son of John and Amelia McBride, was from Grove City, Pennsylvania. He and his wife, Florence Ethel, were graduates of Grove City College. Charles owned a jewelry and watch repair business located at 34 North Main Street and he and his family lived at 27 Hager Street, the present McBride House. (Photograph courtesy of Hubbard Historical Society.)

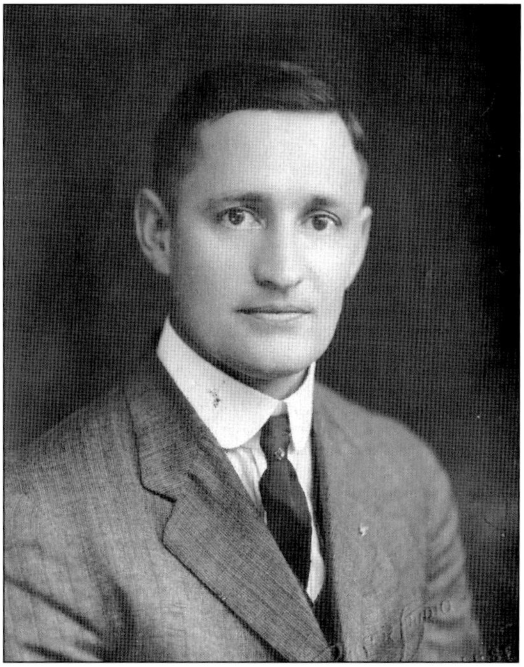

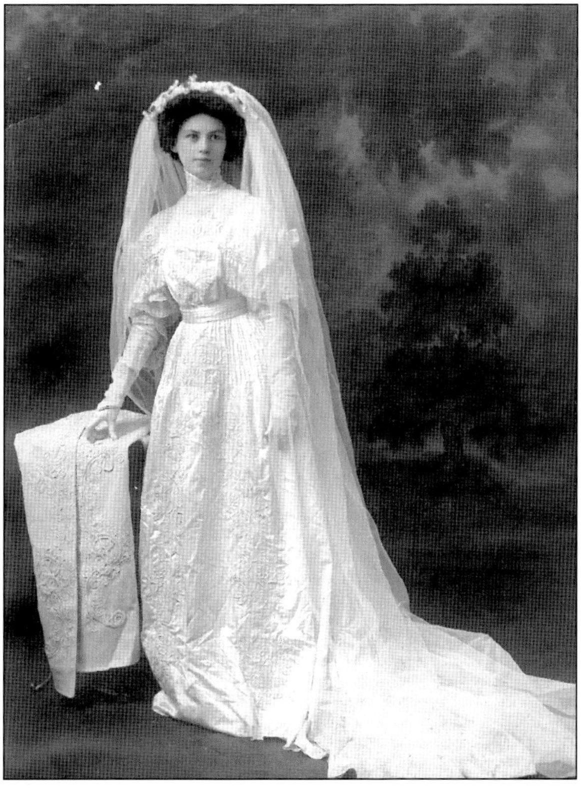

Florence Ethel Lockwood married Charles Gilmore McBride on January 20, 1909, in Zelienople, Pennsylvania. They were both graduates of Grove City College and Florence Ethel had a degree in music. The wedding dress has been donated to the Hubbard Historical Society and can be seen at the McBride House at 27 Hager Street, the society's historical house. (Photograph courtesy of Hubbard Historical Society.)

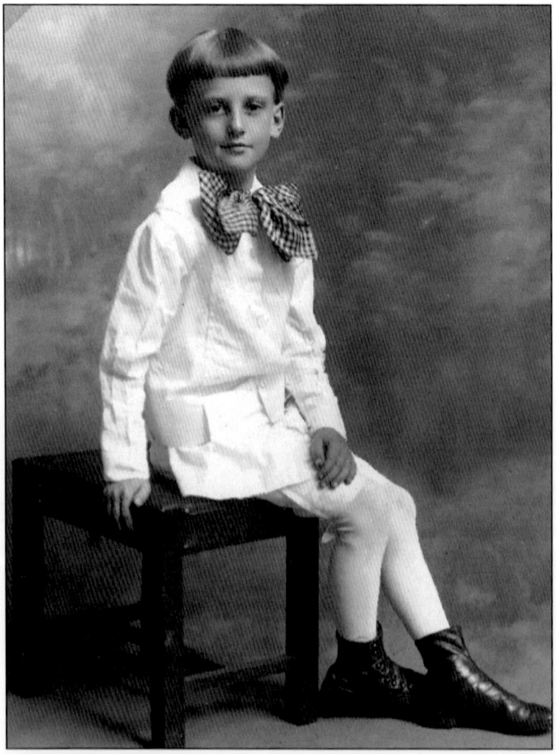

Charles Lockwood McBride was born on August 18, 1910, and was the first child of Charles and Florence Ethel McBride. He owned a grocery business and a service station. He ran for state representative in the early 1950s and in 1951 he ran for mayor of Hubbard on the Republican ticket and lost to Joe Baldine. He lived in Florida from 1953 until 1983 where he operated the McBride Grocery Store. He returned to Hubbard in 1983 and lived with his sister, Margaret, until his death on September 25, 1986. (Photograph courtesy of Hubbard Historical Society.)

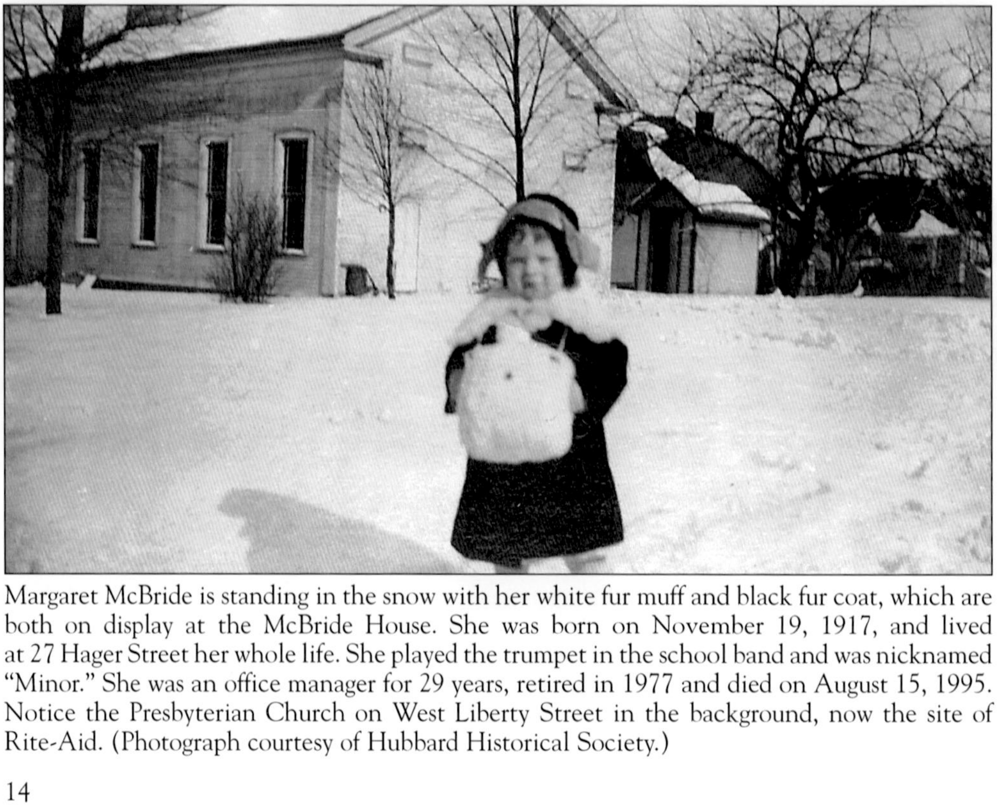

Margaret McBride is standing in the snow with her white fur muff and black fur coat, which are both on display at the McBride House. She was born on November 19, 1917, and lived at 27 Hager Street her whole life. She played the trumpet in the school band and was nicknamed "Minor." She was an office manager for 29 years, retired in 1977 and died on August 15, 1995. Notice the Presbyterian Church on West Liberty Street in the background, now the site of Rite-Aid. (Photograph courtesy of Hubbard Historical Society.)

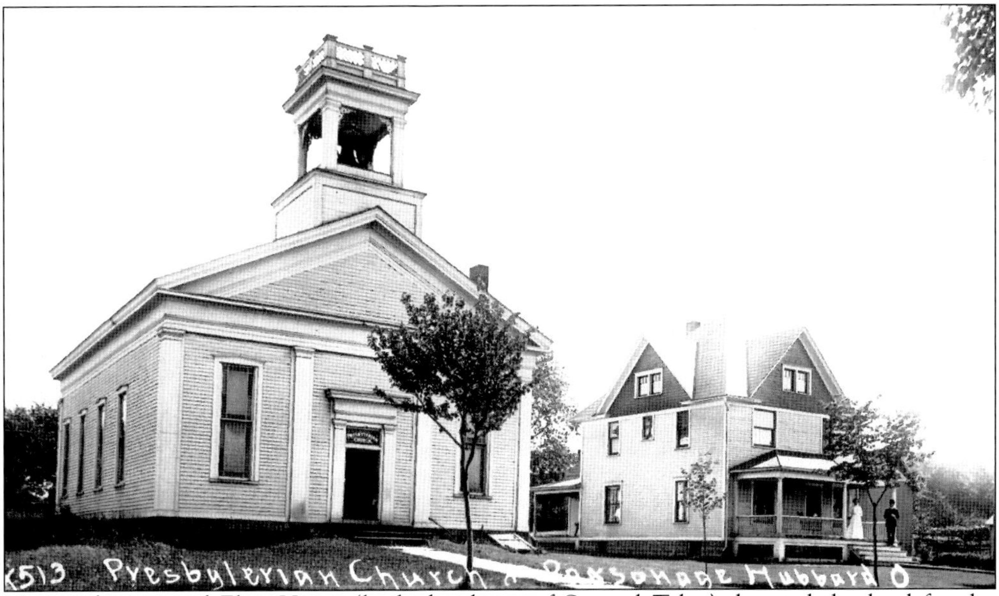

Maria Clingan and Eliza Hager (both daughters of Samuel Tylee) donated the land for the Presbyterian Church, which was built in 1857 on the southeast corner of West Liberty Street and Hager Street. Extensive remodeling was undertaken in 1891 and again in 1923. The current brick First Presbyterian Church was built on Westview Avenue in 1959. (Photograph courtesy of Nancy Gray Silvashy.)

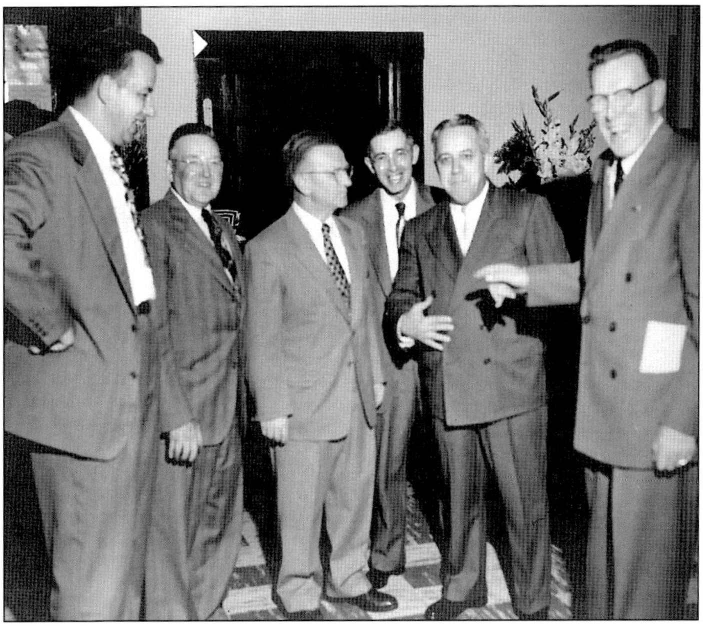

Pictured here, from left to right, are George Guidosh, Howard Thomas, Mr. Metzger, Earl Pettitt, Rev. Paul Gerrard, and Lawrence Stewart in 1940 at the First Presbyterian Church of Hubbard Social Room. Rev. Paul Gerrard served as pastor of the church from 1935 until 1946 and was well loved by his congregation. When he left Hubbard he went to the Lisbon Presbyterian Church from which he retired. (Photograph courtesy of Henry Pettitt.)

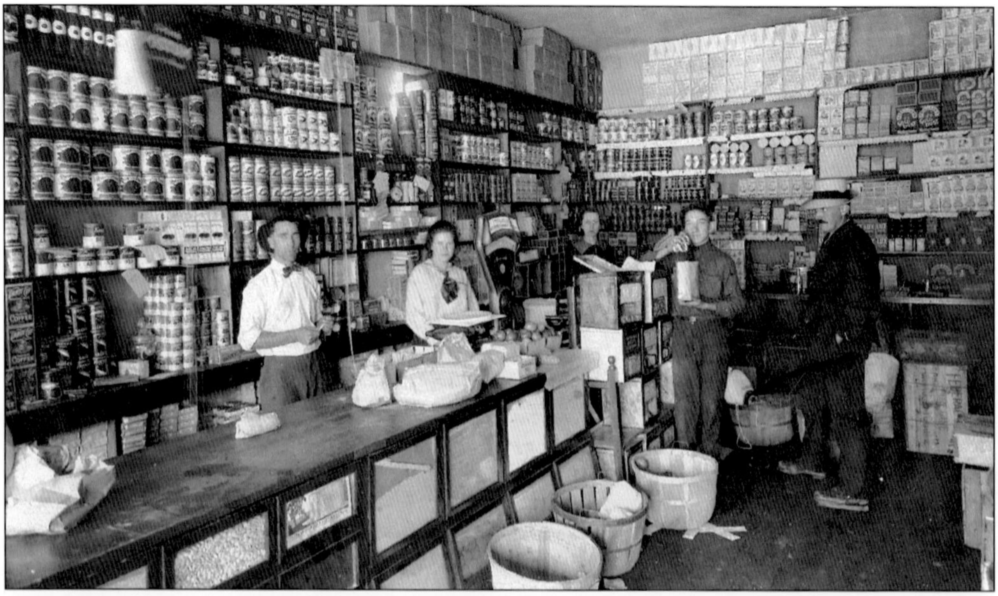

Tom Young had a grocery store in the early 1900s in Hubbard. His original store was located west of the present post office on East Liberty Street. He later moved to a much larger building on West Liberty Street and the top of this building still bears his name, "T.H. Young," along with "Max Schanberg" who had a shoe store. Tom Young, Mariel James Jenkins, and Elisha Snyder were working behind the counter at the store in the early 1900s. (Photograph courtesy of Nancy Gray Silvashy.)

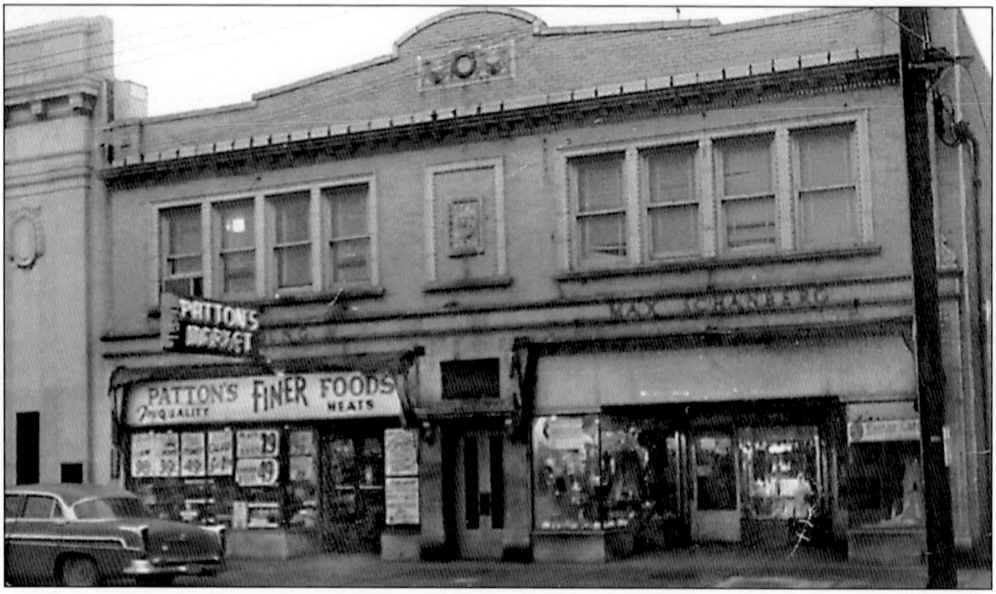

Wilson and Betty Patton opened Patton's Finer Foods in 1942 in Tom Young's building. Wilson had previously worked for The Great A & P Tea Co. He joined the Sparkle Market group and moved his store to 220 West Liberty Street in 1963. In 1984, the store moved to a new 30,000 square feet building at 880 West Liberty Street, the former site of the McConnell family lumberyard and is now called Patton's IGA Supercenter. (Photograph courtesy of Emanuel Mageros.)

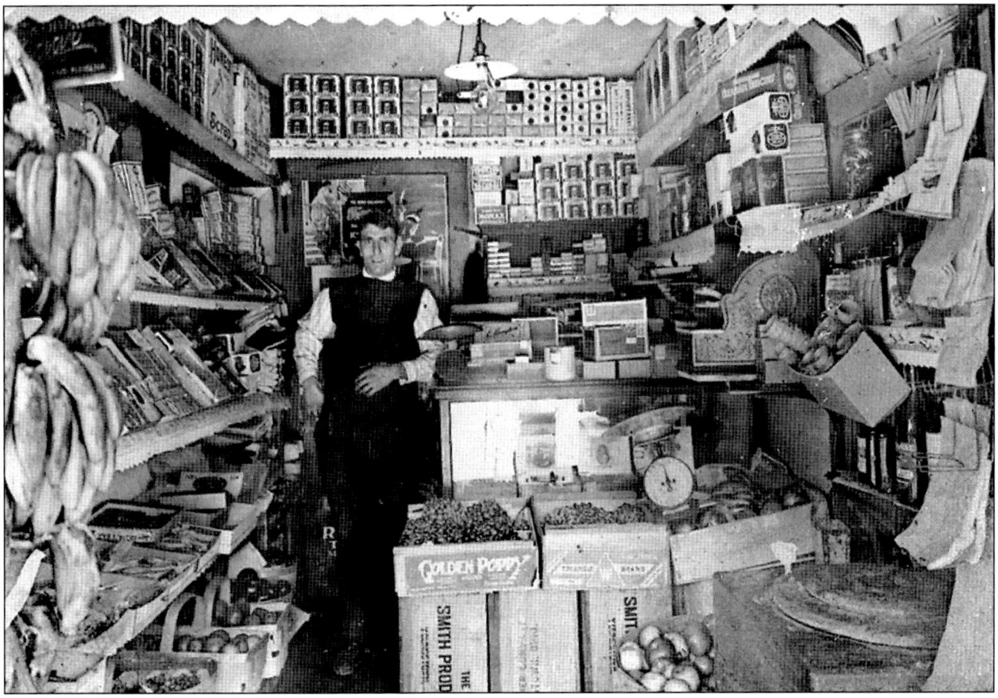

Mike Mageros is shown in his fruit and vegetable store, The California Fruit Market. It was located at 12 North Main Street in Hubbard. The store was started in the late 1920s and operated for 30 years. (Photograph courtesy of Emanuel Mageros.)

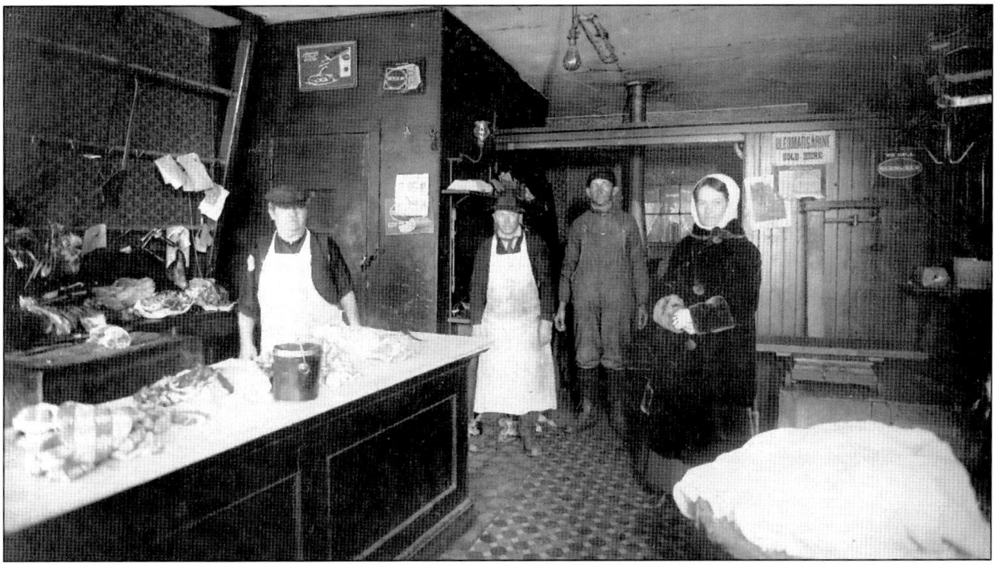

Harry Phillips' Butcher Shop was on the east side of North Main Street (the first block). The meat would be butchered in the morning and peddled all day in the Hubbard area. Pictured here, from left to right, are Harry Phillips, John Phillips (Harry's son), John Wall, and Mrs. Jack Davis of East Liberty Street who was the mother of Chester Davis and David Dale Davis. The new Velma and D. D. Davis garden center at Fellows Riverside Gardens was named after David Dale and his wife. (Photograph courtesy of Nancy Gray Silvashy.)

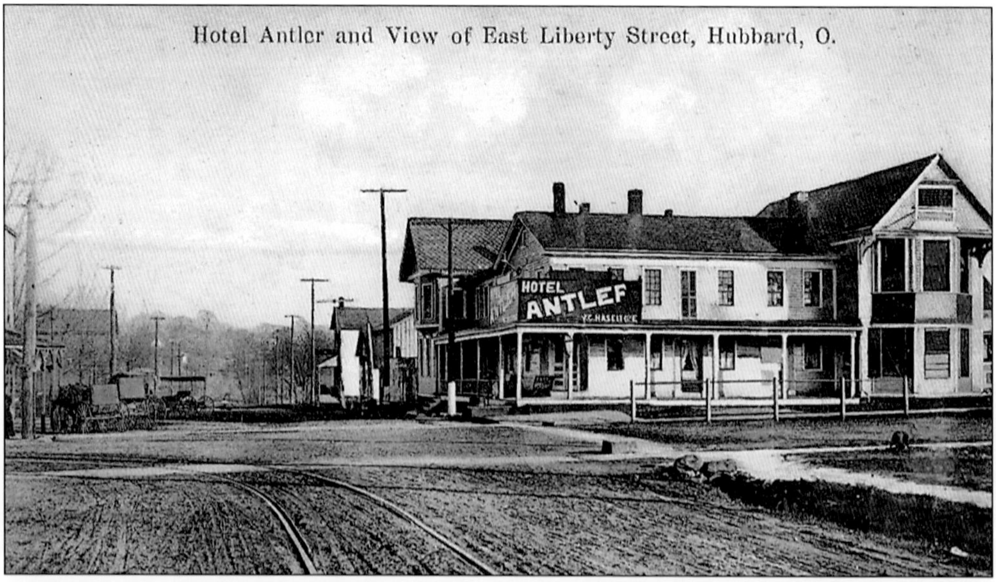

Andrew Gardner built the first hotel in 1828 on the southeast corner of East Liberty Street and South Main Street. It was known by many names over the years including: Rosses Inn, Hamman House, Pew House, and Hotel Antler. In 1893, it attracted not only travelers, but also amateur athletes who used the hotel's large gym. It had a barroom, a restaurant, 13 bedrooms, a lobby, and a livery stable. In 1908, it was remodeled into apartments and later was Livingston's Tire Shop. (Photograph courtesy of Marilyn and Rich Stiver.)

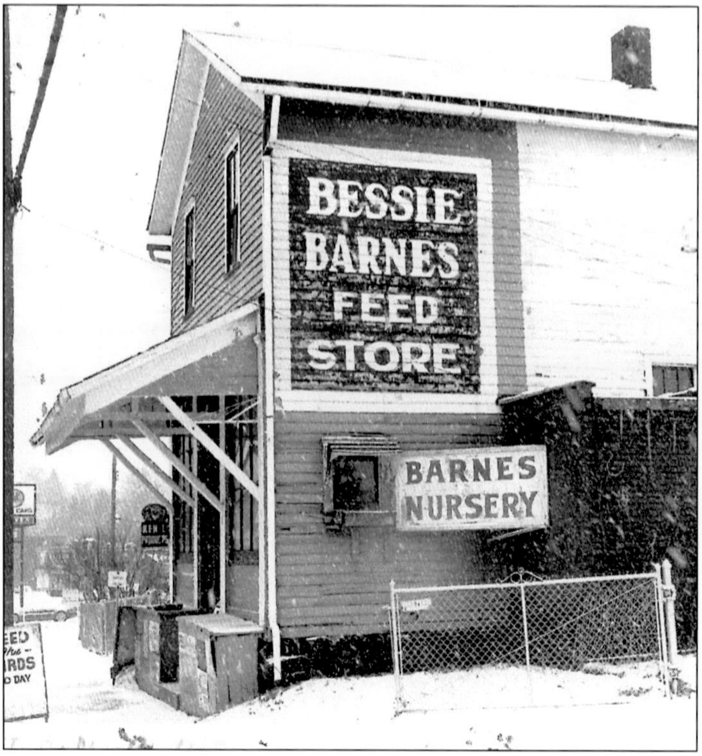

Bessie Barnes's store (originally C. N. Clingan Feed Store) is shown here in the 1970s. William Clingan and his son, William Jr., came to Hubbard from Mercer County, Pennsylvania. They were carpenters by trade and also shipped cattle. William Jr.'s son, Calvin N. Clingan, built the feed store after he returned from the Civil War. The store sold groceries, paint, and animal feed. For a time the Hubbard Band practiced in an upstairs room of the store. They hung their uniforms in the back room. (Photograph courtesy of Emanuel Mageros.)

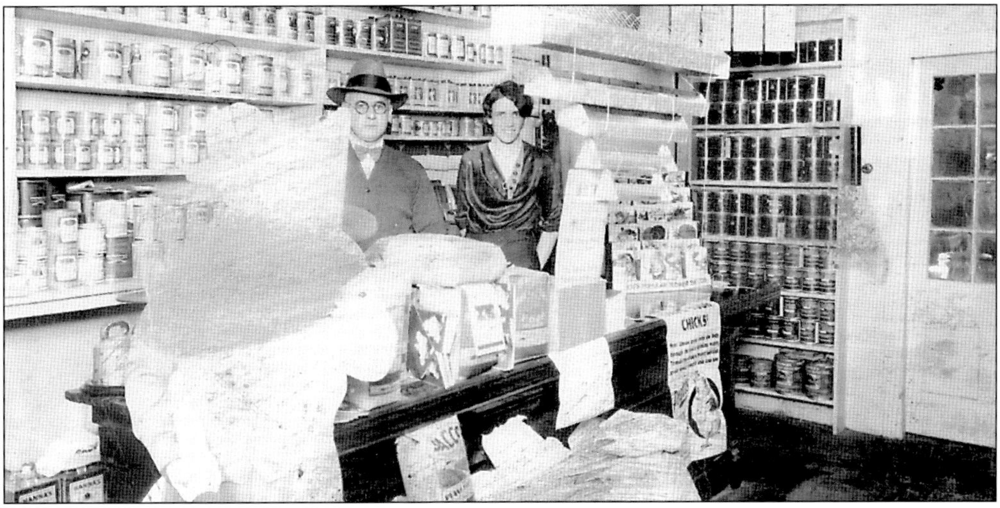

Mr. Calvin N. Clingan is on the left and Bessie Barnes is on the right in this undated photograph of the inside of the C. N. Clingan Feed Store, located at 33 East Liberty Street. Calvin's father, William Jr., bought property located at 6219 West Liberty Street in 1850 when Calvin was seven years old. Governor David Tod purchased the property in 1906, and William Powell, owner of Powell Pressed Steel, purchased it in 1927. It is now the site of Julia's Bed and Breakfast. (Photograph courtesy of Emanuel Mageros.)

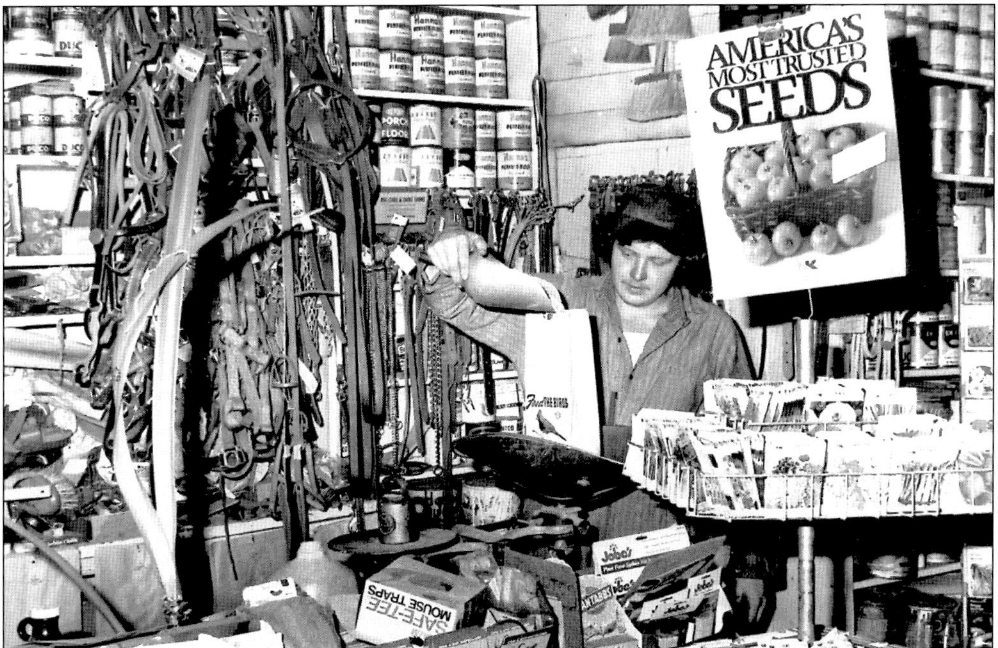

Bessie Barnes worked at the C.N. Clingan feed store for many years, and later bought it. She called on farmers, delivering feed, seeds, and farm supplies. During World War II, as meat was so scarce, she sold 103,000 baby chicks in one year. She married David Austin who worked for the Pennsylvania Railroad and they added a garden center to the store. David died in 1971 and Bessie continued to operate the business until the late 1970s. (Photograph courtesy of Emanuel Mageros.)

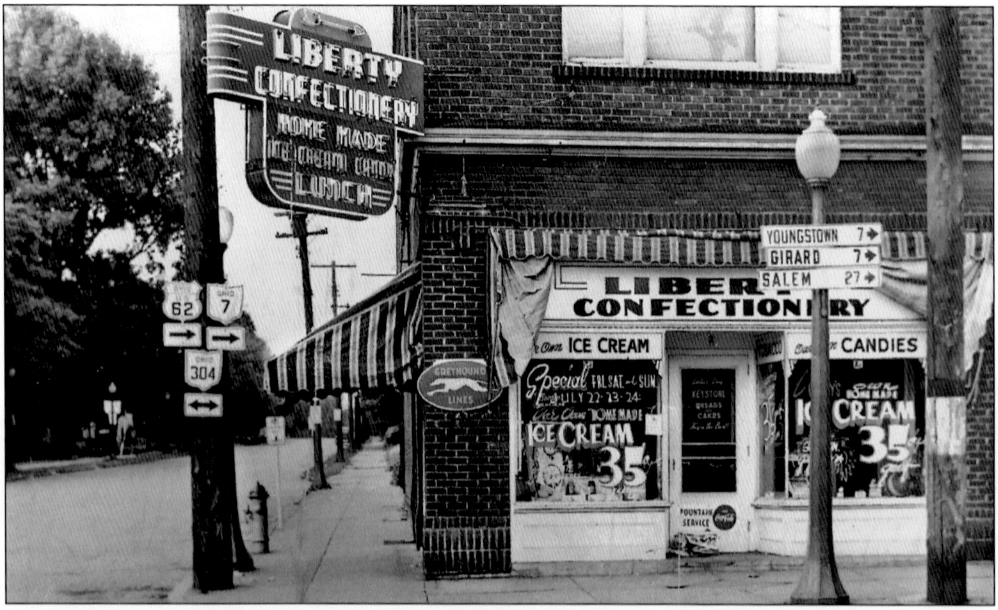

The Liberty Confectionery, located in the IOOF building on the southwest corner of West Liberty Street and South Main Street is shown in this photograph from the early 1950s. Mike Mageros and his brother-in-law, George Mazarakis, owned the business. They served candy, ice cream, and grilled items such as hamburgers and cheeseburgers. The IOOF building is still standing, however, the light fixture is gone. (Photograph courtesy of Emanuel Mageros.)

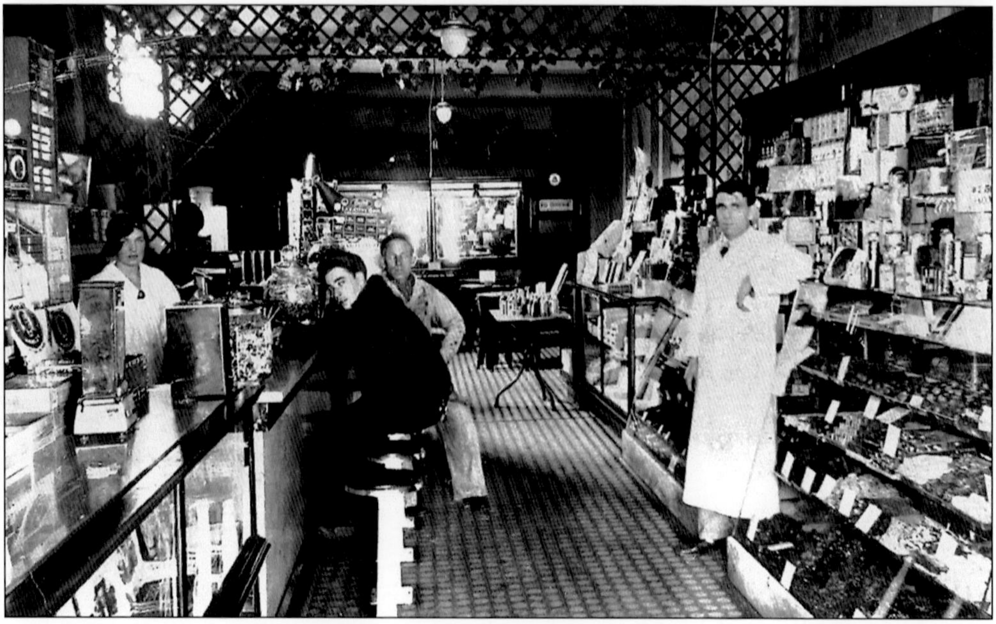

One of the co-owners of the Liberty Confectionery, Mike Mageros, is shown on the right in this photograph from the early 1950s. Mike and his wife, Paska, came to America through Ellis Island around 1918 from Kephida, Greece with their two children, Peter and Thomas. Later, their son Peter and his wife, Helen, opened Mageros Candies at 132 North Main Street. Their son Emanuel and his wife, Debbie, operate the store today. (Photograph courtesy of Emanuel Mageros.)

The Palace Theatre marquee is shown in this photograph taken in 1946. Mr. Wolf (also known as "Pappy" Wolf) had a clothing store in Hubbard on North Main Street and was acquainted with the Warner Brothers who built the Warner Theatre (Powers Auditorium) in Youngstown. He wanted a theatre for Hubbard so he built the Palace Theatre. John Hegfield, his wife Alice, their son Donald, and their daughter Betty (Nehls), were the last owners to operate it as a theater. It was used for storage in its last years, torn down in the late 1970s and replaced with Tylee Park. (Photograph courtesy of Shirley Baker.)

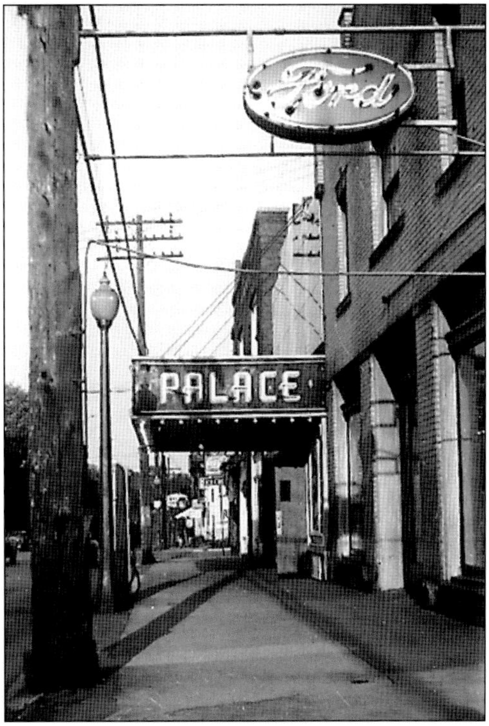

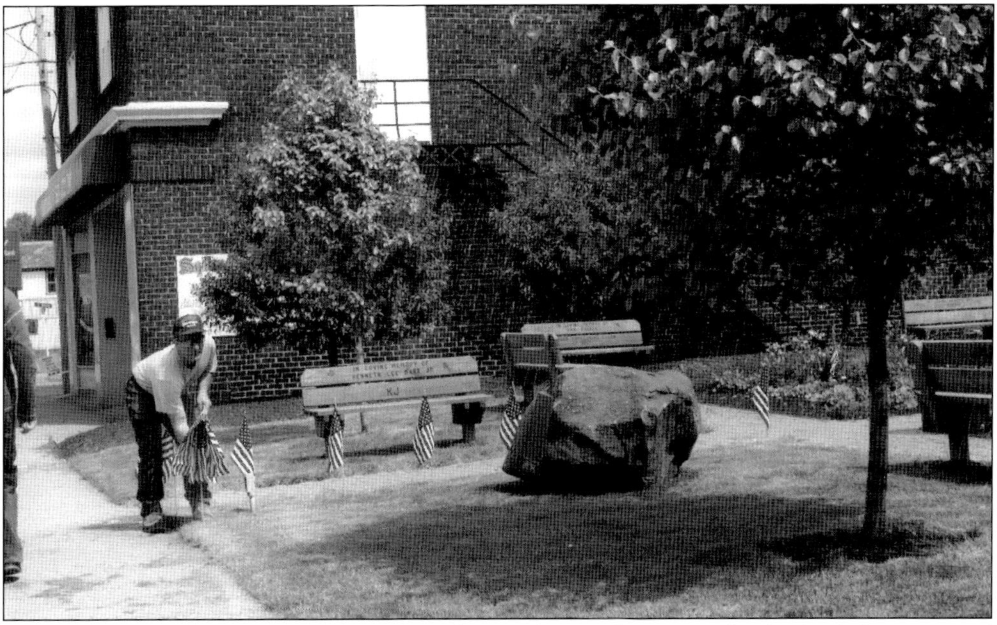

Dave Cook, Street Department worker, is shown placing flags around Tylee Park for Memorial Day, 2003. The beginning of Tylee Park started with Mayor Albert Sauline in 1989 when he held a public meeting to discuss revitalizing downtown Hubbard. This led to the REACH organization raising funds by selling signature bricks to build a small park at the site of the Palace Theatre. Volunteers maintain the park, and in May, the schoolchildren plant flowers.

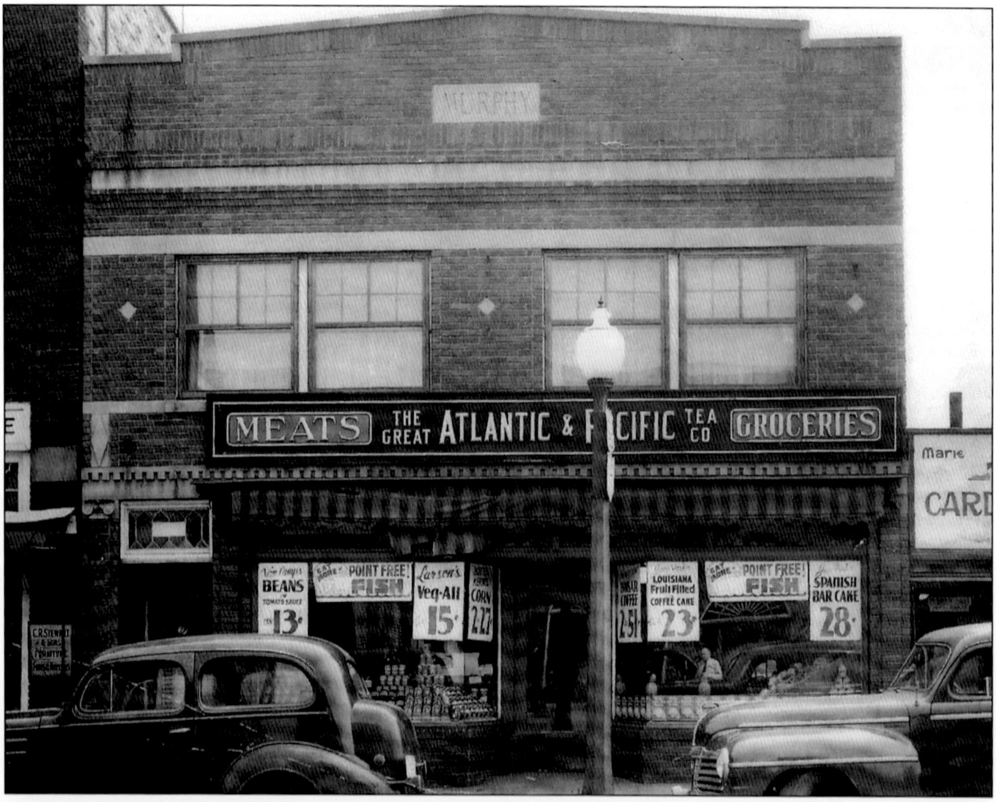

The A & P Store, which sold meats and groceries in the 1930s, was located at 15 North Main Street. Cans of corn are advertised in the windows for two for 27¢. The name, "Murphy," can be seen on the top of the building as it was built by Joe Murphy who had an ice cream, candy, and cigar store in the early 1900s. Golden Glow Tanning is located in the building today. (Photograph courtesy of Emanuel Mageros.)

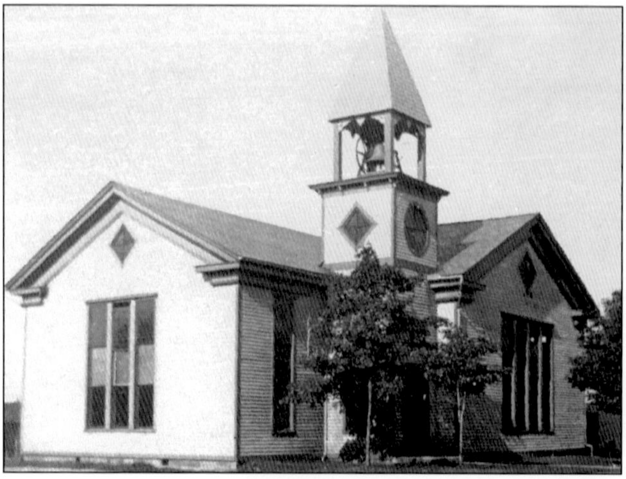

The second United Methodist Church is shown in this picture. Originally, there were two Methodist Churches, a brick church on the southeast corner of West Liberty Street and Bell-Wick Road and the Veach church on Schotten Road. The west and east congregations merged in 1857 after the United Methodist Church was built on Church Street. It was located to the east of the present brick church, which was built in 1925. (Photograph courtesy of Nancy Praznik.)

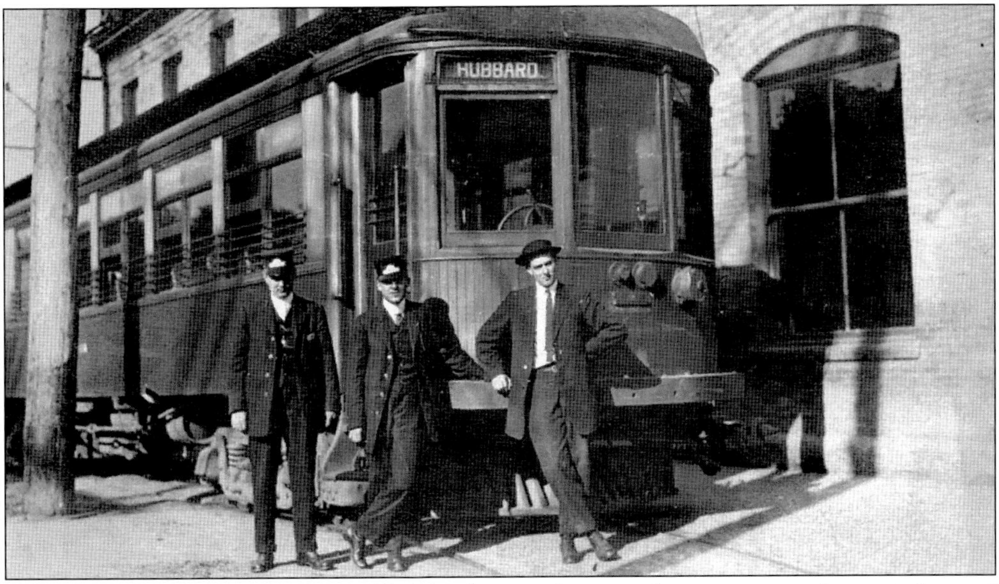

Streetcar conductor William Arnold, left, along with two unknown men is shown in front of the Hubbard streetcar. William's son, William Ellsworth Arnold, known as "Butch," and his buddies would tie firecrackers on the back of the streetcar on the Fourth of July. After lighting them, they would run as fast they could, with Butch's dad running after them. He could never catch them, as he had to go back to work. (Photograph courtesy of Betty Arnold Linebaugh.)

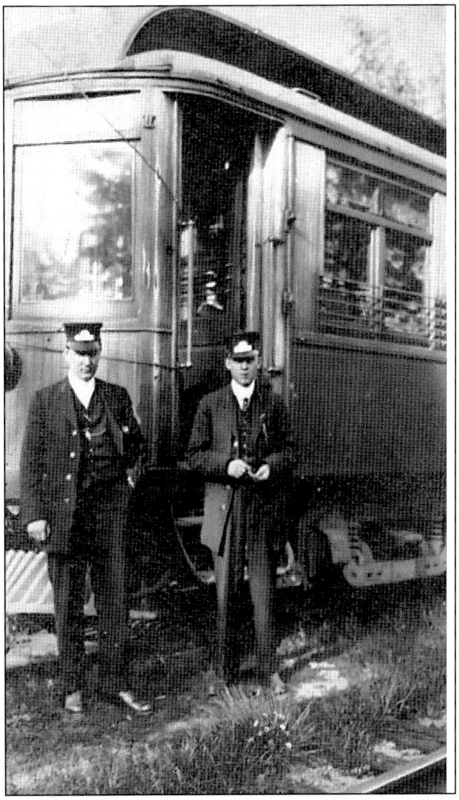

Conductor William Arnold, left, is shown with an unidentified fellow streetcar worker in this photograph from the early 1900s. The streetcars provided transportation for people before the widespread use of automobiles and were operating in Hubbard from 1901 until 1939. The Youngstown-Sharon line went from Youngstown on Jacobs Road to Youngstown-Hubbard Road, then east on West Liberty Street and north on North Main Street where it continued into Sharon, Pennsylvania. (Photograph courtesy of Betty Arnold Linebaugh.)

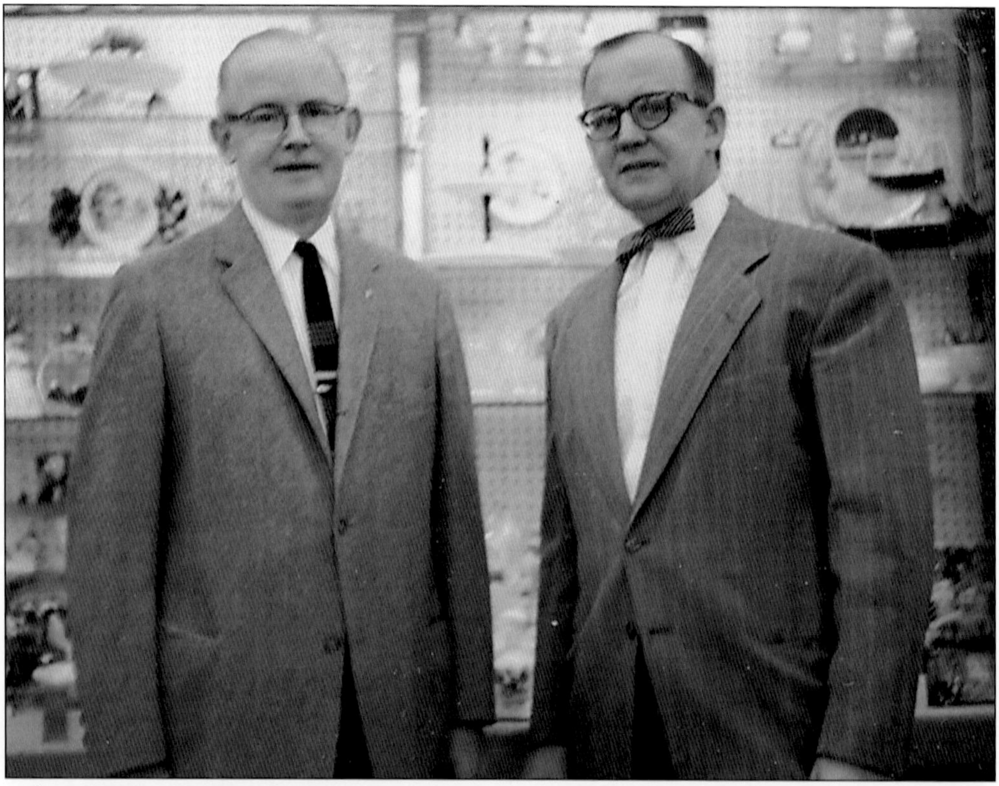

Jack and Robert Diamond are shown in front of a display case full of glass collectibles in their first Hubbard Ben Franklin store located at 51 North Main Street (present location of Hubbard Music). Jack worked at the Ben Franklin in Girard for 13 years and opened his own store in Hubbard in September of 1951. Later, the brothers bought the Girard store and Robert operated that business. The stores carried house wares, hardware, stationery, greeting cards, and toys. (Photograph courtesy of Sally Diamond.)

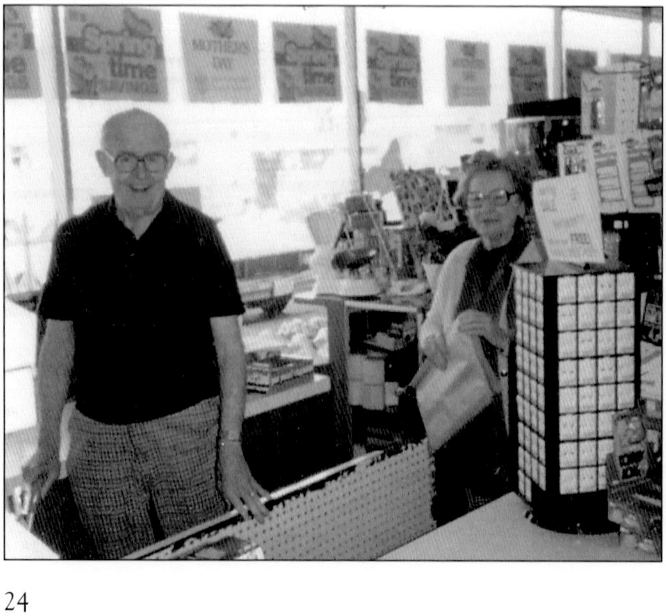

Jack Diamond is shown with employee Evalyn Plumeret in the front of the Ben Franklin store. Jack moved the store in 1964 to 19 South Main Street. Jack's daughter, Sally, worked in the store from the age of 12 years old and when her Dad retired, she became manager of the store. The store moved to Struthers in 1985 after the store lost its lease. Sally opened Sally's Toys and Such at 34 North Main Street in 1999 and sells toys, novelties, cards, and crafts. (Photograph courtesy of Sally Diamond.)

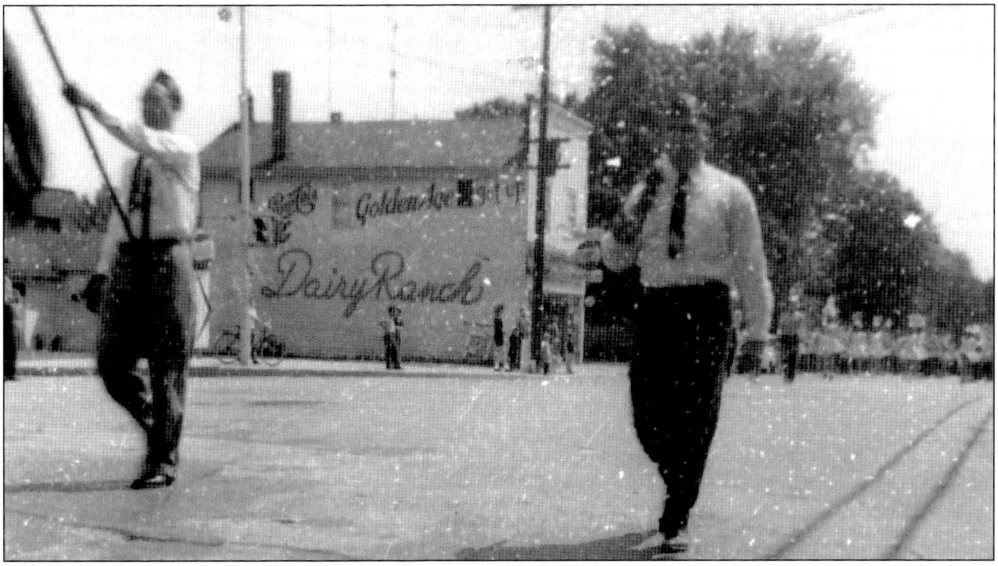

The Dairy Ranch can be seen in the background of this picture taken at a Memorial Day Parade in May of 1958. The Dairy Ranch was located on the corner of North Main Street and East Liberty Street and provided a place for young people to dance and have refreshments. Nancy Ladley Praznik's family lived in an apartment upstairs in 1951 when they first came to Hubbard from the Pittsburgh area. Before the Dairy Ranch opened, Snow Furniture Store was located here. (Photograph courtesy of George and Nancy Praznik.)

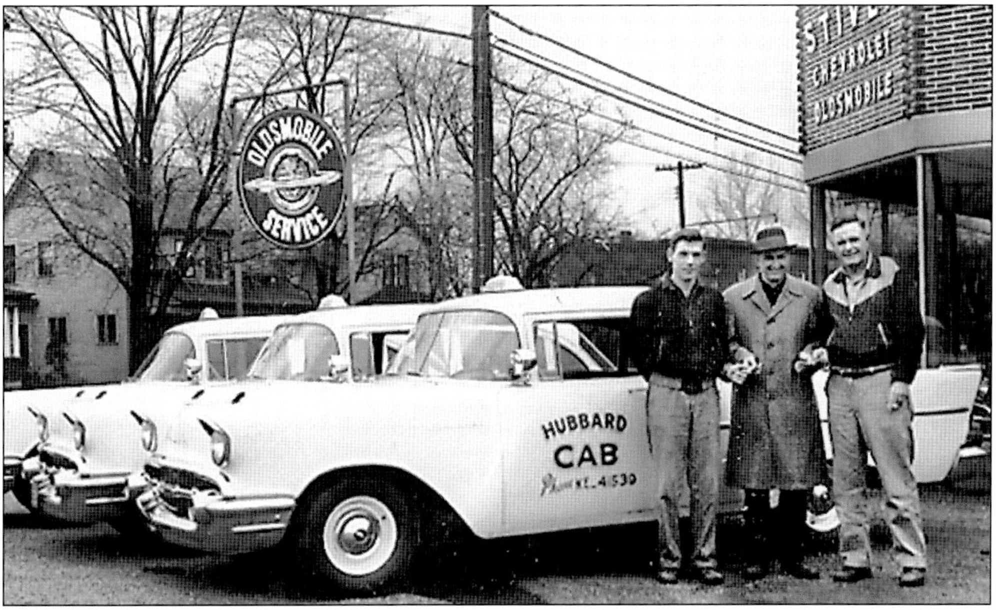

Rich Stiver, center, is shown in this photograph from 1957, handing over the keys to three new 1957 cabs to the Hubbard Cab Company. Frank Kalvoda, who was the owner of the cab company, is on the left and "Judy" Edwards is on the right. Rich worked at the Stiver family business, Stiver Chevrolet-Oldsmobile, at this time and was made a dealer in 1969. Rich, who belonged to many civic organizations, loved Hubbard and Hubbard's history. (Photograph courtesy of Marilyn and Rich Stiver.)

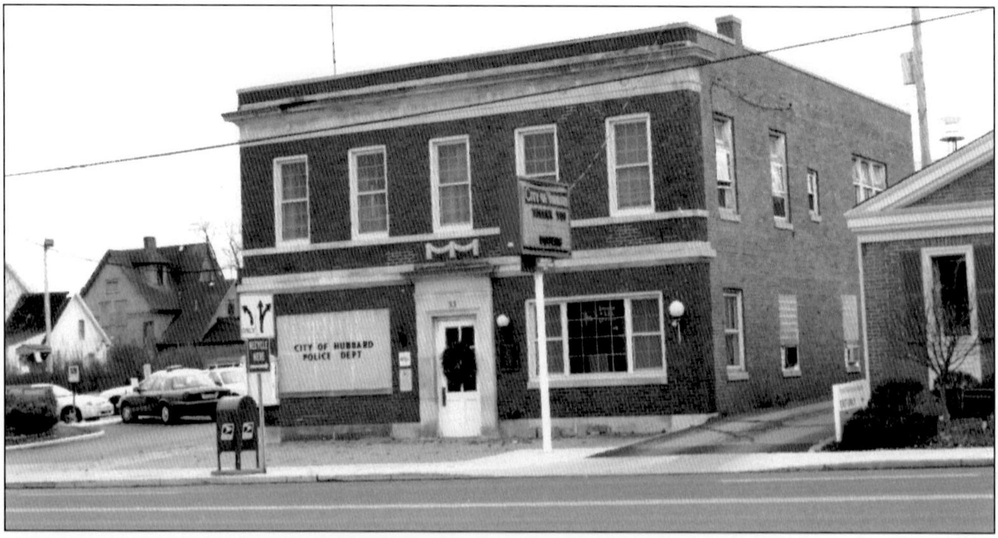

The plaque on the front of the old City Municipal Building and present Hubbard Police Station shows it was built in 1923. C.H. Anderson was mayor, C.P. Creed was clerk, and Carl W. Creed was treasurer at the time. It also lists all council members. The architectural firm that designed the building was the Owsley Company that designed many well known buildings in Youngstown, including South High School, the Home Savings Bank building, the Mahoning County Courthouse, and Youngstown City Hall. (History courtesy of Donna DeBlasio.)

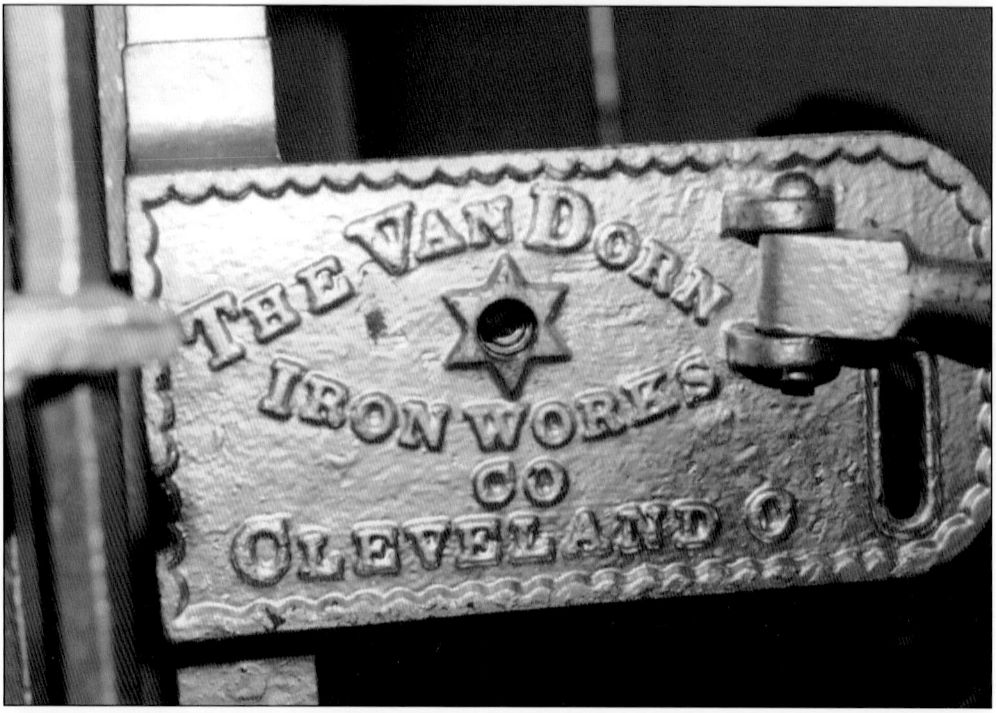

The original door lock on one of the cells in the 1870 Hubbard Jail is shown in this photograph taken in January of 2004. The Van Dorn Iron Works Company in Cleveland, Ohio manufactured the door locks.

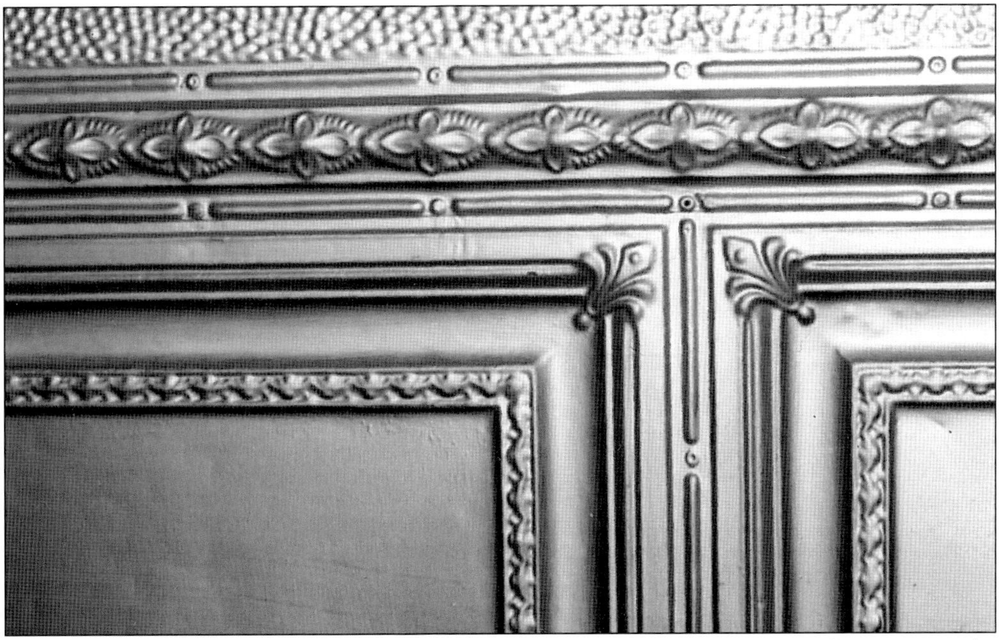

The original embossed tin ceiling is shown in a photograph taken in January of 2004. It can be seen in a closet in one of the offices on the southwest corner of the present Hubbard Police Station. It is notable not only for its beauty, but because it has not been painted and is in its original condition. It is not known what the rest of the tin ceiling's condition is, as it is covered with dropped ceiling tiles.

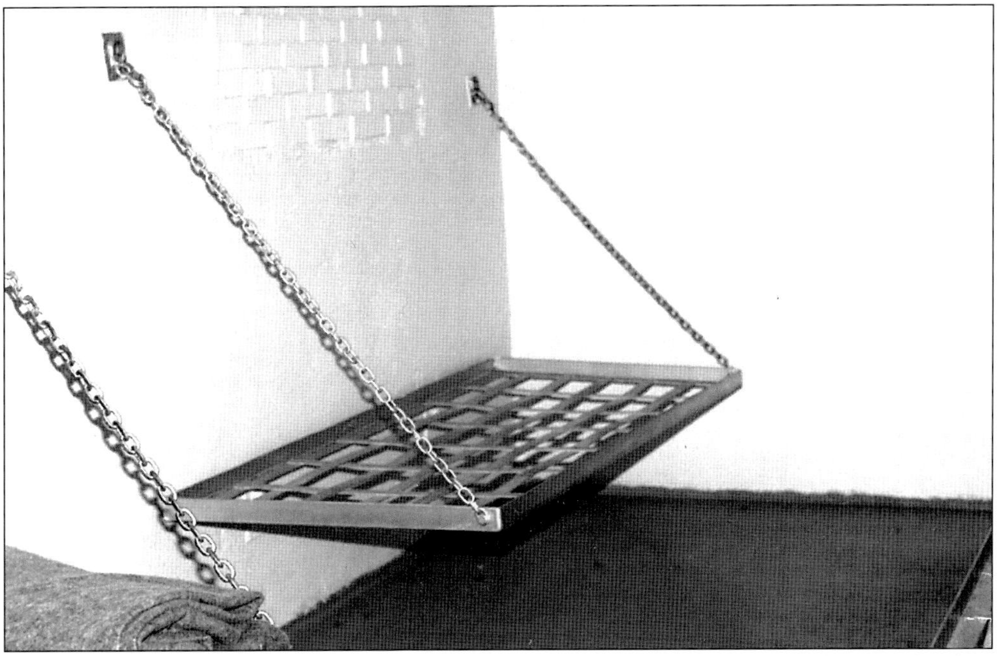

The original hanging beds are still a part of the Hubbard Jail as shown in this photograph taken in January of 2004. The jail was originally built in 1870 and has been kept in very good condition. The metal ceilings of the cells are painted silver.

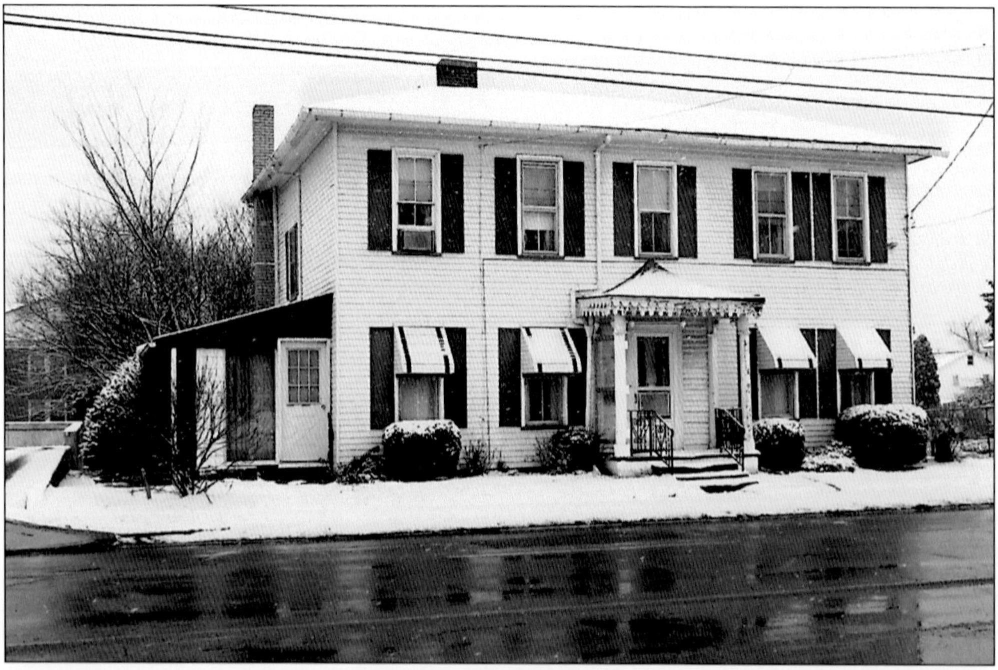

The National City Bank replaced this beautiful frame house located at 70 West Liberty Street in 2002. Hand-made bricks dated 1841 were used in the fireplaces. The last owner of the house was Pat Irwin. Many of the original furnishings can be seen at the Hubbard Historical Society's McBride House located at 27 Hager Street. (Photograph courtesy of Emanuel Mageros.)

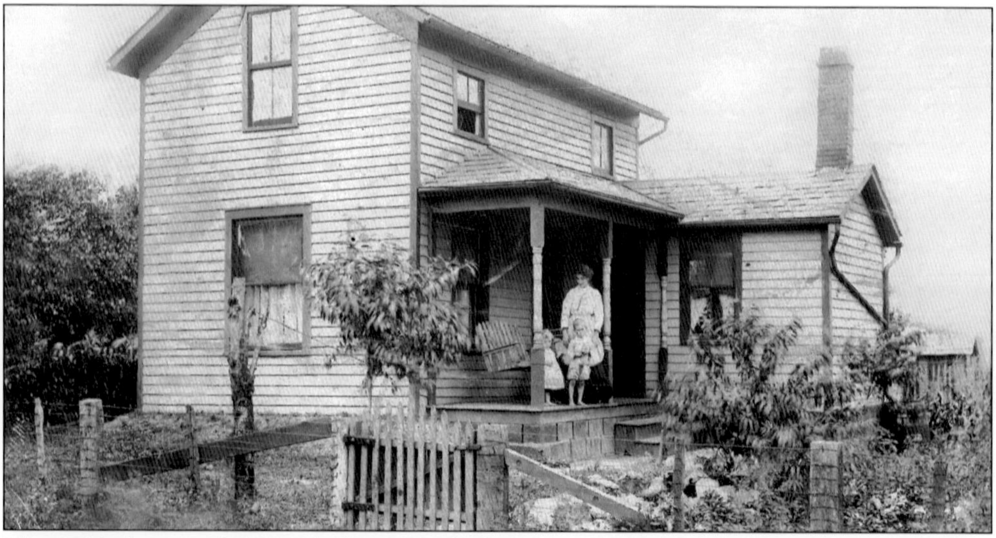

This 1908 photograph shows the homestead of Myron and Mary Ann Jackson, formerly located at 62 West Water Street. Pictured from left to right are Lemuel, Gilbert, and their mother, Florence Jackson Young. Florence's father was Myron Jackson from the lineage of Rebecca Tylee (daughter of Sylvester Tylee) and Cyrus Jackson. Myron's siblings were Caroline and Lemuel. Myron and Jackson Streets, Rebecca, Caroline, Cyrus, and W. Park (formerly Lemuel Street) Avenues were all named after the Jackson family and the area is known as Jackson Heights. (Photograph courtesy of Shirley Baker and Gayle Kerrigan Glasnapp.)

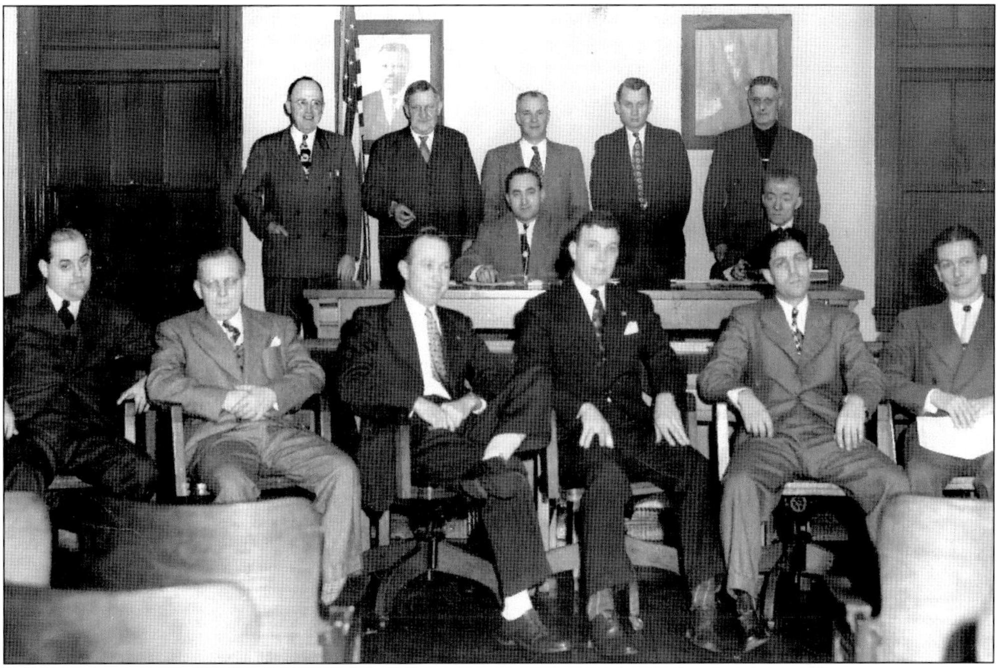

The Hubbard City Council of the mid-1940s included, from left to right: (first row) Bob Allen, Lawrence Coleman, Jim Keenan, Harry Riordan, Leonard Rock, and T.J. Wilson; (seated at the desk) Mayor Joseph Baldine and Doc O'Brien (clerk); (back row) Carl Creed, Fred Brewer, unidentified, John Hainz, and Earl Greer. (Photograph courtesy of Hubbard Historical Society.)

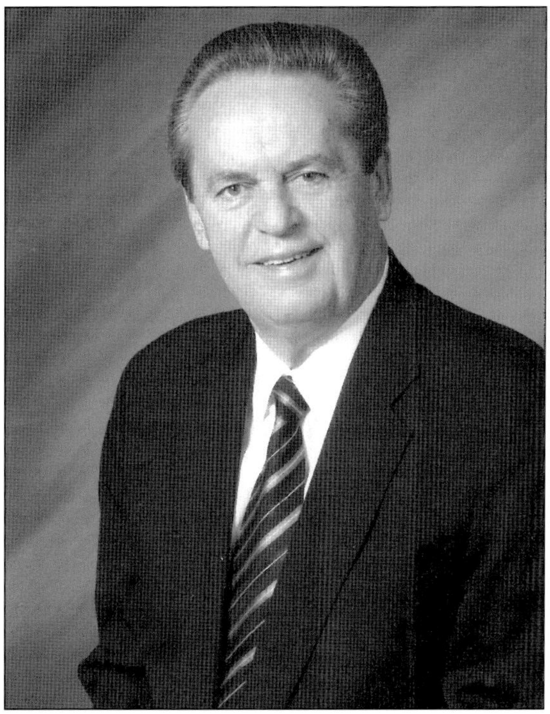

Mayor Arthur U. Magee was elected in November of 2003. He had previously served as a city councilman for over two years and mayor for eight and a half years from June 15, 1974, to January 3, 1983. In 1983, Art was elected Trumbull County commissioner and served for 16 years, the longest elected commissioner in county history. He is a 1954 graduate of Hubbard High School. (Photograph courtesy of Arthur U. Magee.)

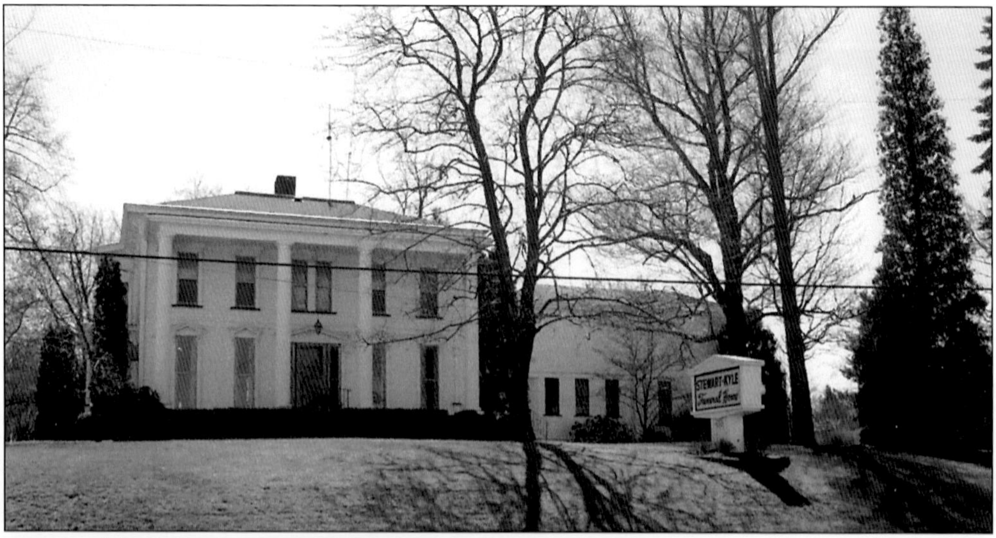

Joel Smith built the house at 407 West Liberty Street in the late 1860s, which the Jewel family purchased. In 1927, the Stewart family purchased the property for their funeral business, the Stewart Funeral Home. In 1947, Wilber and Bernice Kyle purchased the funeral home, naming it the Stewart-Kyle Funeral Home. In 1956, their son, A. Ray, purchased the business. Today, his sons, Timothy and David, own and operate the funeral home. The viewing room ceiling still has the original design of painted birds and leaves, edged in scroll molding. (Photograph courtesy of Diane and A. Ray Kyle.)

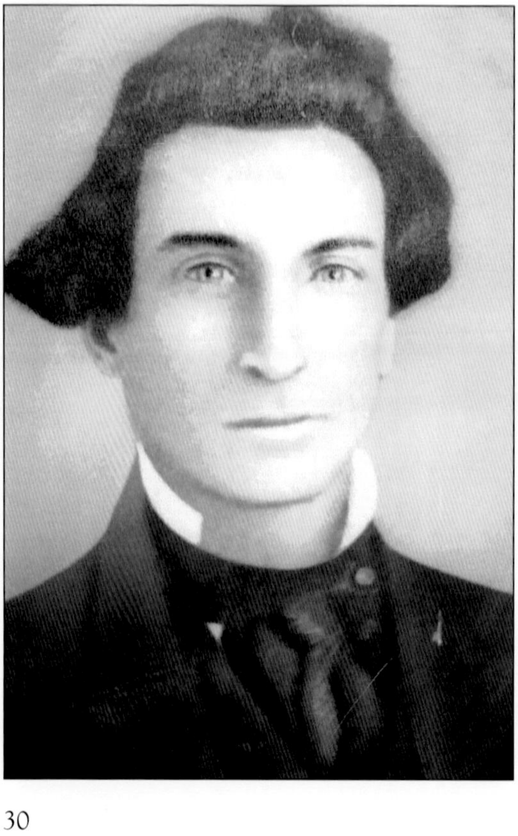

Alexander Lowry Stewart was married to Lorena Clingan. Lorena was the daughter of Maria A. Tylee (youngest daughter of Anna and Samuel, first settlers of Hubbard) and Jehiel Clingan. Alexander was a cabinetmaker and casket maker. He measured the bodies and custom built the caskets to fit them. His business was in operation from 1850 until 1890. (Photograph courtesy of Karen Simmons, history courtesy of Ruth Stewart Logerquist.)

Calvin R. Stewart, Alexander Lowry Stewart's son, started the C.R. Stewart and Sons Furniture Store, which was originally located next to the family residence on West Liberty Street, across from the current Stewart-Kyle Funeral Home. Calvin also operated a funeral business at this location, with people holding funerals in their homes. In 1917, the current furniture store was built on North Main Street. (Photograph courtesy of Betty Stewart Patton, history courtesy of Ruth Stewart Logerquist.)

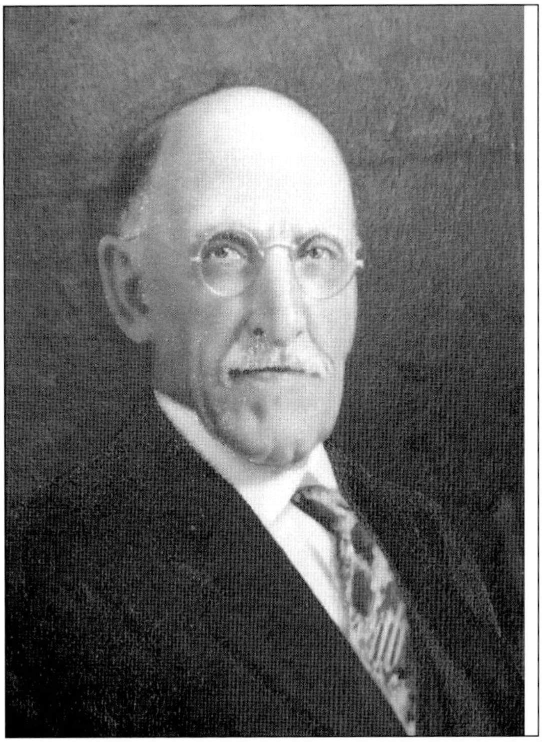

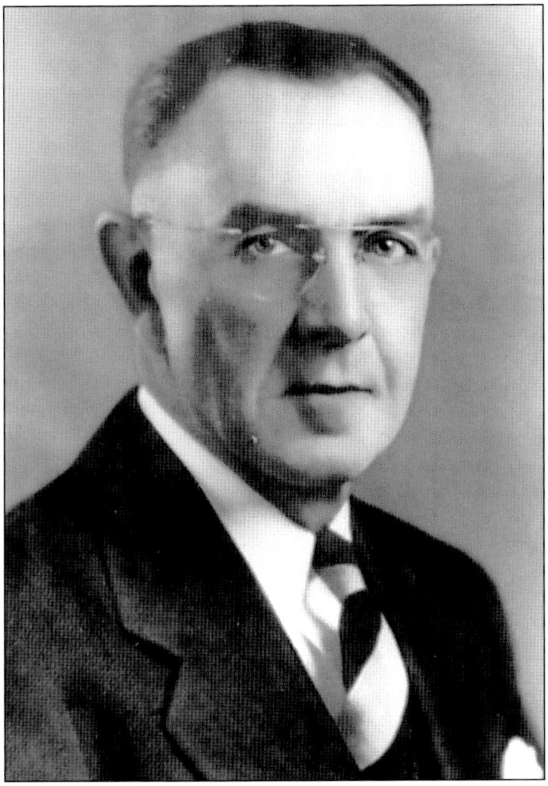

Earl S. Stewart, son of Calvin, took over the family funeral business in 1936. His sister, Lorena, said that as a child, Earl didn't want to sleep in the bedroom that overlooked the barn, the original location of the morgue. Ironically, it was Earl who went into the funeral business! He established the Stewart Funeral Home as ideas were changing about having funerals in private homes. He was successful because the community trusted and respected him. (Photograph courtesy of Betty Stewart Patton, history courtesy of Ruth Stewart Logerquist.)

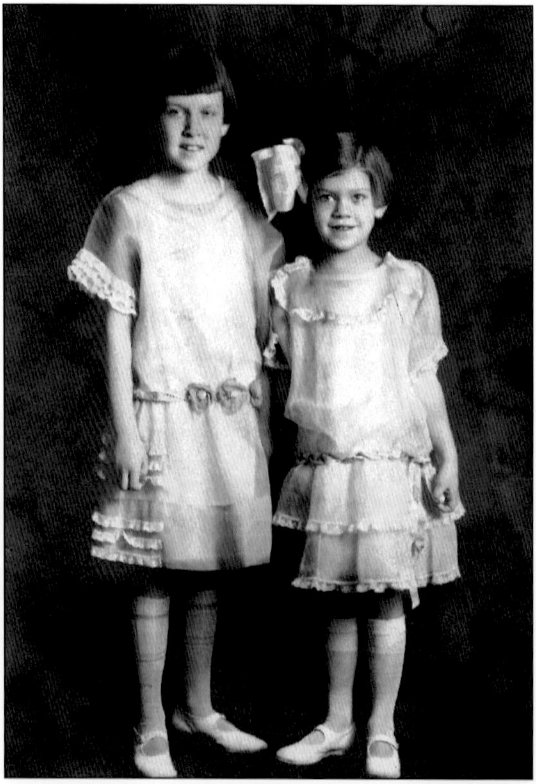

The daughters of Earl and Della Stewart pose in 1920. Ruth, on the left, was a musician and sang, played the piano and the organ, and later gave piano lessons to local children. Betty was the worker in the family, and washed the small windowpanes of the east porch for a penny a pane. Betty slid down the banisters of the staircase, and pretended that the middle hallway was an elevator. (Photograph courtesy of Betty Stewart Patton.)

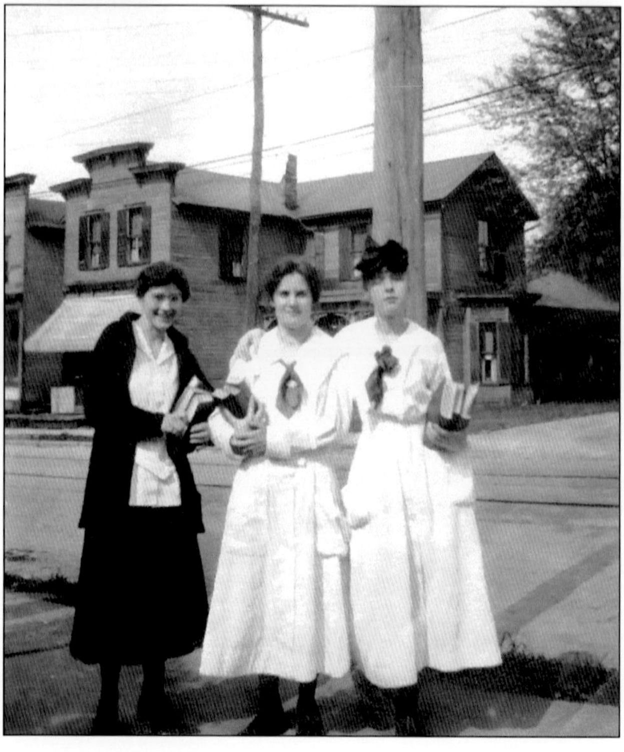

Bessie Brown Lehn, Florence Mitchell Carter, and Mabel Stewart, from left to right, are shown in a photograph from 1917. Mabel was a missionary to India and came home after she contracted tuberculosis. She was nicknamed "Kidder." One time she was lying on the porch of the family home, across from the Stewart Funeral Home, and narrowly missed being injured in a freak accident. One of the funeral cars rolled down the driveway, almost running her down. (Photograph courtesy of Betty Stewart Patton.)

Wilson and Betty Patton are shown in the early 1940s after Wilson was drafted into the army during WWII. Just before being drafted and sent to Fort Worth, Texas, Wilson bought Tom Young's store, leaving Betty to raise four children and manage the store with the help of a store manager, a meat manager, and a cashier. He stayed in the Army for over a year, at which time he was honorably discharged because of the point system. (Photograph courtesy of Betty Stewart Patton.)

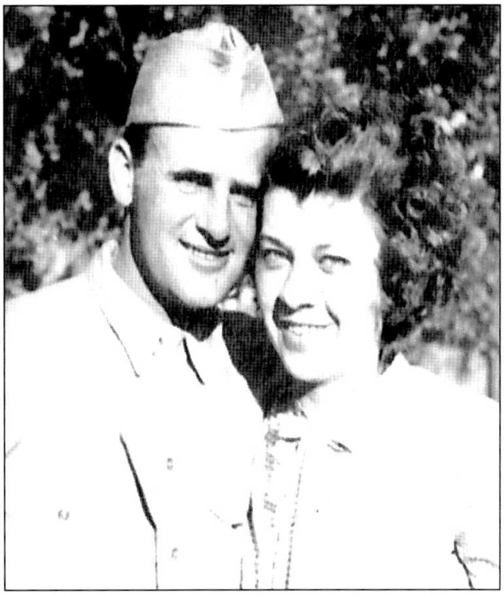

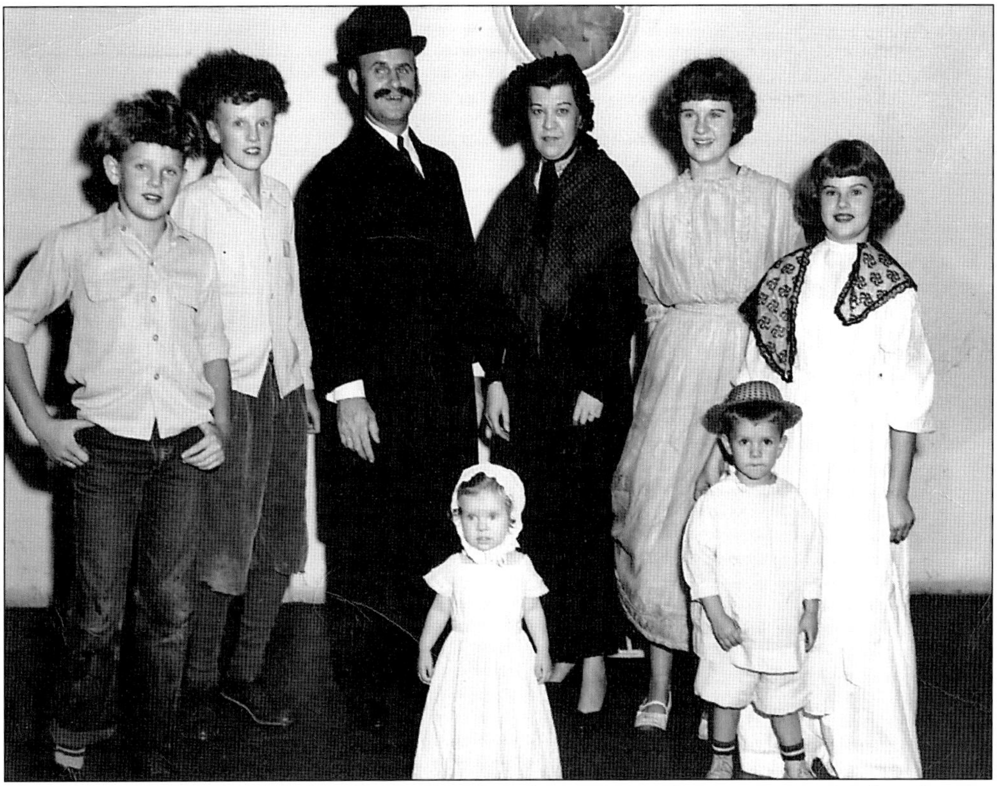

The Patton family was dressed as pioneers for Historical Pantomime Night for the 150th anniversary of the First Presbyterian Church, celebrated on September 19, 1954. In the back row, pictured from left to right, are Richard "Dick," David "Dee," Wilson, Betty, Beth Ann, and Mary Jane. In the front row, from left to right, are Nancy and Robert "Rob." David died at the age of 53 in 1994 from asbestosis, contracted when he was in the Navy. (Photograph courtesy of Betty Stewart Patton.)

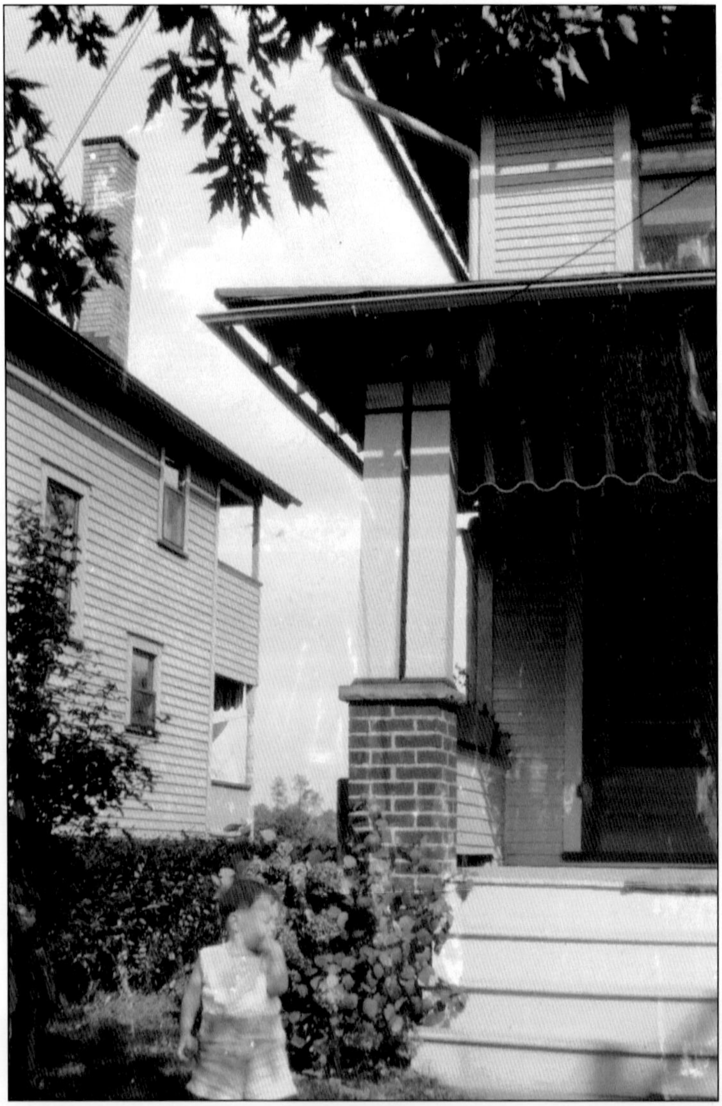

Don Creed, at around one year old, is shown in front of his family's home at 47 Mackey Street in 1931. The home is worth mentioning because it was a Sears Catalog home. Sears sold homes that could be ordered by catalog from 1916 through 1933. The homes would arrive by train in two boxcars with all the lumber ready-cut and numbered. In looking through a reproduction of the Sears, Roebuck 1926 House Catalog, the Creed home can be seen on page 48 and was called "The Gladstone." It was an Honor-Bilt home, No. P3222, "Already Cut" and fitted and sold for $2,029. The "Honor Bilt" modern homes were better quality than the "Standard Built" homes. Incredibly, in looking through the catalog, some of the homes did not include bathrooms. However, The Gladstone included a bathroom in the upstairs, along with three bedrooms. The downstairs had a living room on the front left side, a dining room on the front right side, and the kitchen behind the dining room. In 1937, Don Creed's father, Carl, altered the house somewhat, as the left side of the porch was added onto the living room. Also, his father dug a basement out under the porch by hand to make a shop and a fruit cellar. Imagine him digging all that dirt out by hand and taking it by wheelbarrow up the basement steps. Carl Creed worked as a cashier at the Hubbard Banking Company. (Photograph courtesy of Don Creed.)

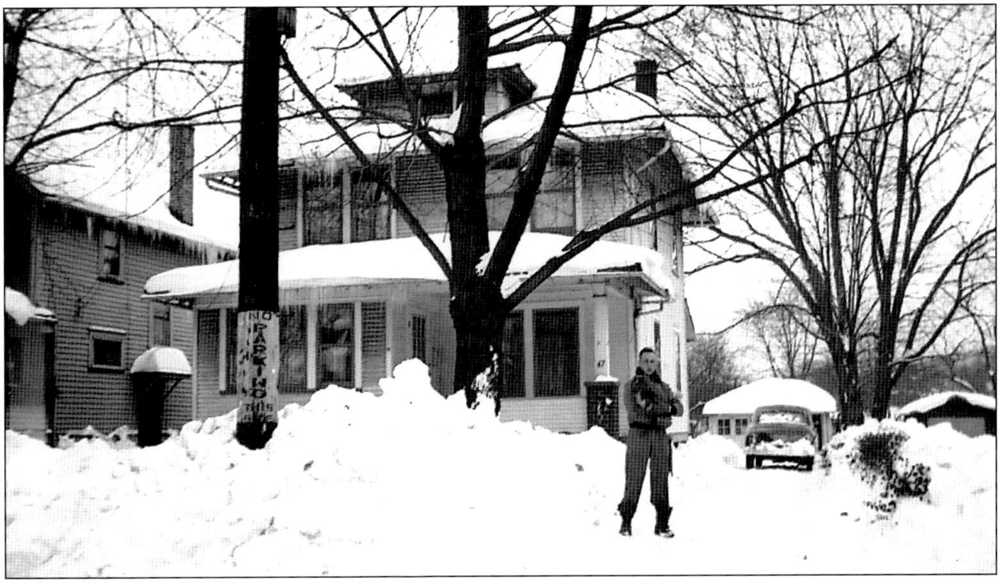

Don Creed stands in front of his house on 47 Mackey Street after the big Christmas 1950 snowstorm. It was a "Winter Wonderland" until Don's mother, Mary, decided that she needed to have some things from Patton's Grocery Store. Don made it there and back using his sled to transport the groceries home. The next day the snow was piled up 10 feet in front of stores with only a path dug from the street to the doors. (Photograph courtesy of Don Creed.)

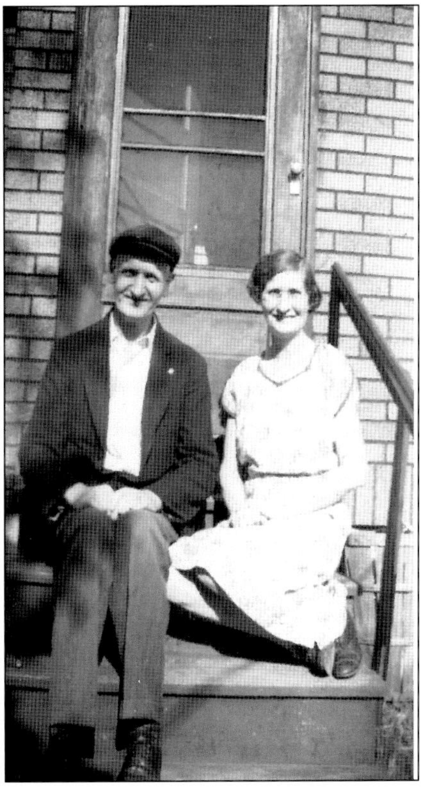

Mike and Lottie Zileski are shown sitting on their back porch at their home on 52 Mackey Street. Mike came from Poland when he was only six months old and his wife, Lottie Vogel Zileski, who was German and Polish, came at age 16. After sailing to New York, she rode a train to Youngstown, and then walked to Hubbard where she had relatives. Mike and Lottie's children included John, Ambrose, Katheryn, Clara, Margaret, Eleanor, Florence, Agnes, and Lucille. (Photograph courtesy of Gerald and Mala Smith.)

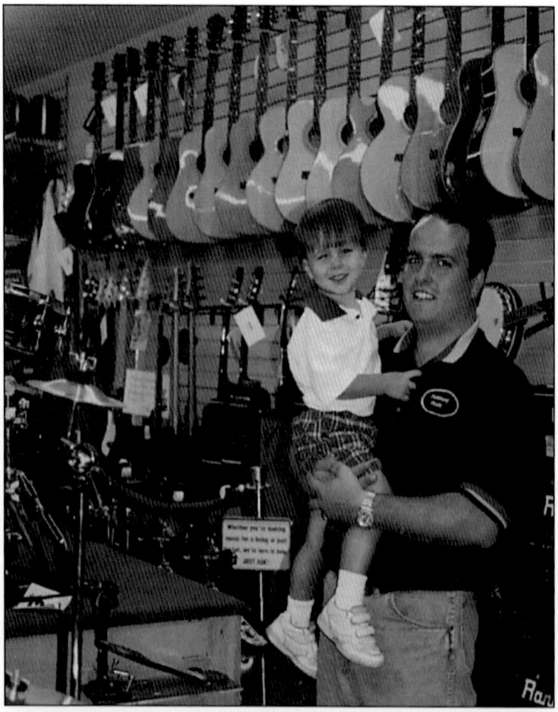

Mark Tirabassi, co-owner of Hubbard Music, is shown in 1998 with his two-year-old son, Nate. Mark opened his store in 1990. There were 10 to 15 students taking music lessons per week at first, but today, teachers provide music lessons to 233 students per week. Many students perform at the annual Hubbard Music Recital, held at the Hubbard High School Auditorium. Parents Marge and Mario Tirabassi help with lesson scheduling and maintenance. (Photograph courtesy of Mark Tirabassi.)

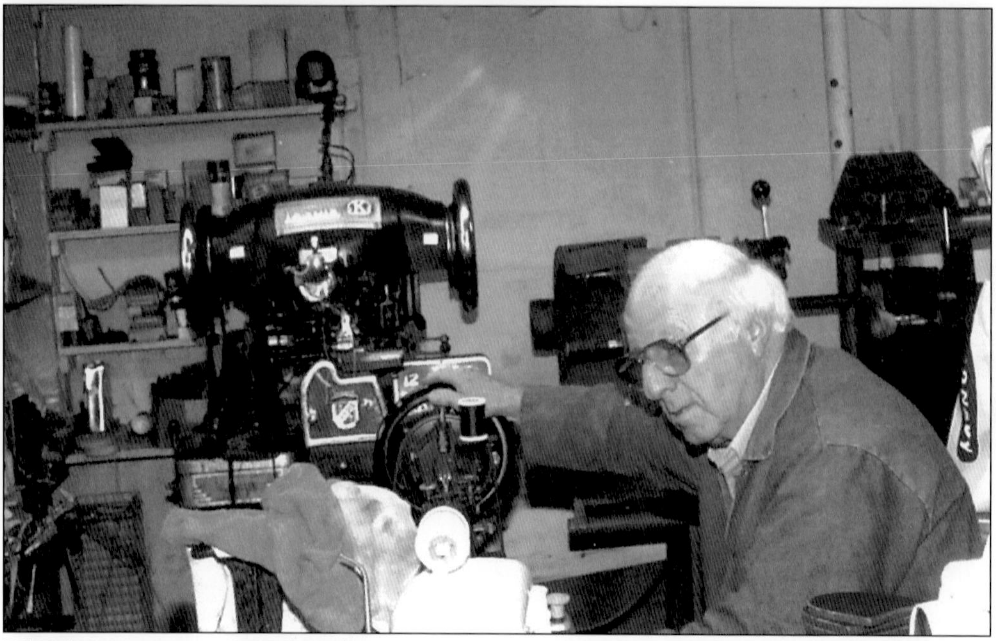

Ed Palestro, owner of Frank's Shoe Repair, 512 North Main Street, is repairing items with equipment that was purchased by his father, Frank, in 1942 for $4,000. Frank emigrated from Italy when he was 17, learned the shoe repair trade in New York City, and came to Hubbard, opening his business in the barn of the Huff farm after purchasing the property for $2,500. The horses had been kept downstairs and the hay upstairs. Ed took over the shop when he retired from Federal Wholesale in 1993. (Photograph courtesy of Ed Palestro.)

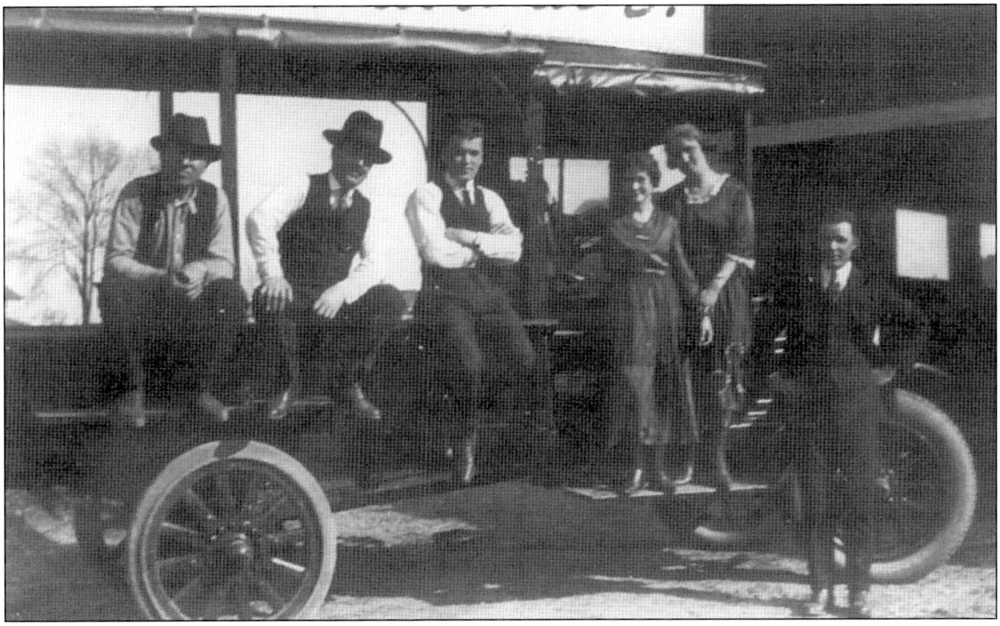

Pictured in this photograph from 1921, from left to right, are Nick Moga, Eli Curia, John Antinie, Mrs. Antinie, Carolina Poparad, and John Lupu, the "Ice Man." John delivered ice to homes and businesses for their iceboxes. Before the electric refrigerator, people used iceboxes to keep their food cold. A company from Farrell, Pennsylvania supplied John's ice. Two of his biggest customers were the New York Central Railroad Company's dining cars and the hotel that was located near the roundhouse at Coalburg Yard. (Photograph courtesy of Eli Moga.)

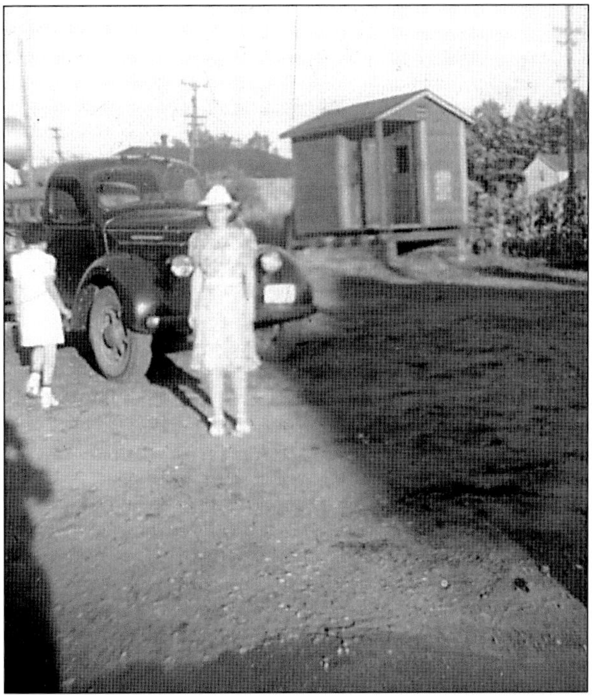

The icehouse can be seen in this picture from the mid 1930s, when kindly Mr. John Lupu delivered ice to homes for iceboxes. People would put a sign in their window to indicate how many pounds of ice they needed. Mr. Lupu would chip the ice off his block of ice, leaving slivers of ice that neighborhood boys would take. Mr. Lupu would shoo them away, but later would give the ice slivers to the girls, who were better behaved. The girls in the picture are Dolly Brownlee Hardin and Betty Brownlee Malin, daughters of Lloyd and Hazel Brownlee. (Photograph courtesy of Dolly Brownlee Hardin.)

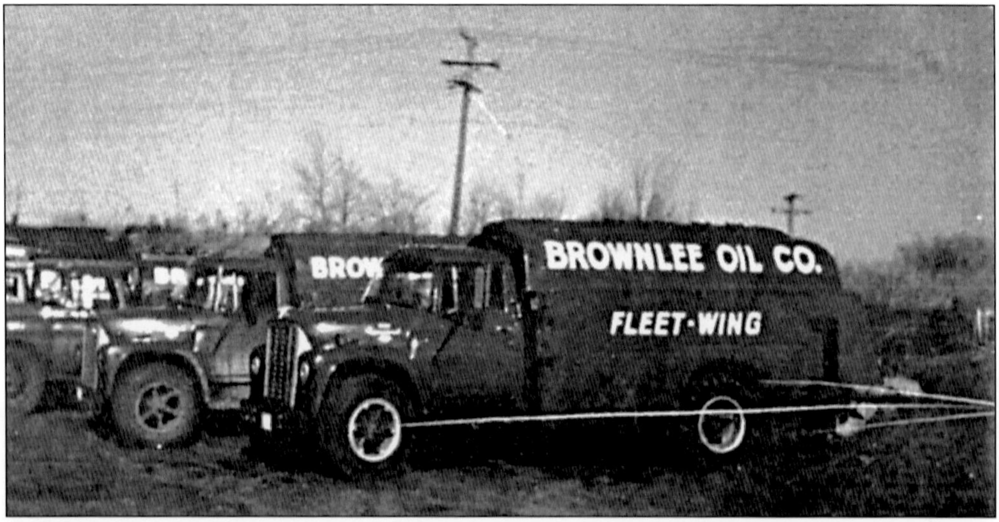

Lloyd and Hazel Brownlee purchased the gas station at 757 North Main Street that was owned by French Clingan in the early 1930s. The Brownlee Oil Company sold Fleet-Wing brand fuel oil and kerosene, sold gas at the "filling station," and repaired cars at their company for approximately 40 years. In 1975, Pennzoil bought the business as they had bought out Fleet-Wing. Later, Pennzoil sold the business to the Jugenheimers. The building is now used for storage. (Photograph courtesy of Dolly Brownlee Hardin.)

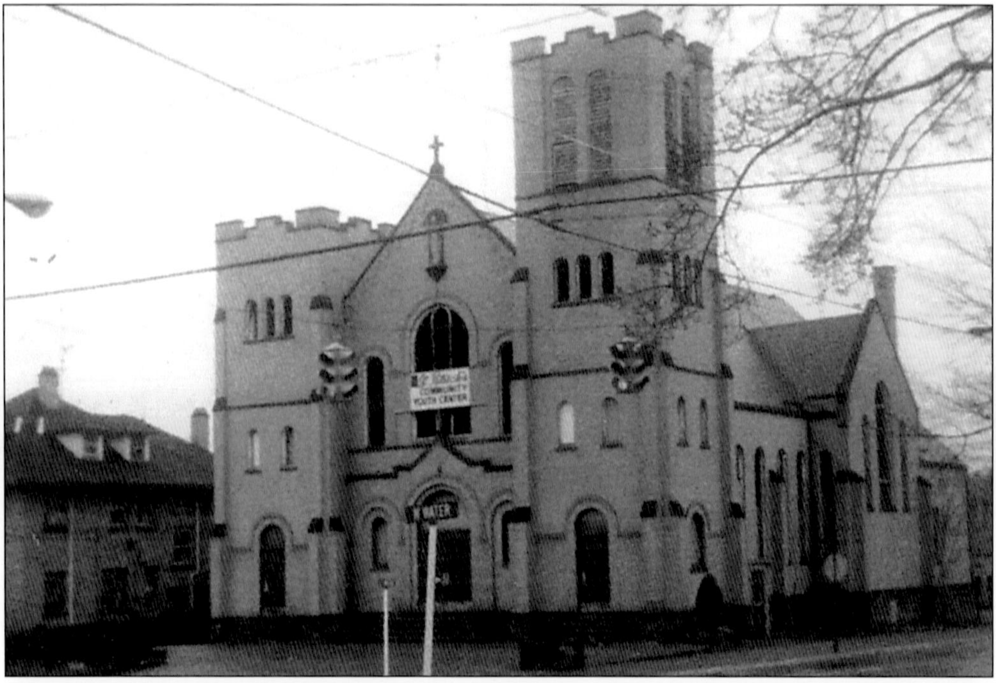

The yellow brick St. Patrick's Church was built in 1908 and located on the corner of North Main Street and East Water Street. An earlier frame church was built in 1867 on the west side of North Main Street across from the present church, which was built in 1967. The yellow brick church was used for a time as a community youth center, but eventually was demolished to make way for a parking lot. (Photograph courtesy of Jim and Imogene Deiwert.)

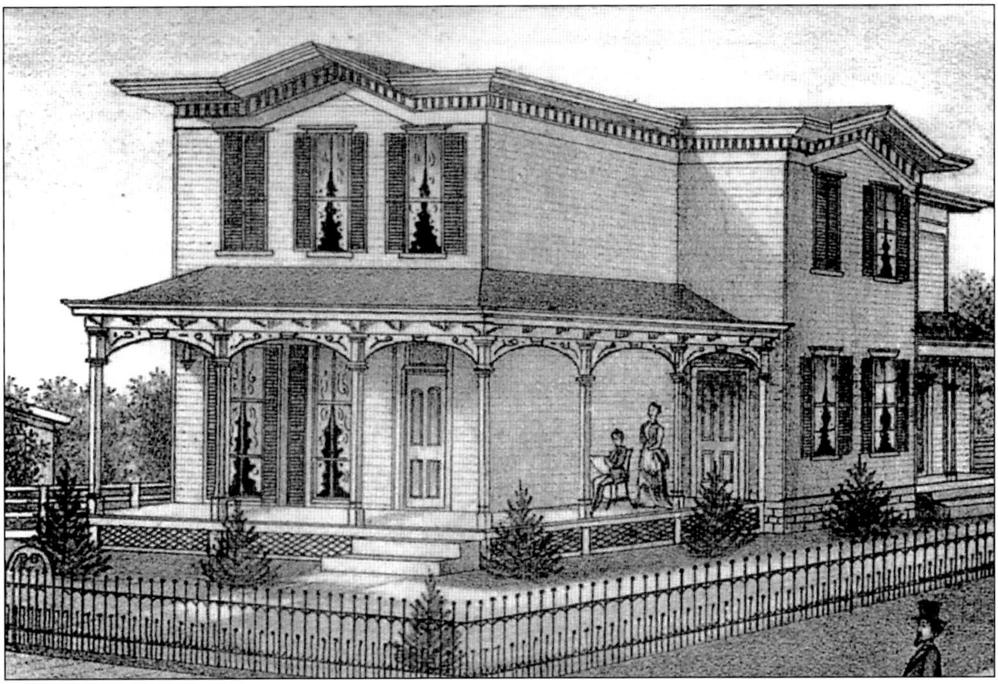

A.P. and Rebecca Flaugher built their home on North Main Street in 1873 on the northwest part of original Lot No. 46. A.P. Flaugher was the founder of the Hubbard Iron Company. John Anderson purchased the Flaugher home in 1905 for his business, the Anderson Funeral Home. In 1943, Clyde Kelley purchased the business and in the 1950s his son, C. Robert Kelley, joined him. In June of 1989, Dennis Robb purchased the business and it is now called the Kelley-Robb Funeral Home. (Photograph courtesy of Dennis Robb.)

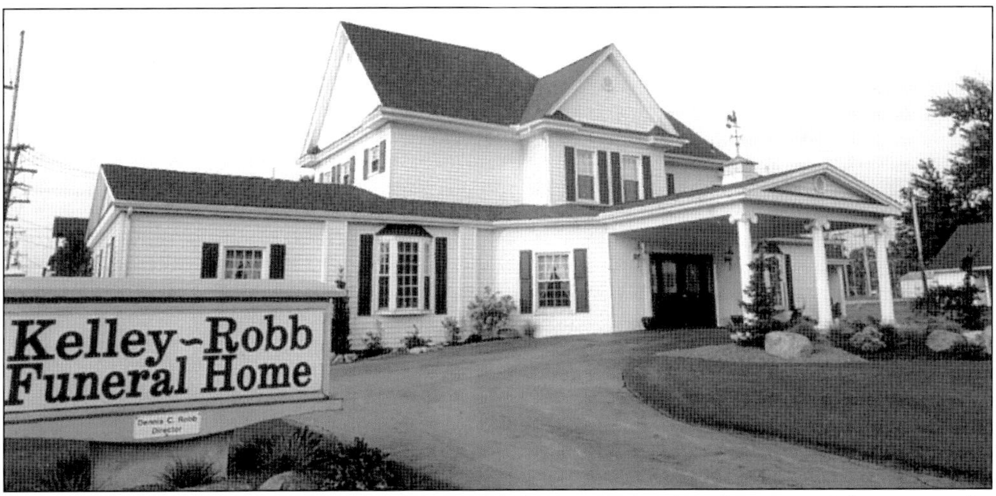

Dennis Robb grew up in Hubbard, and returned after 20 years of working out of the area in the mortuary field. The Kelley-Robb Funeral Home has been remodeled many times. The original Italianate-style roof is no longer visible as it was completely remodeled into a steeper roofline. There was a new room added onto the front of the house, which encompasses both the porch and front door area of the house. The original front door of the house is now inside the funeral home. (Photograph courtesy of Dennis Robb.)

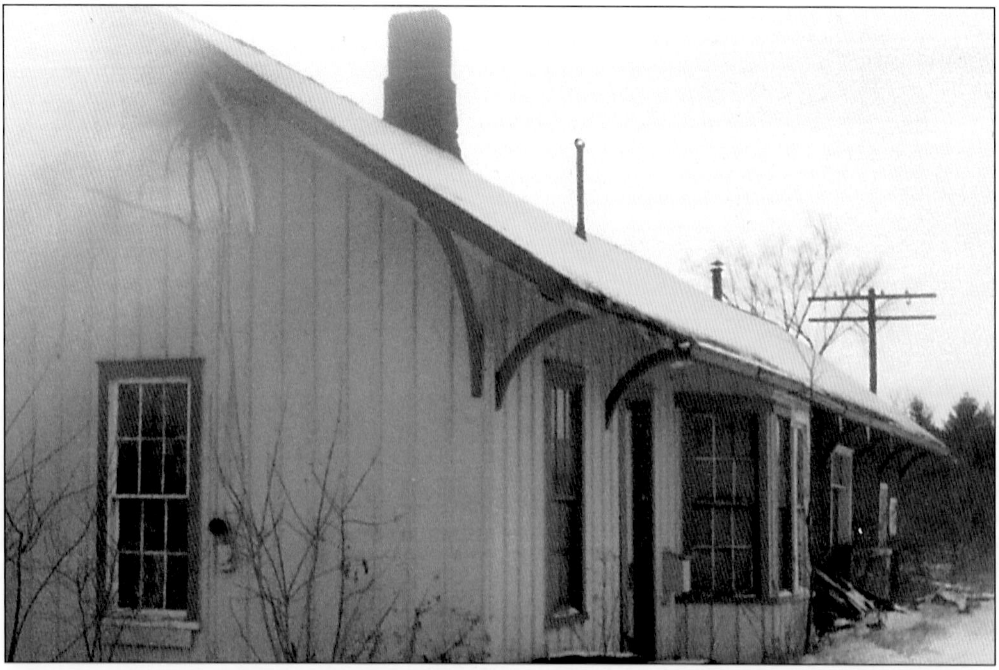

The old Pennsylvania Central Station, formerly the Lake Shore and Michigan South Station, was built in 1887. Used by passenger railroads in the past, it was later used for billing freight accounts. (Photograph courtesy of Hubbard Historical Society.)

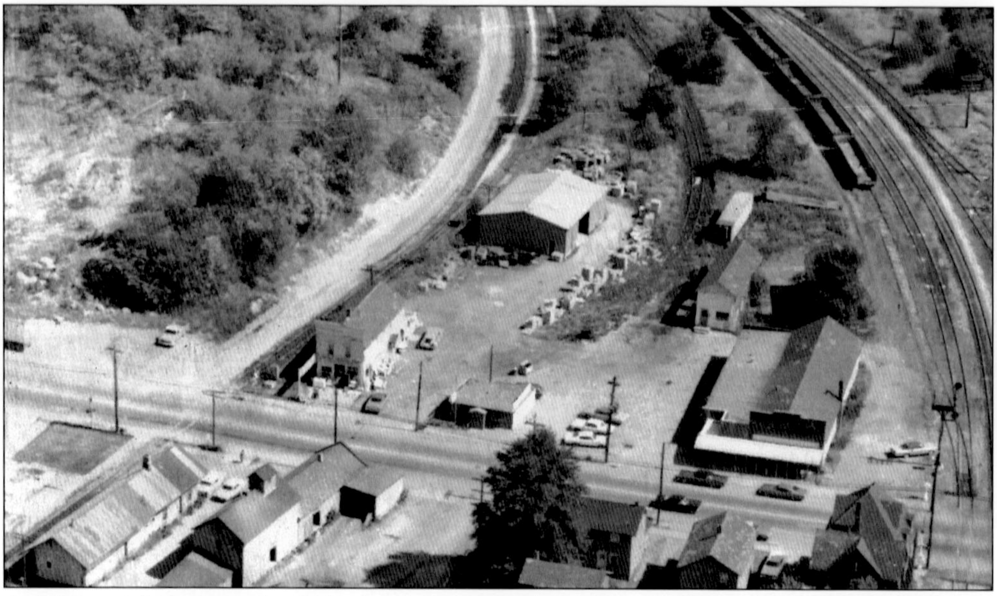

A 1973 aerial photograph of North Main Street shows the old Pennsylvania Central Station next to the Penn Central Railroad tracks (which have been removed) and to the right is the Hubbard Coal and Supply Company. Across the street is the Trading Post and at the bottom right is the Marconi Lodge (Collier's Hotel and Bar in the early 1900s). To the far right is the building that was once the McKelvey Store Company, which currently houses several businesses. (Photograph courtesy of Dave Barlett.)

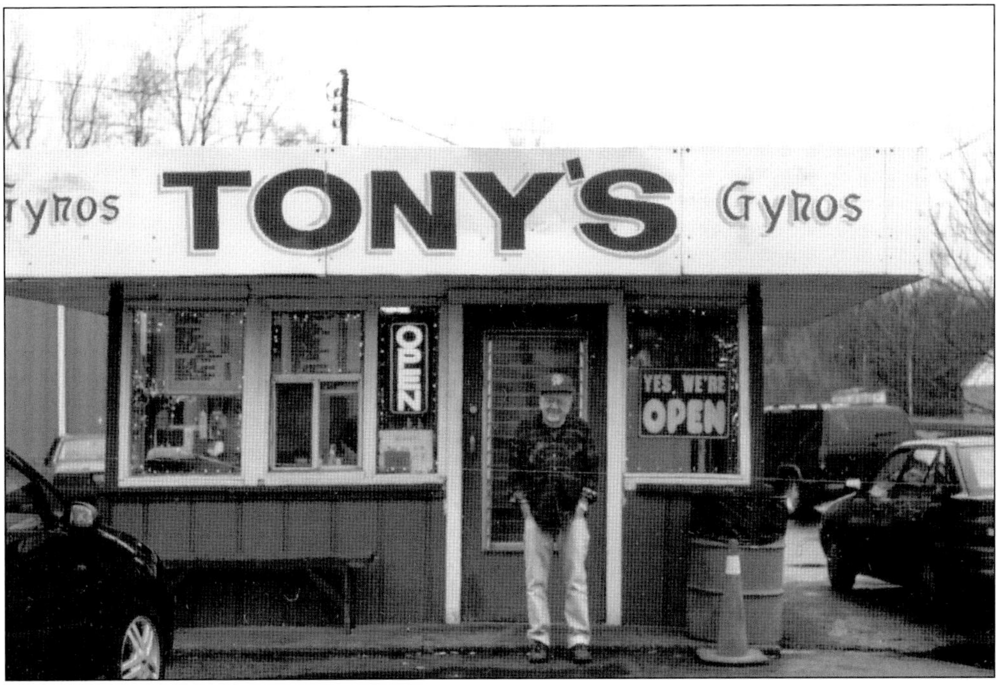

Tom Gast, shown, was a fireman with the New York Central Railroad Co. when he first came to the area from McKee's Rocks, Pennsylvania. When diesel engines replaced steam engines in 1954, Tom became an engineer. He bought Tony's Sandwich Shop in 1964 and retired as an engineer in 1986.

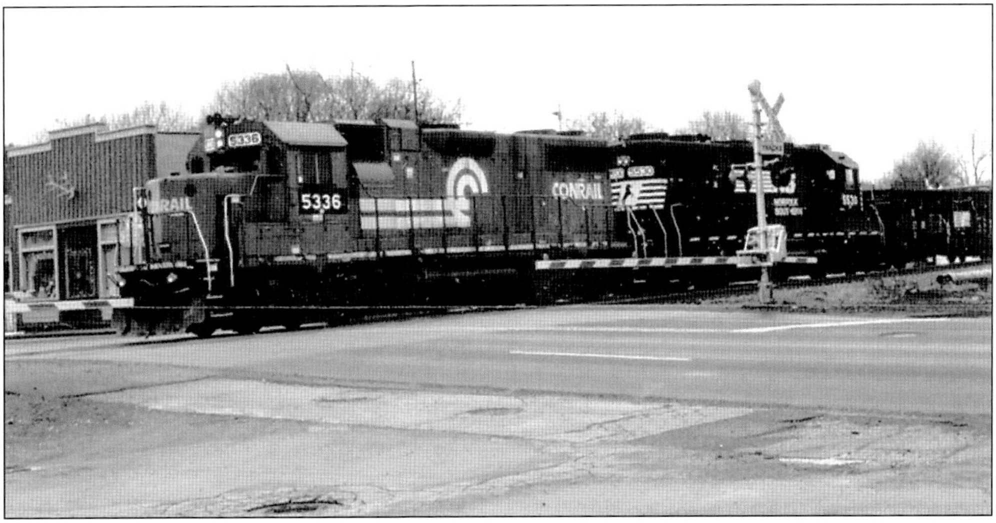

Conrail and Norfolk Southern locomotives cross North Main Street. In 1968, the New York Central and Pennsylvania Railroad merged to form Penn Central. In 1976, the federal government merged the Erie Lackawanna, Penn Central, and other railroads to form Conrail. In June of 1999, the CSX and Norfolk Southern Railroads bought Conrail, dividing it between them. The tracks on North Main Street travel east and north to Meadville, Pennsylvania, and west and south to Youngstown or west and north to Ashtabula. There is also a spur track that provides service to local industry in Hubbard and Masury.

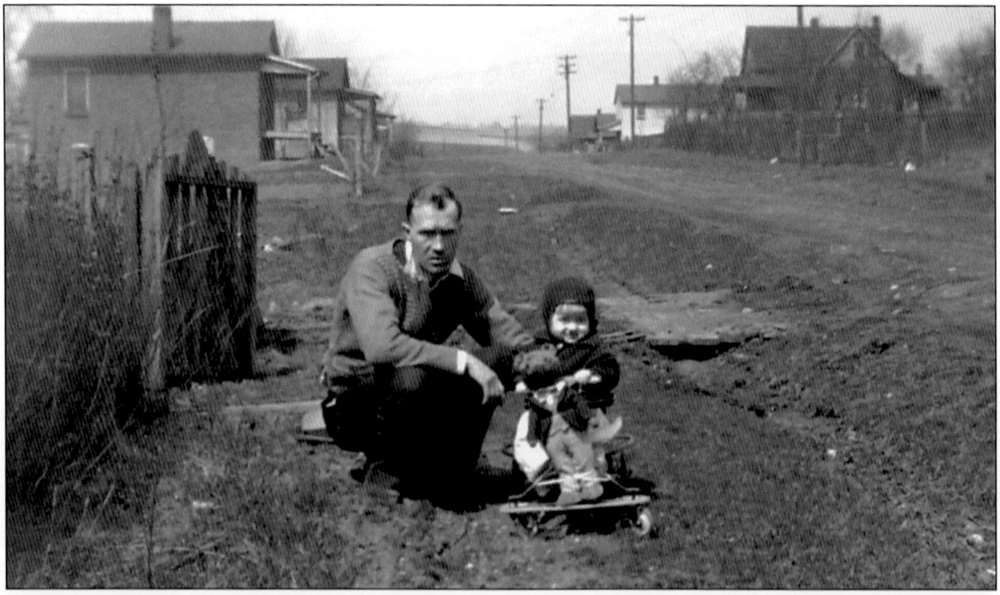

Anthony Halicki and his daughter, Ruth, are pictured in this 1937 photograph of Woodland Avenue. There was a neighborhood pump in the street that can be seen just to the left of the white house in the background. Since Hungarian and Polish immigrants settled on Woodland Avenue, it was known as "Little Budapest." (Photograph and history courtesy of Ruth Halicki Means.)

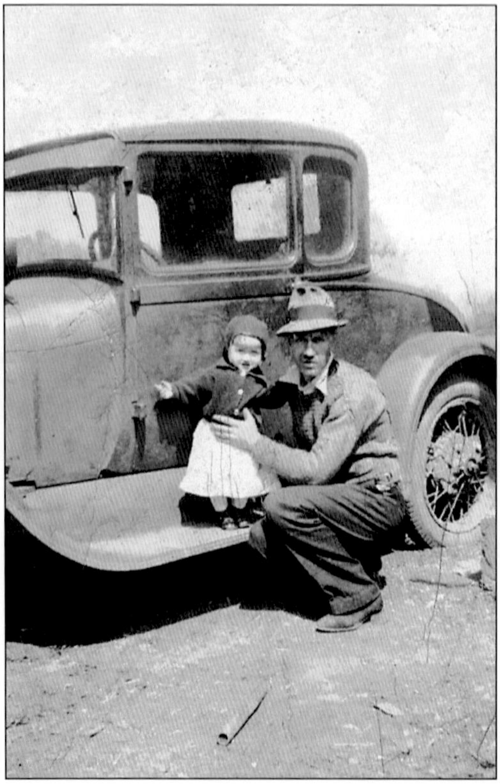

Anthony Halicki, proudly showing off his little one-year-old daughter Ruth, worked at Powell Pressed Steel Company on Erie Street. Ruth and her mom, Anna Kuty Halicki, would crawl under the fence that surrounded the plant in order to take lunch to Anthony. Anthony drove the tow motor, welded, and worked in the paint booth. At that time Powell Pressed Steel Company was a defense contractor and made parts for airplanes, invert bins, and fenders for boat trailers. (Photograph courtesy of Ruth Halicki Means.)

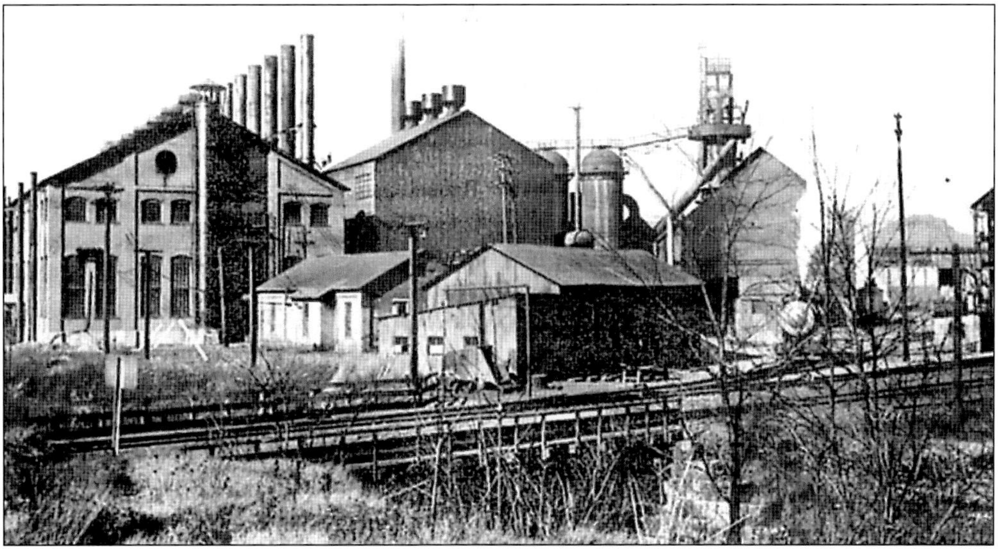

The Andrews and Hitchcock Furnace No. 1 was built in 1868 and Furnace No. 2 was built in 1871. Mules were used to supply power to charge the furnaces in the beginning. Iron was poured into molds and called pig iron. Youngstown Sheet and Tube bought the furnaces in 1914; they closed in 1959, and were dismantled in 1967. (Photograph courtesy of Emanuel Mageros.)

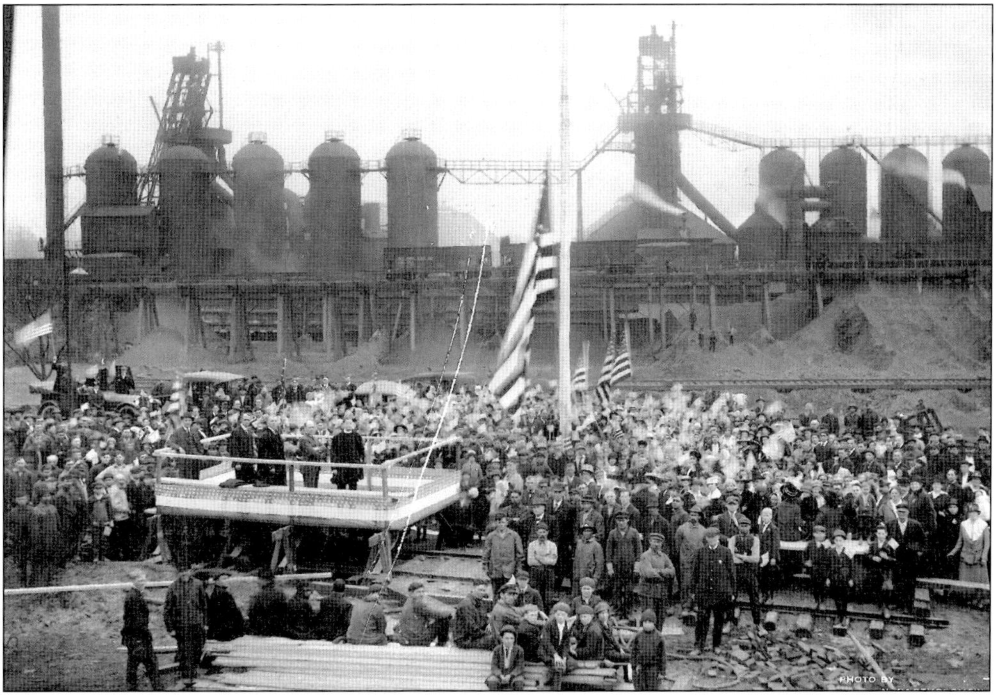

The Hubbard Furnace Reunion of 1918 is pictured in this photograph. A skip car took iron ore, limestone, and coke to the top of the furnace, where it was heated to a temperature of 1,600 degrees. It was then cast into sand or ingot molds. High school boys were hired to test the iron for the proper specifications, answer the phone, and sweep floors. The furnace produced 500 tons of iron per day. (Photograph courtesy of Nancy Gray Silvashy, history courtesy of Henry Pettitt and Don Hardin.)

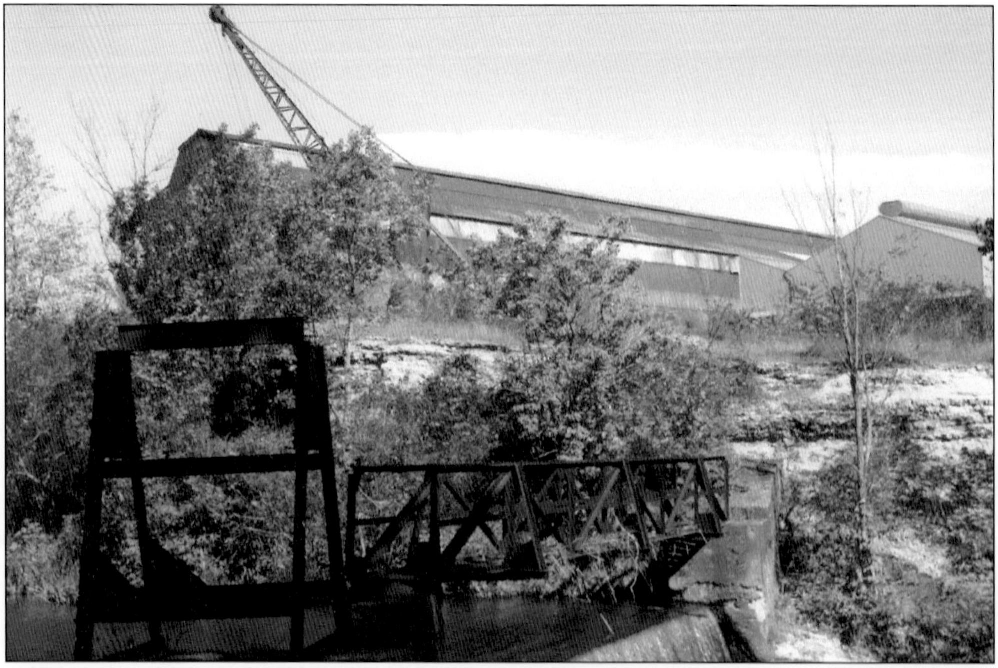

Ellwood Engineered Casting Co. at 7518 Masury Road bought Valley Vulcan Mould Company in 1991. They produce ingot mold products and highly engineered castings for various companies as well as for their steel ingot producing division. They have three 55-ton coreless induction furnaces that melt 900 tons of iron per day and a 140,000 square-foot foundry that turns molten iron into precision castings.

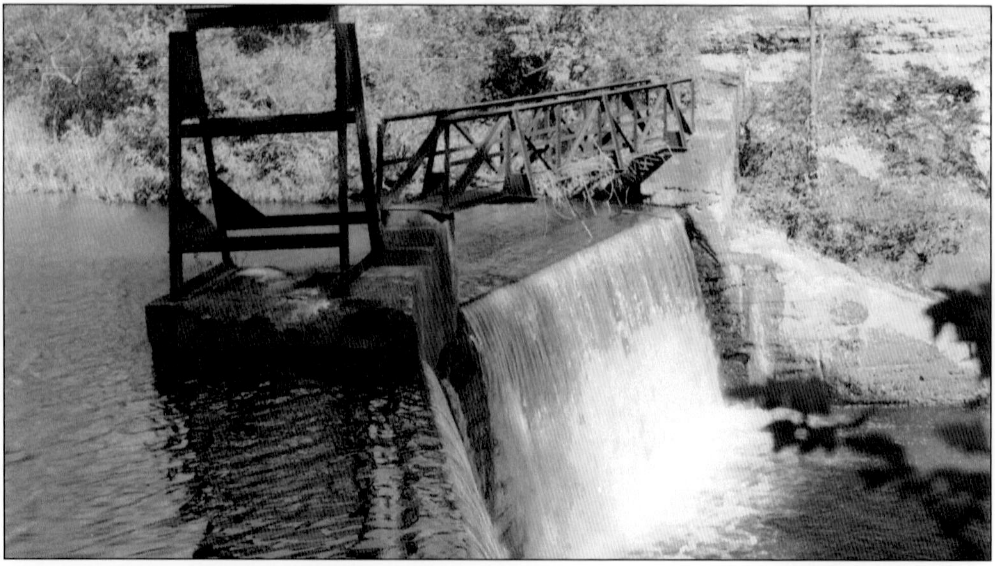

The dam behind the Ellwood Engineered Casting Company was used to provide water to the Hubbard Furnace many years ago. After the July 27, 2003 flood, Hubbard filed an application to request funding to breech the 100-year-old dam on Little Yankee Run as it was thought to be impeding the natural flow of water. The dam's drop is 10 to 14 feet; however, the lake is shallow due to sediment, which is an environmental concern.

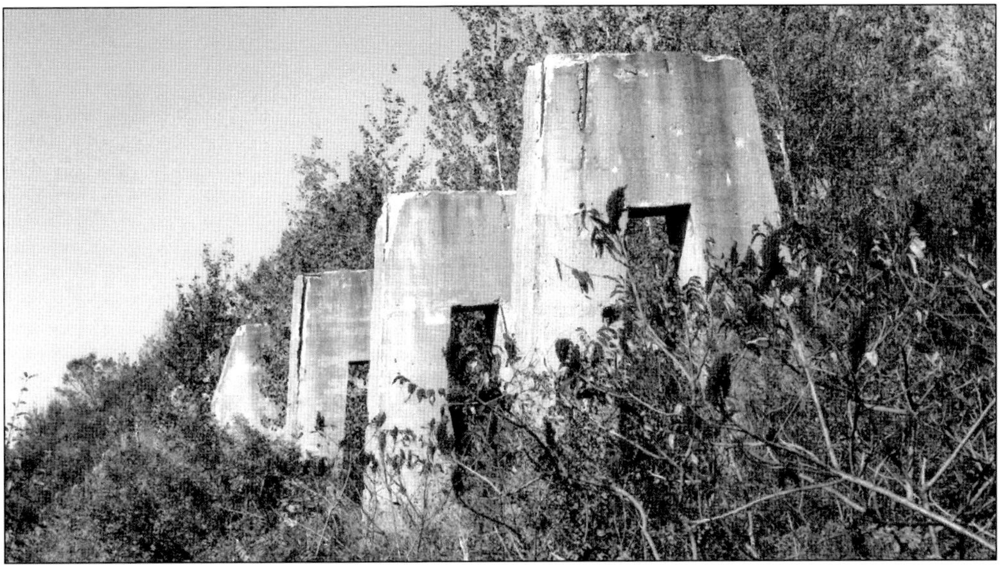

The trestles that run parallel with the railroad tracks on Elmwood Drive Extension are all that remain of the Sintering Plant that was built in the 1880s. On the top of the trestles, a railroad track ran that was used to dump the iron ore into containers below. The Sintering Plant recycled iron ore from the Hubbard Blast Furnace by dredging the lake behind the furnace or reclaiming iron ore from the smoke emitted from the furnace. At times, houses near the plant would turn red from the smoke that was produced by the plant.

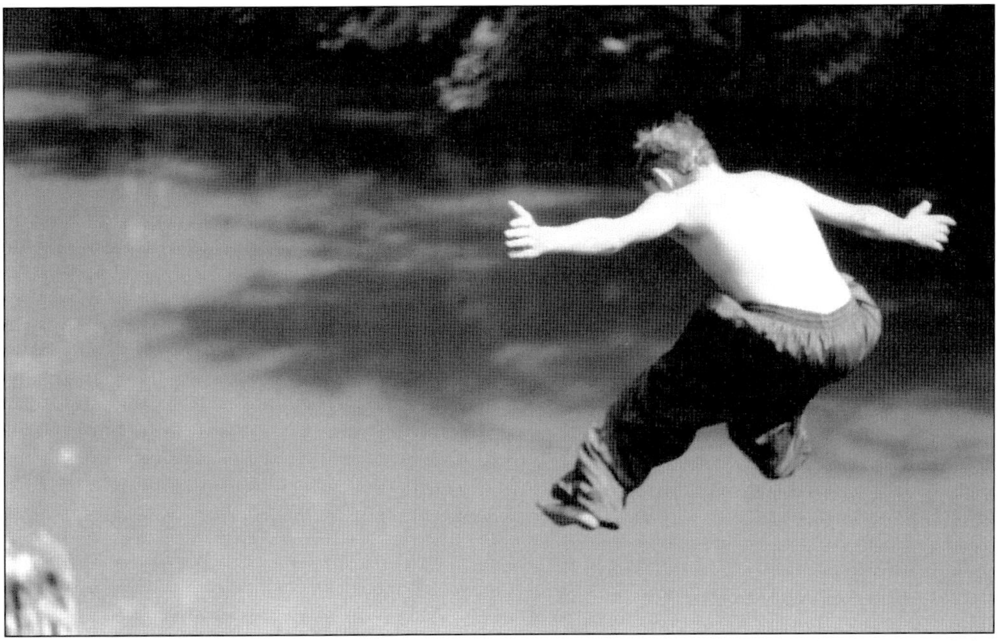

A dam was built on Little Yankee Creek to provide water for the old Hubbard Furnace and the lake still exists, even though the furnace is gone. Children enjoyed swimming in the lake, especially in the water that came from the furnaces, as it was so warm. Neighborhood children are still attracted to the lake, as shown in this photograph taken in the summer of 2004. (Photograph courtesy of Kurt Emch.)

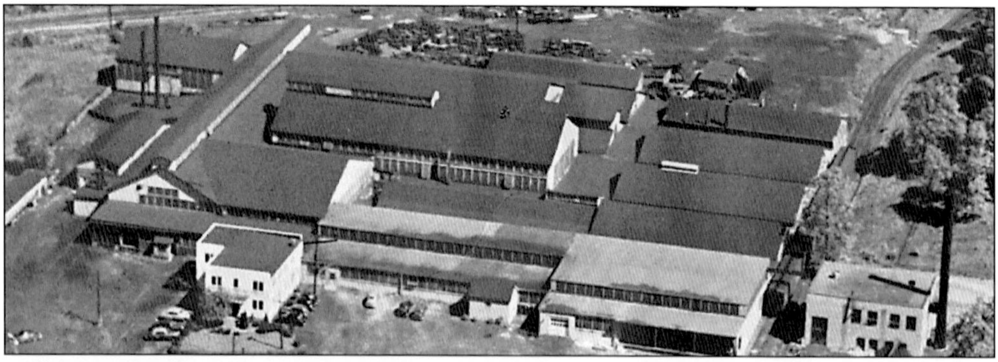

William J. Powell established Powell Pressed Steel Company on Erie Street in 1920. They made pressed steel products. During World War II, production went into making armor for vehicles, shell casings, and rocket caps. Later, they produced steel corrugated containers, bumpers, fuel tank supports, and a variety of steel stampings. Eli Moga's father, Nicolae (Nick) Moga who came from Romania in 1906 when he was 19 years old, started working as a laborer at Powell Pressed Steel in 1922. One day one of the hinges on a corrugated door broke from strong winds and Nick forged some new hinges and put the door back in place. When Mr. Powell asked who fixed the door, someone said, "that Romanian over there!" Mr. Powell pointed his finger at Nick and said, "Tomorrow, you'll start out as foreman in the assembly and welding department." Nick worked there more than 40 years. It closed in 1982 due to high labor costs, and was torn down in 1991 except for the shipping and machine shop. (Photograph courtesy of Emanuel Mageros.)

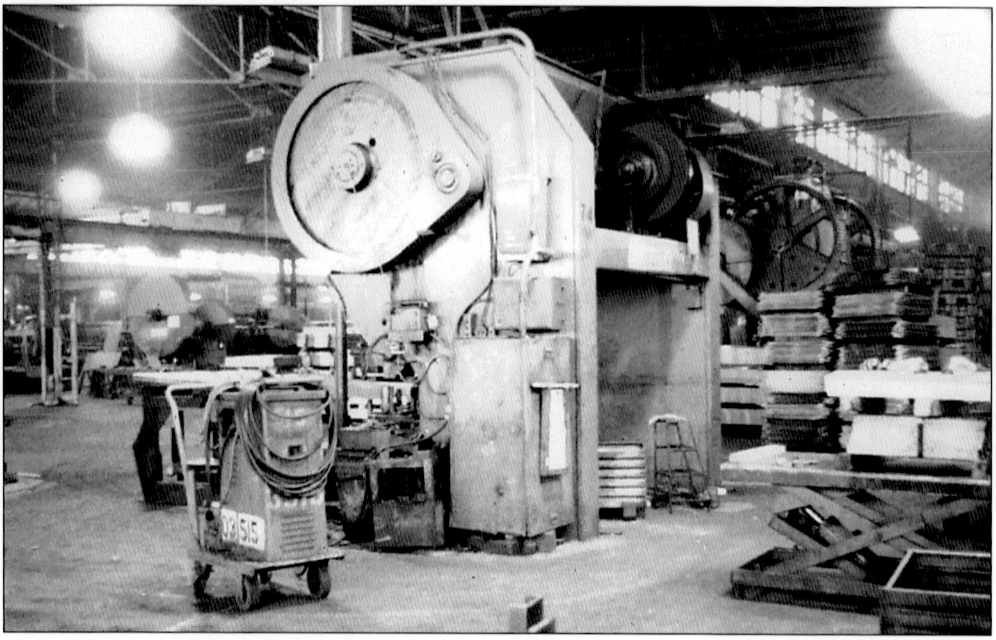

This 1980-photograph taken inside the Powell Pressed Steel Co. shows a large press that was used to make corrugated boxes. A die was placed into the press to corrugate a piece of steel, and then another press would flange the top. A die would go into the original press to flatten the flange. Another press would place a 90-degree angle in the steel, which would be sent to the welding department. The welders finished the box by welding the two box sides and the bottom together. (Photograph courtesy of Emanuel Mageros.)

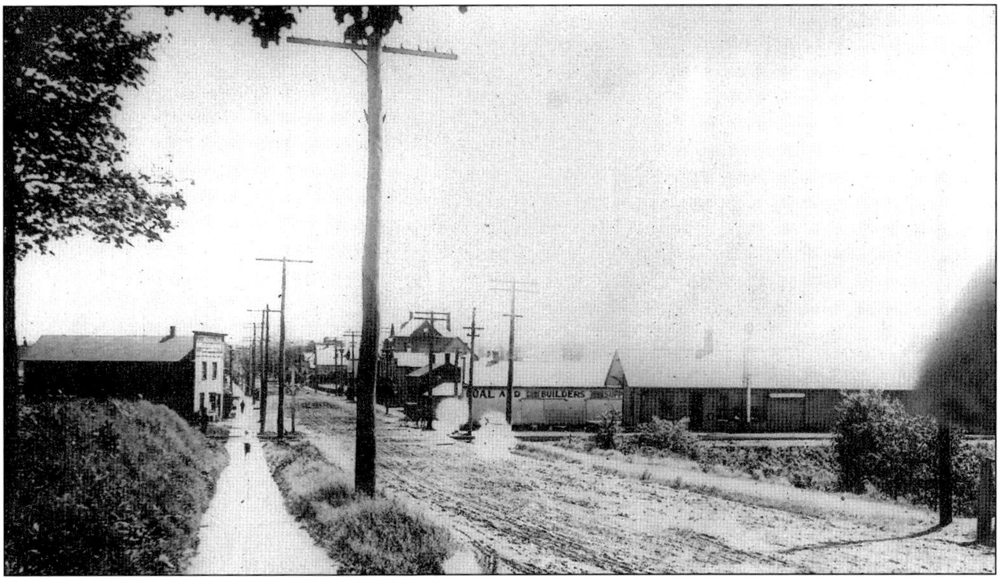

The Pennsylvania Central Railroad Depot and Hubbard Coal and Supply are shown in this 1910 photograph of North Main Street looking south. A long-time Hubbard resident remembered cattle being driven down North Main Street, which was nothing but mud, after being unloaded from cattle cars at the Erie Depot, located south of the Penn Central Depot. Any available men or boys would help in the drive. Their destination was a slaughterhouse on East Liberty Street behind the old Stiver/Greenwood Chevrolet. (Photograph courtesy of Dave Barlett.)

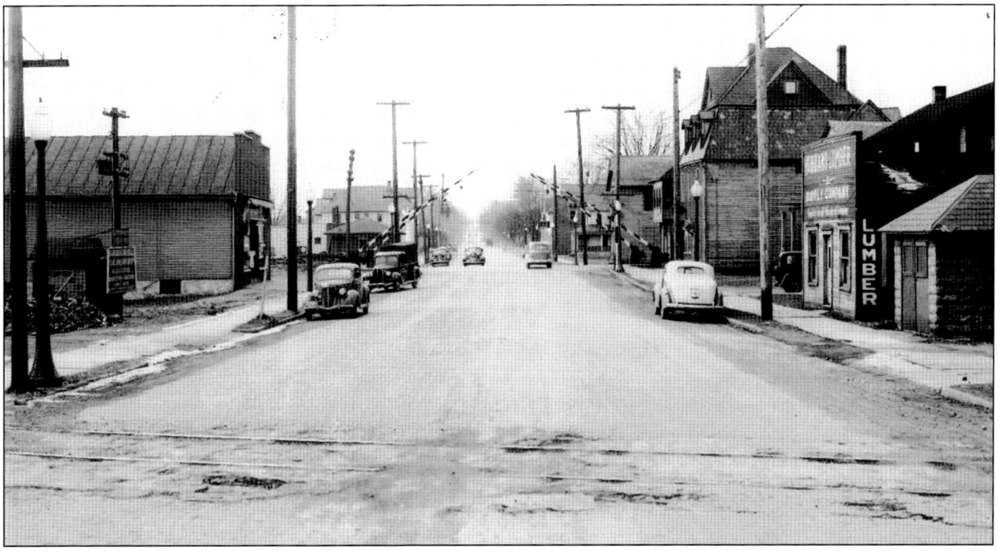

The G. M. McKelvey store, on the left in this late-1930s photograph, opened in September of 1877 and sold groceries, dry goods, and animal feed. In 1891, the building was the site of the Hubbard Store Company, a "company store" owned by Andrews and Hitchcock who operated the Hubbard Blast Furnace. Local coal miners were paid here in cash. In 1957, James Devine opened Devine's Super Market here. New York Central Railroad tracks are seen in the foreground (taken out in the middle 1960s); the Erie Lackawanna Railroad tracks are seen in the background. (Photograph courtesy of Emanuel Mageros.)

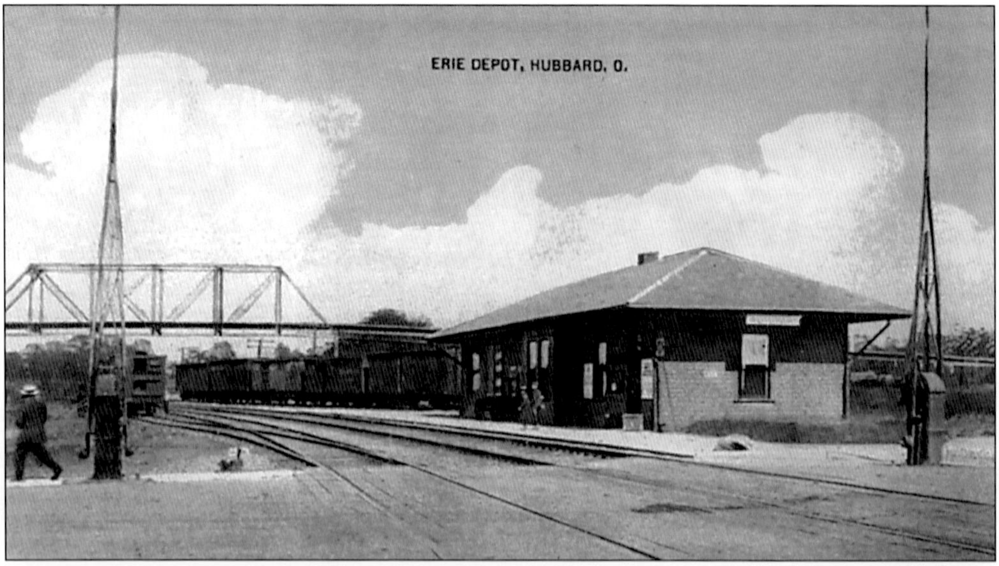

The streetcar viaduct (elevated streetcar tracks) can be seen in the background in this picture of the Erie Depot on North Main Street from the early 1900s. Erie Street is on the right. The viaduct crossed over Erie Street, the Erie Railroad train tracks, and the Pennsylvania Central tracks to the east of North Main Street and would take passengers to New Castle, Sharon, and Youngstown. (Photograph courtesy of Vince Pompili.)

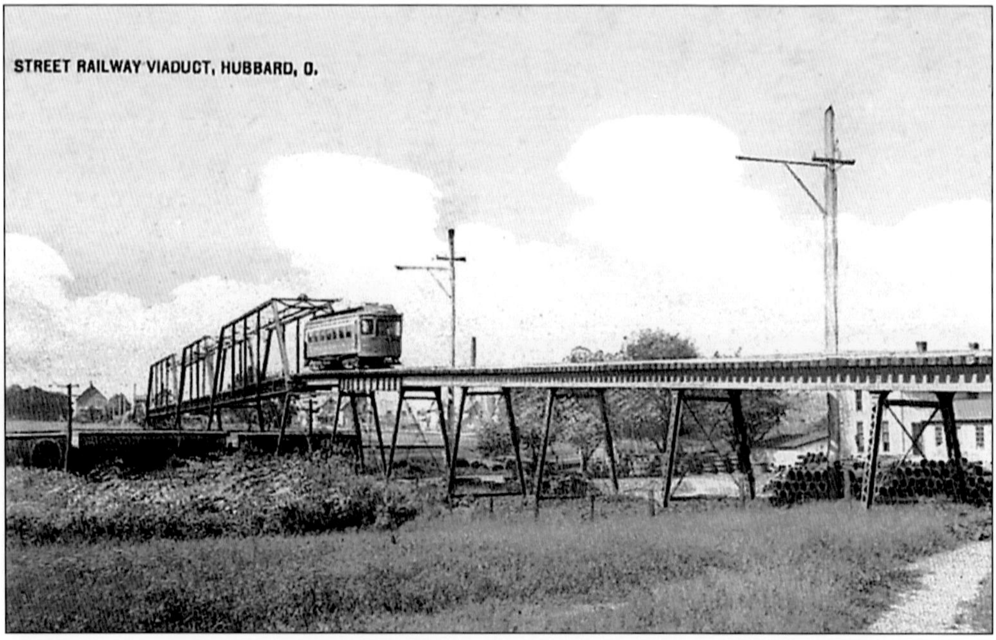

The streetcar viaduct crossed over the Pennsylvania Central tracks, the Erie Railroad tracks, Erie Street, and connected to the Hubbard-New Castle line which traveled south, and the Hubbard-Sharon line which went north to Sharon and south to Youngstown. Houses on Henry Street can be seen to the left of the viaduct. Remnants of the tracks can still be seen on Henry Street. (Photograph courtesy of Hubbard Historical Society.)

A 1912 photograph of the C & C Coal Company shows Lillian Lucille Campbell Struble on the left with two of her coworkers. Lillian was born on December 12, 1893 and died on January 30, 1975. Bill Stevenson bought the company in 1929 and changed the name to Hubbard Coal and Supply Co. Tom Cooksey owned the store until August of 1999 when Dave and Cathy Barlett bought the store. The Barletts added carpets and floor coverings to the inventory. (Photograph courtesy of Dave Barlett.)

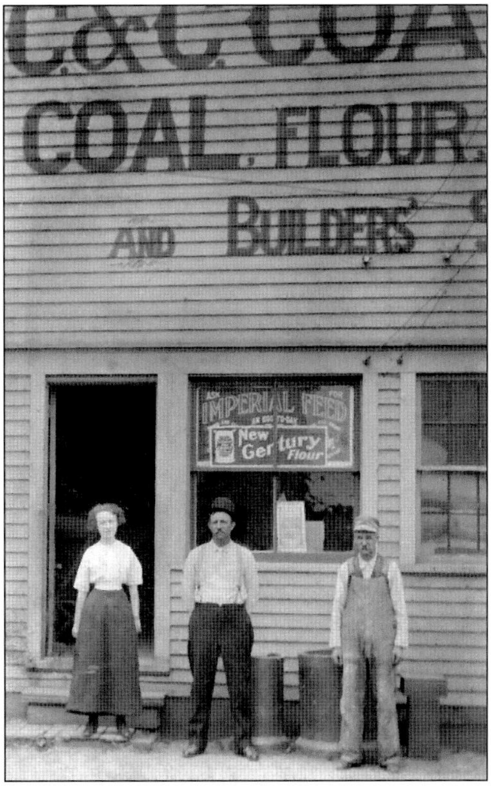

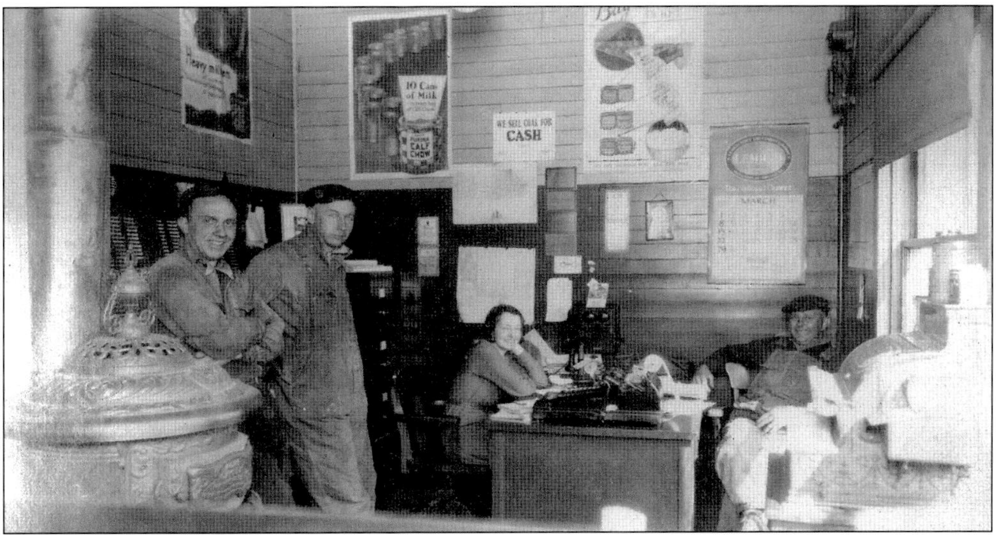

Shown, from left to right, are Frank Anderson, William C. Stevenson, S. Hayman, and Lawrence Weiser Sr. in 1931 at the Hubbard Coal & Supply. Lawrence drove the truck, mixed feed, and delivered coal to people's houses. Occasionally, while delivering coal, he would startle homeowners who would be in their basements, taking baths. Lawrence's son, Art, started working in the store in 1948 and mixed feed for customers. A feed mix of salt, molasses and other nutrients would be added to ground crushed corncobs and oats. (Photograph courtesy of Dave Barlett, history courtesy of Art and Violet Weiser.)

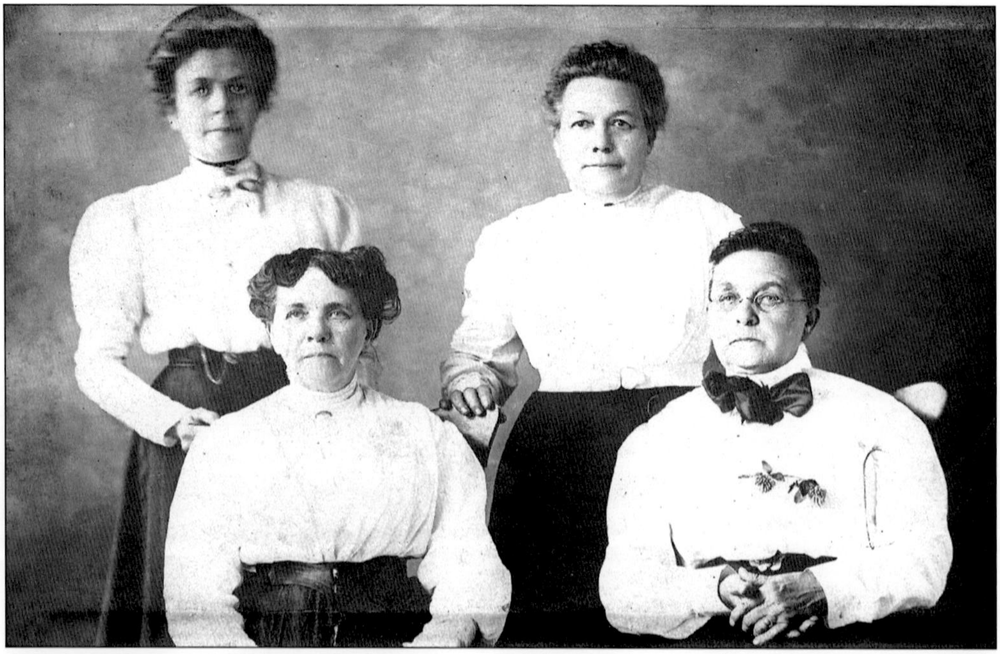

A picture taken in 1895 shows, clockwise from top left, Lois Flint Veach (wife of Norman Veach), Isabelle Flint Cook, Sara Flint Murphy (who was married to John Murphy), and Ruth Flint. Sara was the mother of Anna Murphy, Jack Wilson's great grandmother. (Photograph courtesy of Jack Wilson.)

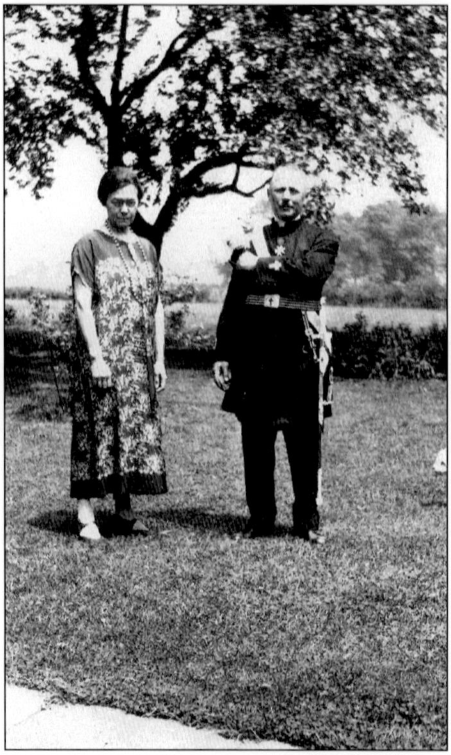

Anna Murphy Kashner and John S. Kashner are in the backyard of their home at 335 Drummond Avenue. John is in his Masonic uniform. He was a 32nd degree Mason—the second highest level a Mason can attain in America. Anna and John had four children, Irene, Lenore, Stanley, and Laverne. (Photograph courtesy of Jack Wilson.)

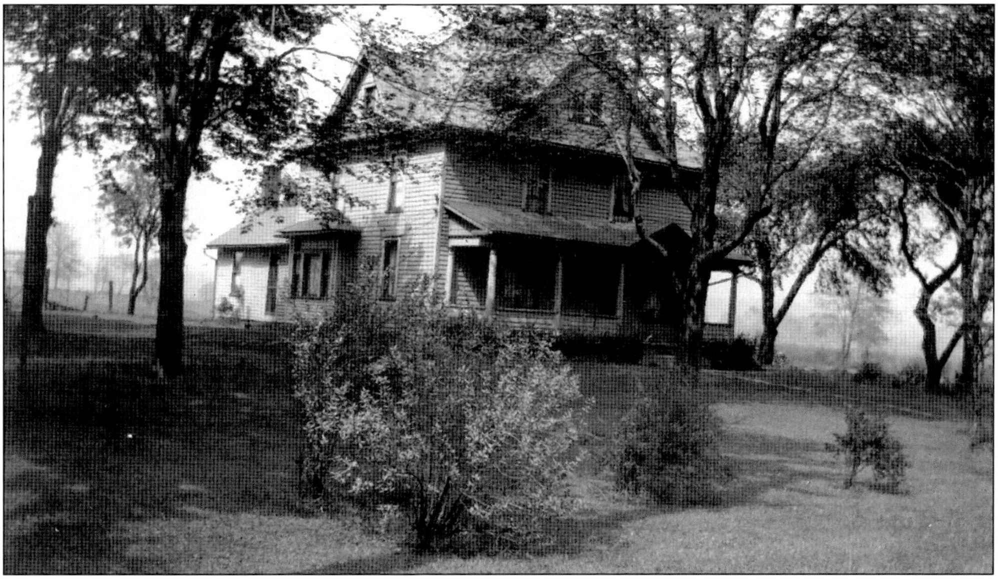

The house located at 335 Drummond Avenue was home to Anna Murphy Kashner and John S. Kashner and their four children, Irene, Lenore, Stanley, and Laverne. Laverne was Jack Wilson's mother. (Photograph courtesy of Jack Wilson.)

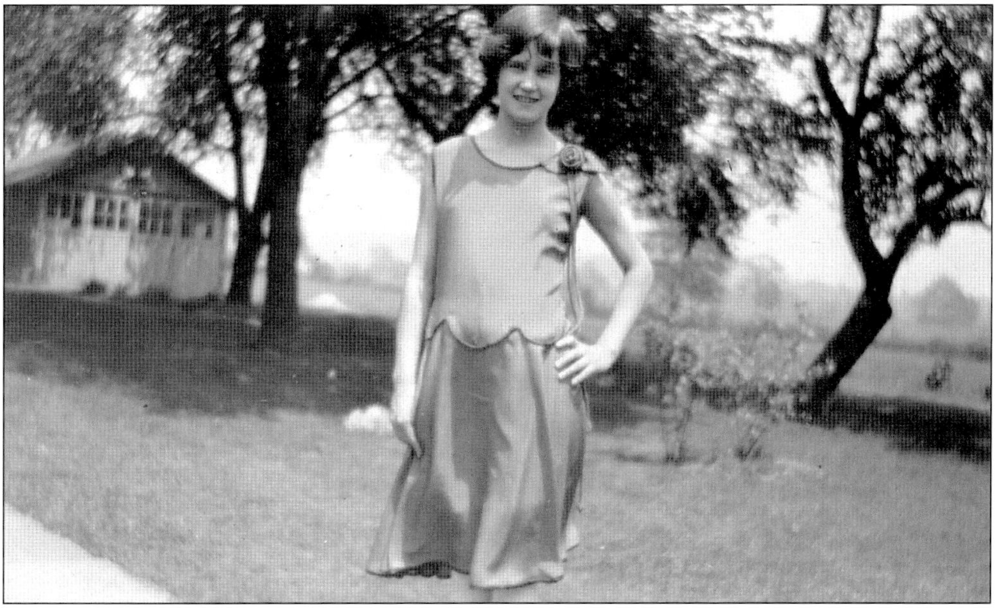

Laverne Kashner is seen here in front of the family garage at 335 Drummond Avenue. She was probably around 12 years old in this picture. She married T.J. Wilson from New York State who was a tool and die designer for Powell Pressed Steel and later worked for Commercial Shearing. They moved to 136 Christian Avenue, the former G.M. McKelvey home. (Photograph courtesy of Jack Wilson.)

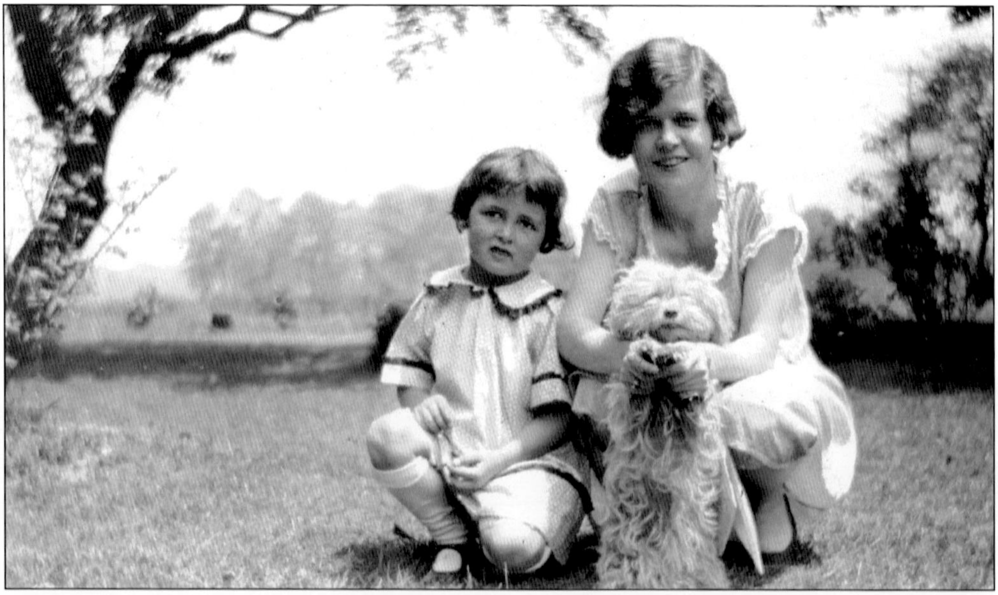

On the left is Evelyn Jones Sinn (daughter of Lenore Kashner) and her aunt, Irene Kashner, with Rags the dog at the family home at 335 Drummond Avenue. (Photograph courtesy of Jack Wilson.)

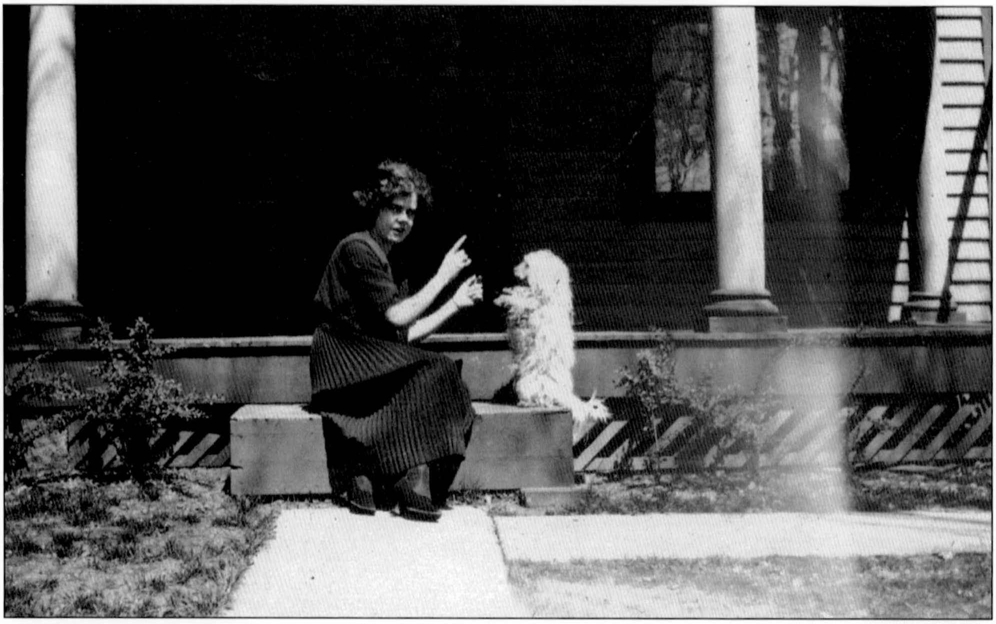

Irene Kashner is seen with Rags the dog on the porch of the family home on 335 Drummond Avenue. Irene was executive secretary to Mr. Beeghley, chairman of the Board of Standard Slag Co. in Youngstown. (Photograph courtesy of Jack Wilson.)

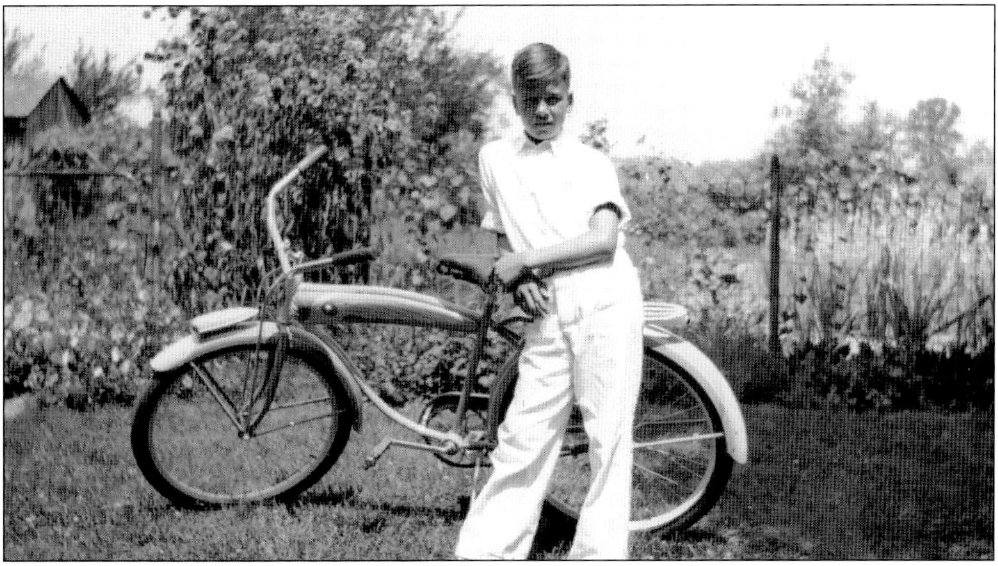

Jack Wilson, pictured here at the age of 12, often rode his bicycle from his home on Christian Avenue to the railroad crossing on North Main Street and waited patiently for the train to come by. The steam locomotive engineer stopped the train, which was going around five miles per hour, and picked up Jack for a ride to Valley Mould and back. They were carrying hot ladle or molten iron, which they had picked up at the furnaces in Youngstown after the Hubbard Furnace closed. (Photograph courtesy of Jack Wilson.)

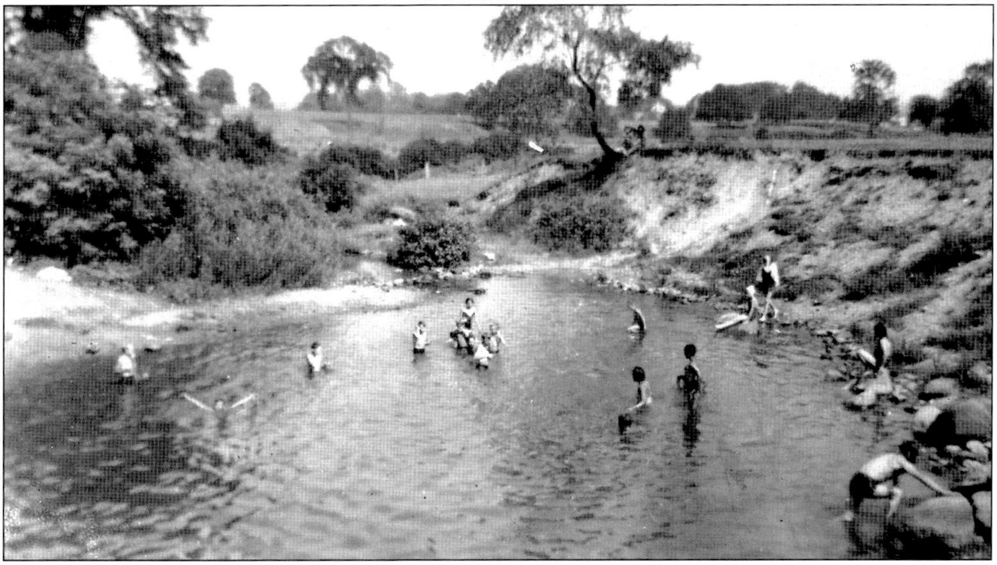

Clay Banks was a popular swimming hole for children who lived in the Drummond Avenue area. It was located to the east of where Drummond Avenue extension makes a sharp bend to the west. There was a sandy beach on the east side. Sometimes the boys would go skinny-dipping and when the girls wanted to swim, they would yell for the boys to get their clothes on. George Praznik swam there with his brothers, Frank and Nick, and sisters, Ann and Bernice. (Photograph courtesy of George and Nancy Praznik.)

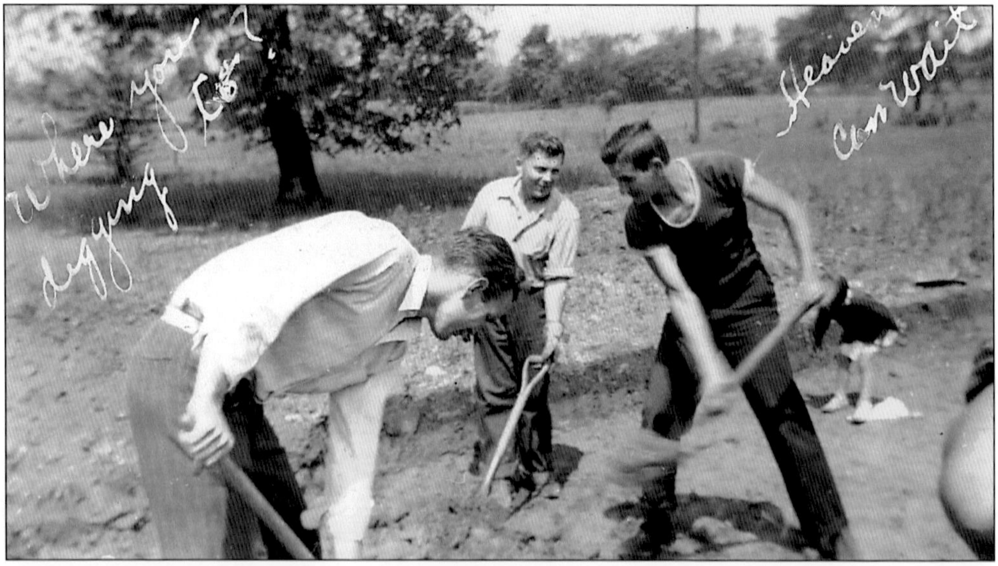

Pictured here, from left to right, are Pete Matovina, George Praznik Sr., and Paul Vukovich, who were hand digging the basement of the Praznik's new house in the 1940s. George Praznik Sr. and his wife, Katherine, came from Yugoslavia in the 1920s as young adults. George Sr. worked at Republic Steel in Youngstown, Ohio and they lived in Coalburg until they built their home at 481 Drummond Avenue. They had four sons, Joe, Frank, Nick, and George Jr. and two daughters, Ann, and Bernice. (Photograph courtesy of George and Nancy Praznik.)

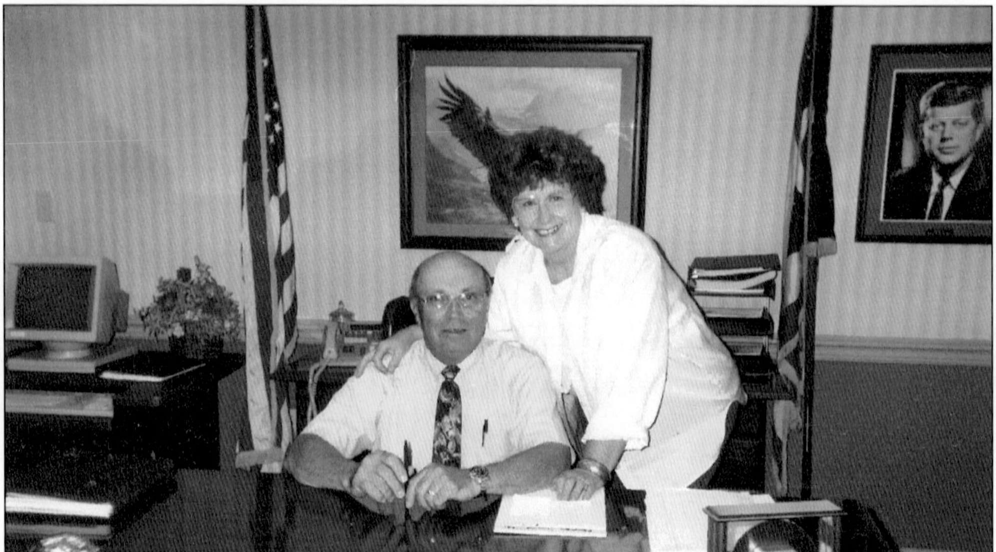

Council members voted George Praznik Jr. into office as mayor of the City of Hubbard in 1996 after Mayor Albert Sauline resigned to work in the private sector. George served three and one half years of that term and was elected to a full four-year term in November of 1999. He obtained funding for completing a waterline-looping project, paving West Liberty Street and North Main Street, installing new sidewalks and storm sewer improvements. George and his wife, Nancy, are shown in this photograph taken in January of 2000. (Photograph courtesy of George and Nancy Praznik.)

Two

North and East Hubbard Township

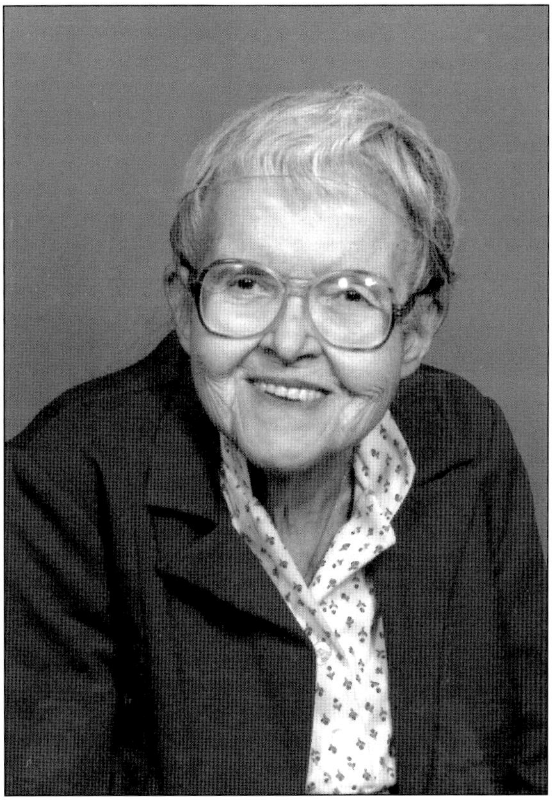

Marvel Hibler Walker was 82 years old on March 25, 1987. She was born in 1905 to older parents who had lost a child four years earlier. She was married to Mr. Freiheit and when he passed away, she married Ed Walker. In 1963, when her house and property were taken by the state for Interstate 80, she moved two miles east to old Route 62 on June 1, 1963. She passed away on July 8, 1991. (Photograph courtesy of Robert Walker.)

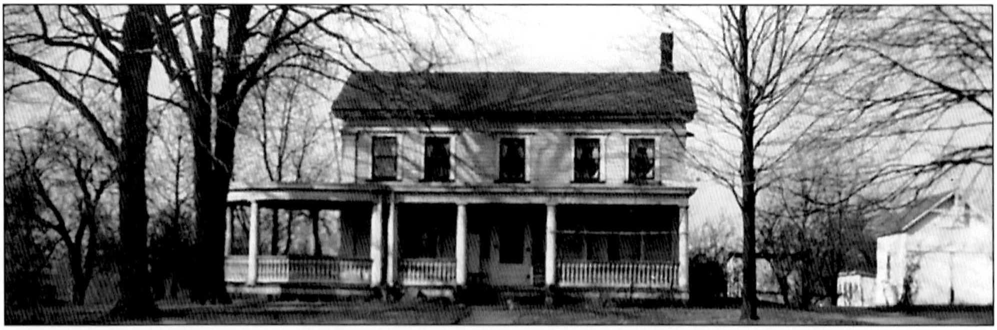

Marvel Hibler Walker's home, shown in a photograph dated November 10, 1949, was located north of Little Yankee Creek on the west side of State Route 7/US 62. Currently, there is a small evergreen tree with a sign that says "Welcome to Hubbard" where her house was located. In a 1985 oral history tape, Marvel said every year in the springtime all the woolen carpets were taken up in the house, beaten with rug beaters, the floors cleaned, and fresh wheat straw placed under the carpets to keep the floors warm. (Photograph courtesy of the Hubbard Historical Society.)

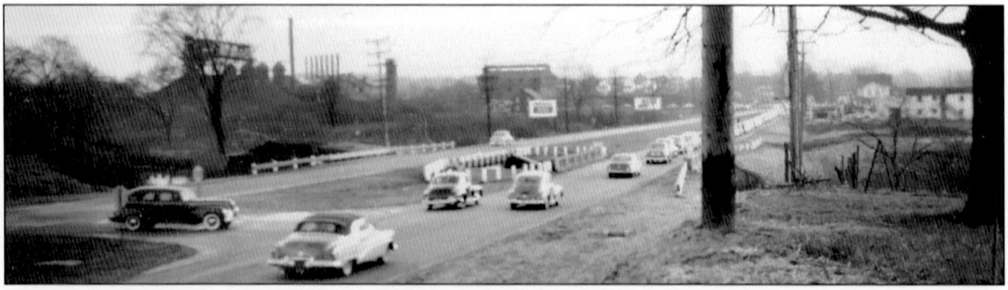

The Youngstown Sheet and Tube Hubbard Furnace is shown in the left background of this picture from the early 1950s, taken from the front yard of Marvel Hibler Walker's house. The entrance to the furnace was located on a road that was just to the right of the present Wholesale Fireworks Company, which is at 2665 North Main Street. A small bridge spanned Little Yankee Run in order to get to the furnace. (Photograph courtesy of Hubbard Historical Society.)

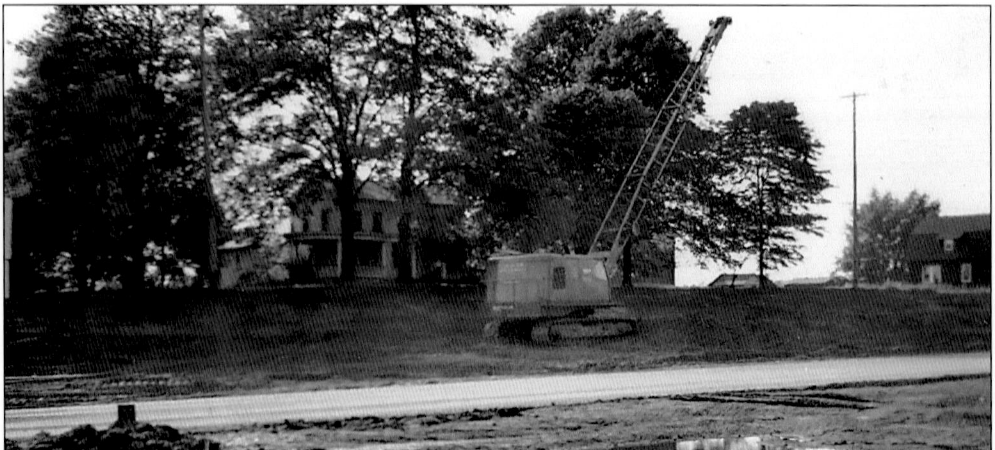

This 1953 photograph shows Marvel Hibler Walker's home during the construction of the new State Route 7/US 62. In 1963 when Interstate 80 was built, her house was taken through eminent domain. (Photograph courtesy of the Hubbard Historical Society.)

Ron Wright is shown in 1960 with his 1953 Ford Coupe Centennial in the driveway of his home at 22 Meadow Lane, a street that was replaced in 1962 by the entrance ramp to westbound Interstate 80. It had only two houses, 22 and 24 Meadow Lane. Both homes were on the north side of the street, now occupied by the back parking lot of McDonald's. In the background, the McFarland house, the Karcher home and Tarr's house, which were all on North Main Street, can be seen. (Photograph courtesy of Ron Wright.)

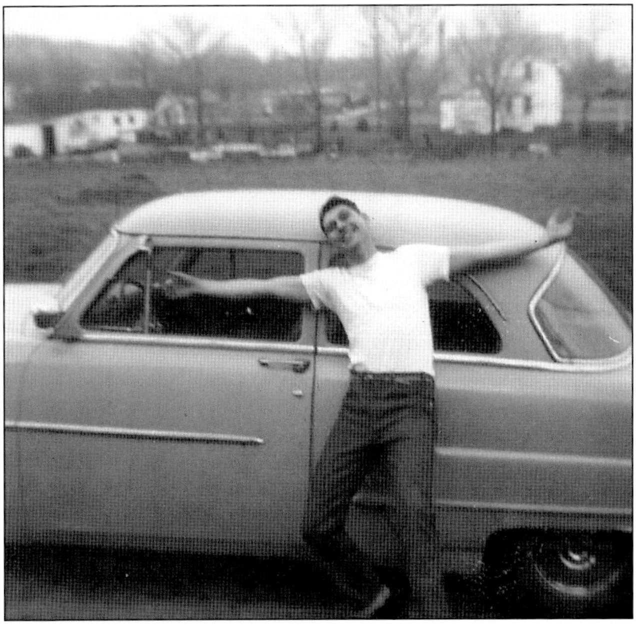

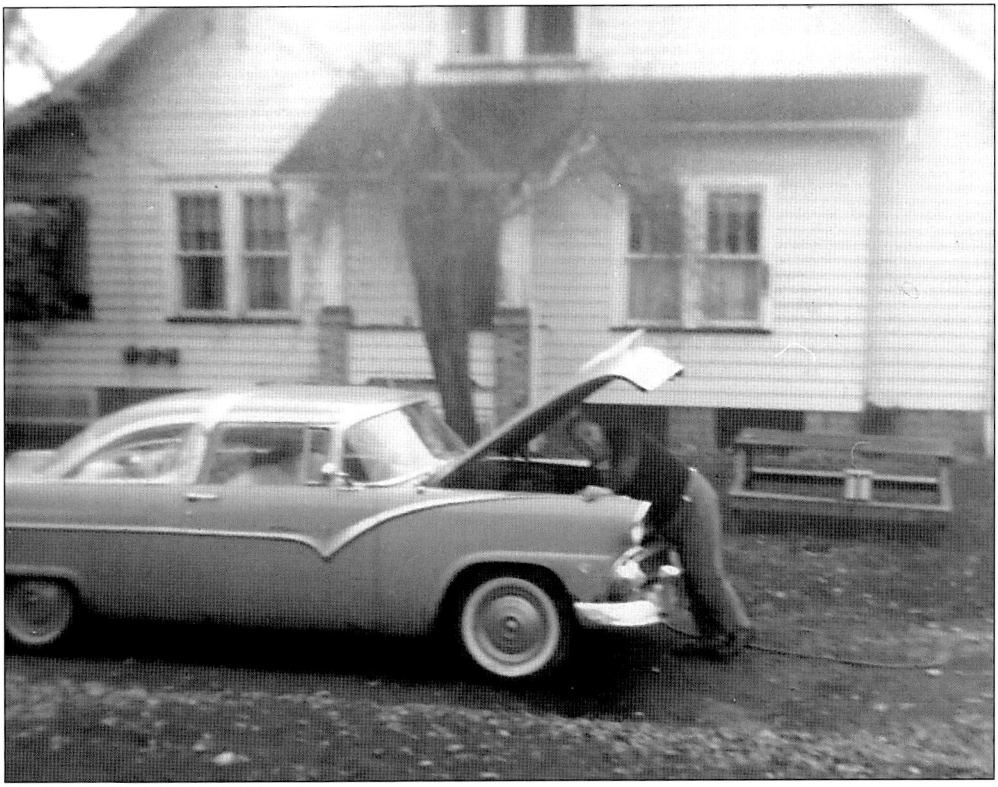

Glenn Young is shown working on his car in November of 1961 in front of his house, which was located at 24 Meadow Lane. This was one of only two homes that existed on this street. Within approximately one year, this house would be gone to make way for Interstate 80. (Photograph courtesy of Ron Wright.)

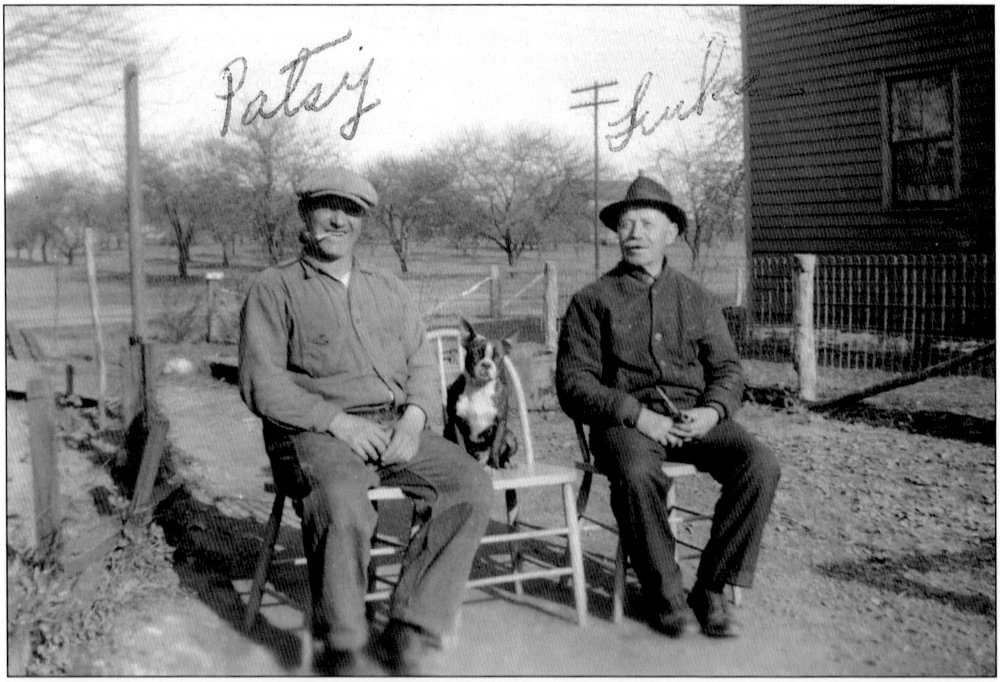

Luke Palumbo Sr., Patsy Sansota, and Jiggs the dog are seen here enjoying themselves on a sunny day in 1938. Patsy's son, Frank Sansota owned Frank's Auto Wrecking. The old, dirt Hubbard-Brookfield Road, which would later become State Route 7/US 62, can be seen in the background. John B. Palumbo's house was later built in the orchard across the street, which eventually became the location of Truck World. (Photograph courtesy of Carole Palumbo Williams.)

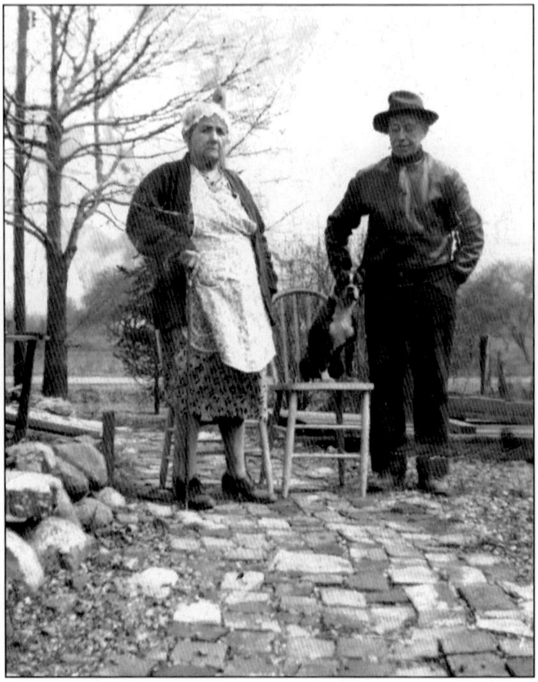

Angelique and Luke Palumbo Sr. are shown at their home, which was located on the west side of Hubbard-Brookfield Road (now State Route 7/US 62). The apple orchard, which eventually became John B. Palumbo's property and later the location of Truck World, can be seen in the background. (Photograph courtesy of Carole Palumbo Williams.)

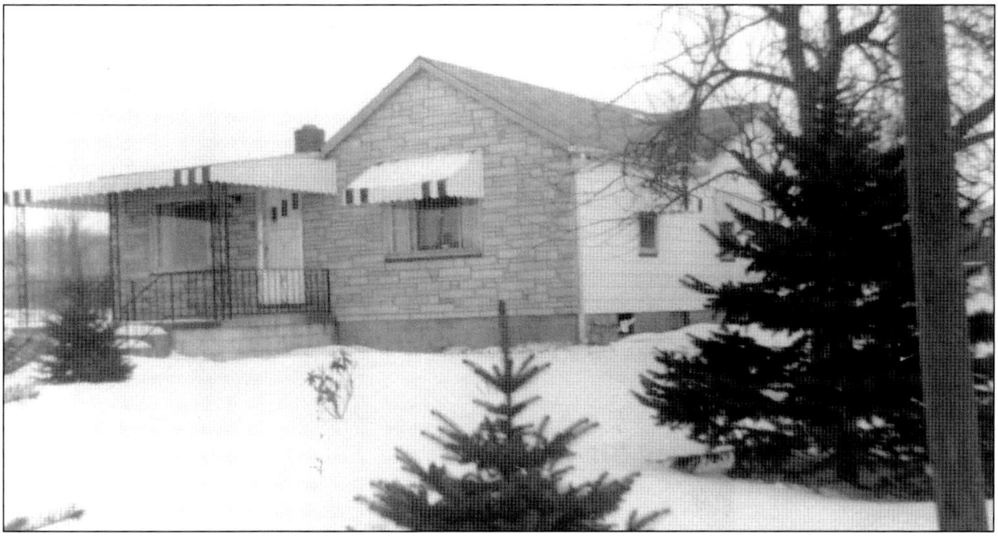

The home of John B. Palumbo and family, shown here in February of 1960, was originally the site of an apple orchard. The address was 69 Brookfield Road (now State Route 7/US 62) and was later demolished to make way for the building of Truck World. (Photograph courtesy of Carole Palumbo Williams.)

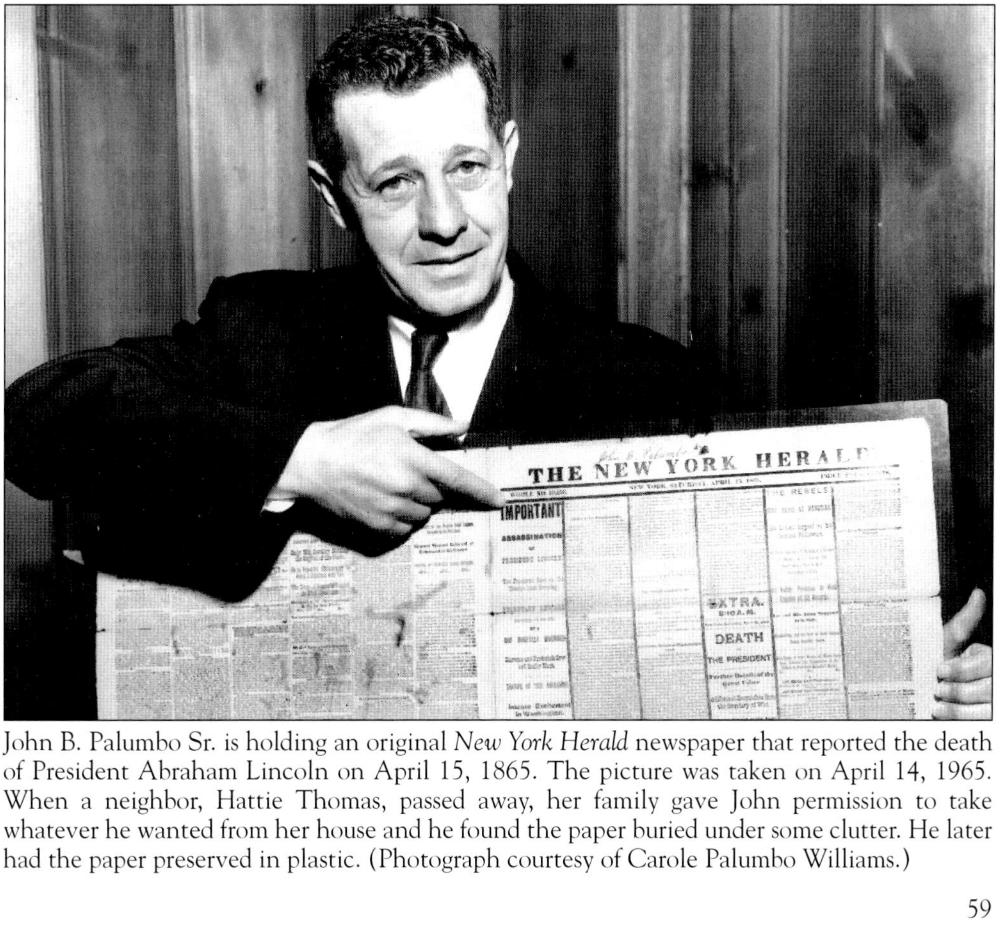

John B. Palumbo Sr. is holding an original *New York Herald* newspaper that reported the death of President Abraham Lincoln on April 15, 1865. The picture was taken on April 14, 1965. When a neighbor, Hattie Thomas, passed away, her family gave John permission to take whatever he wanted from her house and he found the paper buried under some clutter. He later had the paper preserved in plastic. (Photograph courtesy of Carole Palumbo Williams.)

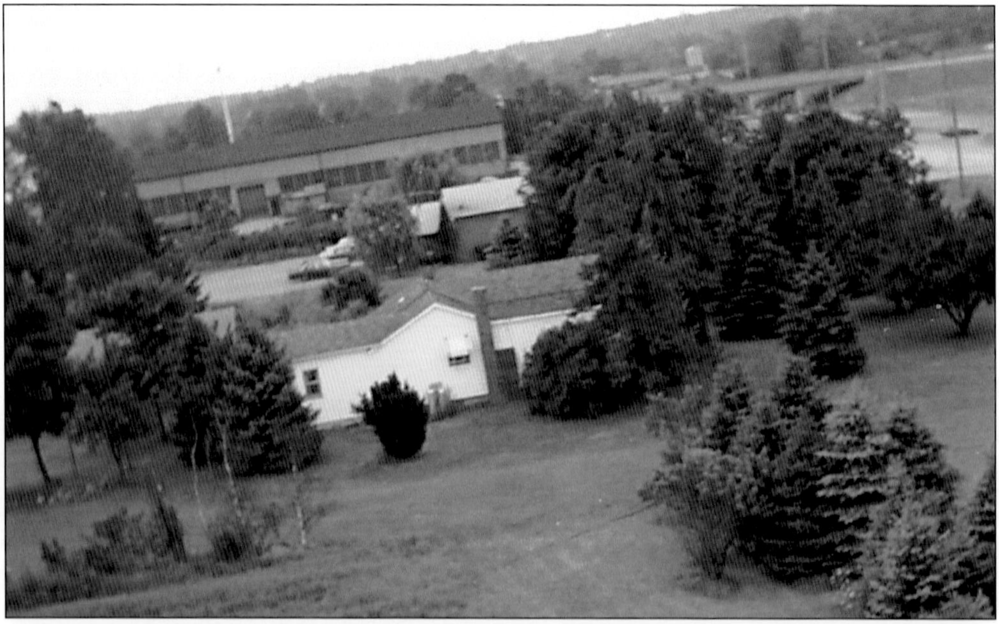

This is an aerial view, taken in 1972, of John B. Palumbo's house, which was located at 69 Brookfield Road (now State Route 7/US 62), in Hubbard. In the 1960s, the address was RD 1, Hubbard. The property was later sold to developers who built Truck World. (Photograph courtesy of Carole Palumbo Williams.)

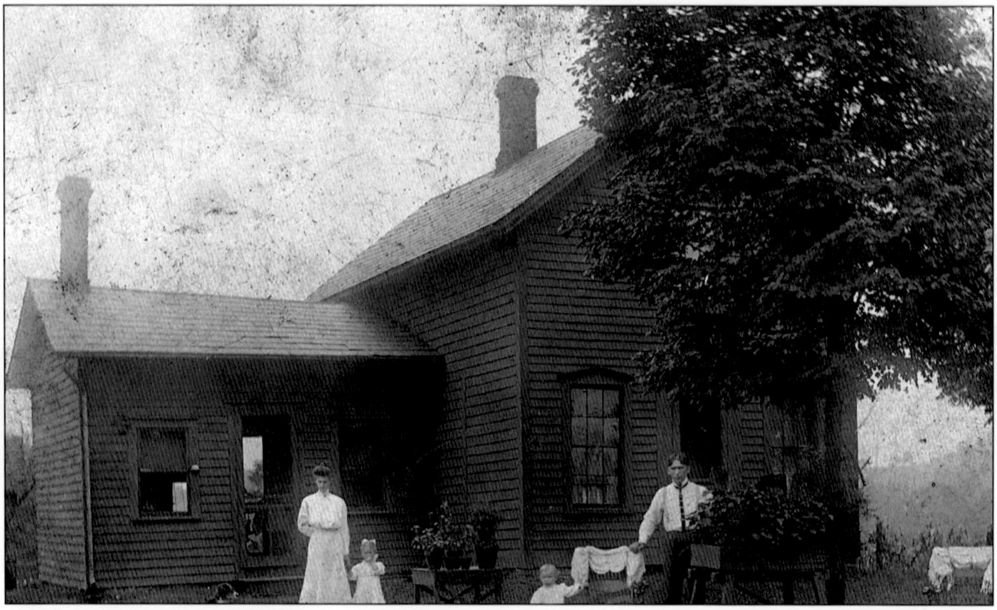

Emma L. Ryser married Plummer L. Corll on July 18, 1906. Their home was located at the present location of the Flying J Truck Plaza on North Main Street in Hubbard. Their first child was Esther and then a son, Oscar, was born. Later children included Helen, Edward, and Lewis. Emma's parents, Frederick and Elizabeth Ryser came from Switzerland and settled in Hubbard. Their children included Nellie, Emma, Frederick Jr., Florence, Edward, Lucy, Lewis, Mary, and Albert. Plummer's father was Freeman Corll. (Photograph courtesy of Susan Corll Parkany.)

William (Bill/Willy) Palumbo is pictured in his WWII Army uniform. He owned Bill's Bike Shop, which was located on Youngstown-Hubbard Road just past Lewis-Seifert Road on the way to Youngstown on the right side. The company later relocated to North Main Street and Ruth Street, which is the street across from the Flying J Truck Plaza. (Photograph courtesy of Carole Palumbo Williams.)

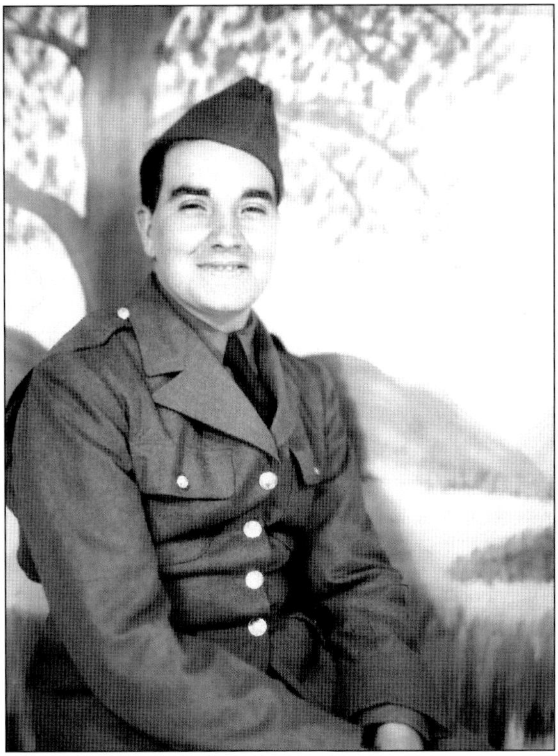

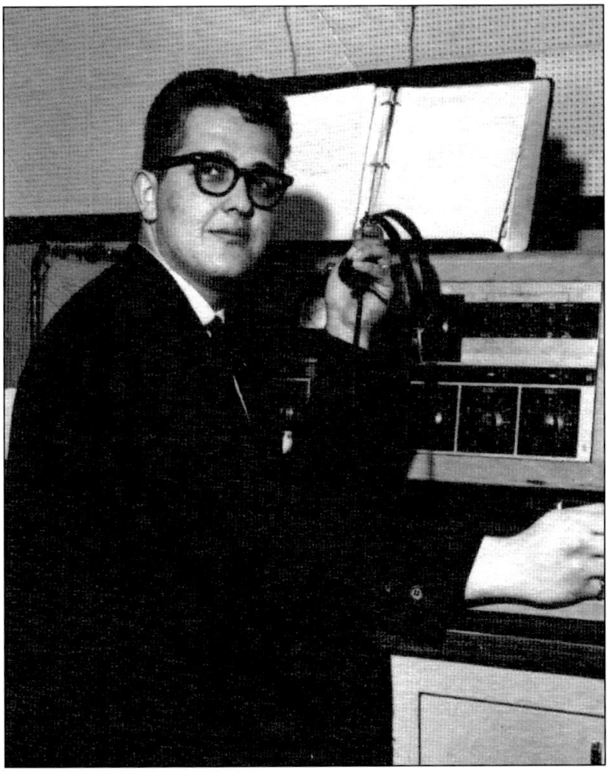

Bob Palumbo used the name "Bobby Shannon" when he worked for WNIO as a DJ in the 1960s and 1970s. He was an early founder of the Van Dykes Boys Club, which held dances as fundraisers for charities. In the 1980s, he was self-employed as a disc jockey, known as "Boppin Bob" and he played music of the 1950s, 1960s, 1970s, and 1980s. (Photograph courtesy of Carole Palumbo Williams.)

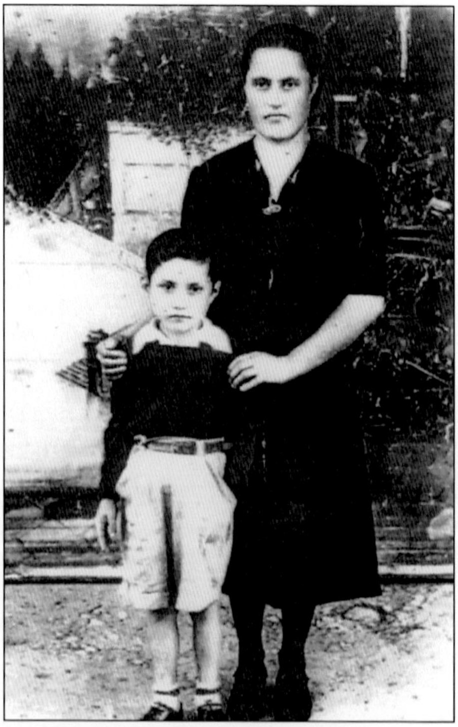

Antonio (Tony) DiTommaso, seven years old, and his mother, Gemma Ginocchi Di Tommaso are pictured in approximately 1950. They lived in the Italian town of Baia and Latina. In 1945, when Tony was 1 1/2, his father died. In 1951, Gemma met Jim Condi, who had come from America to visit, and they were married. They could not bring 7-year-old Tony with them to America until they could secure papers for him, so he was left behind with his Aunt Stephanie Russo. Tony resented the attention his aunt gave to her own son so he left their home and ran away. He jumped on a horse drawn mail cart and traveled 35 miles to Naples. He survived on the streets with other runaway or orphaned children by stealing, begging, and selling things that he stole. He slept on the streets, in doorways, or on park benches. Occasionally, someone might take him in for the night. In June of 1954, Tony's mom sent his aunt the papers for him to immigrate to America. His aunt went to Naples and found Tony, who was by this time a month shy of 11 years old. Tony's mother had given him his father's wedding suit, which was cut down to fit him for his trip to America so the crotch of the suit was down to his knees. He wore the suit on the boat, never taking it off for the entire 13-day-long trip; he had no other clothes. He left Italy on June 12, 1954 and arrived at Ellis Island on June 25, 1954. He remembers the pipe rails on either side of the line to be checked by authorities. No one was allowed to leave the line and Tony waited in line all day long. He passed his physical, which was fortunate because otherwise he would have been sent back to Italy. He was put on a ferryboat, which took him to the mainland of New York City and was met by an interpreter who asked him, "Where are you going?" Tony said he didn't know and he showed her the papers. She put him in a taxi and he arrived at Grand Central Station, scared to death. He was put on a train and rode all night. Early the next morning, a porter tapped him on the shoulder. Tony didn't understand, but showed him the papers. When the train stopped in Youngstown, he was tapped on the shoulder and the porter pointed to the door. When Tony didn't move, the porter tapped him again, more forcefully and he walked out and there was no one at the train station to meet him. After many hours his mom came and took him to his new home in America, at the southeast corner of Chestnut Ridge Road and Old Route 62. He arrived in Hubbard on June 27, 1954, and was 11 years old on August 5, 1954. (Photograph courtesy of Tony DiTommaso.)

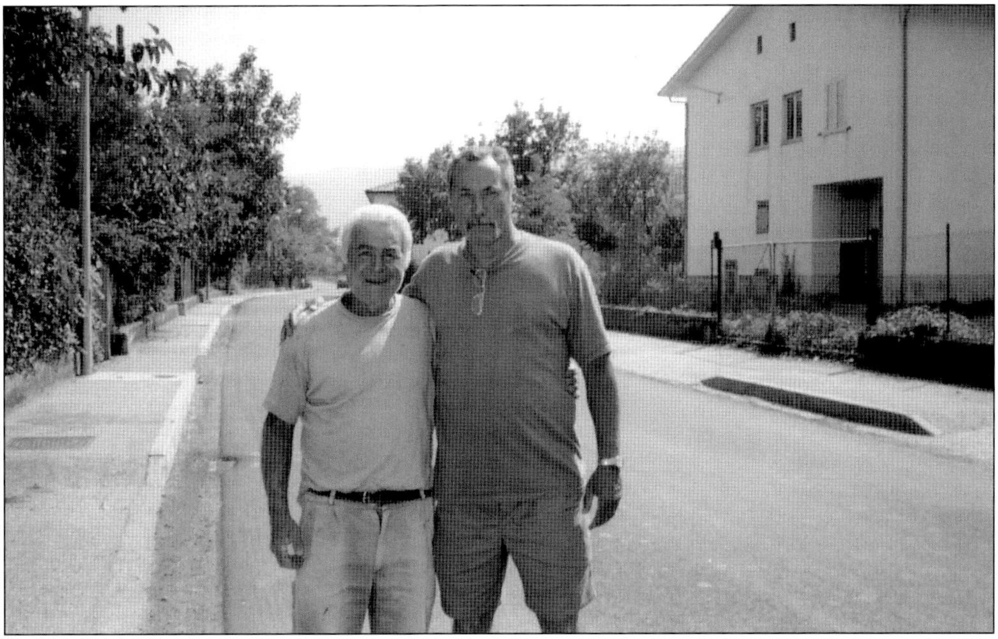

Tony DiTommaso decided to return to Italy in September of 2000, but didn't tell anyone he was coming. His family was shocked, but very happy to see him. Everyone remembered him. His Uncle DiCerbo took him to see his aunts and uncles and on the way they saw two men who were working on some scaffolding. Uncle DiCerbo asked them "Do you remember this guy?" Akilo, on the left, who was Tony's cousin, said "Oh my God, that's Tony!" (Photograph courtesy of Tony DiTommaso.)

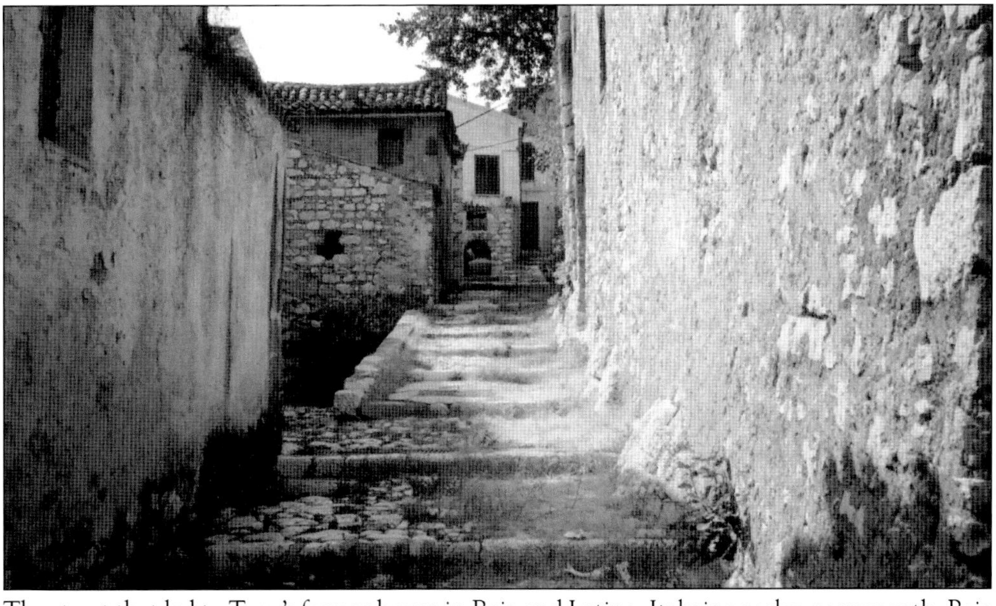

The street that led to Tony's former house in Baia and Latina, Italy is a rocky, narrow path. Baia and Latina are actually two towns that are joined by a cemetery. He later visited his family's home, which was not inhabited and in poor condition. The home had only two rooms, a combination living room/bedroom and a kitchen. (Photograph courtesy of Tony DiTommaso.)

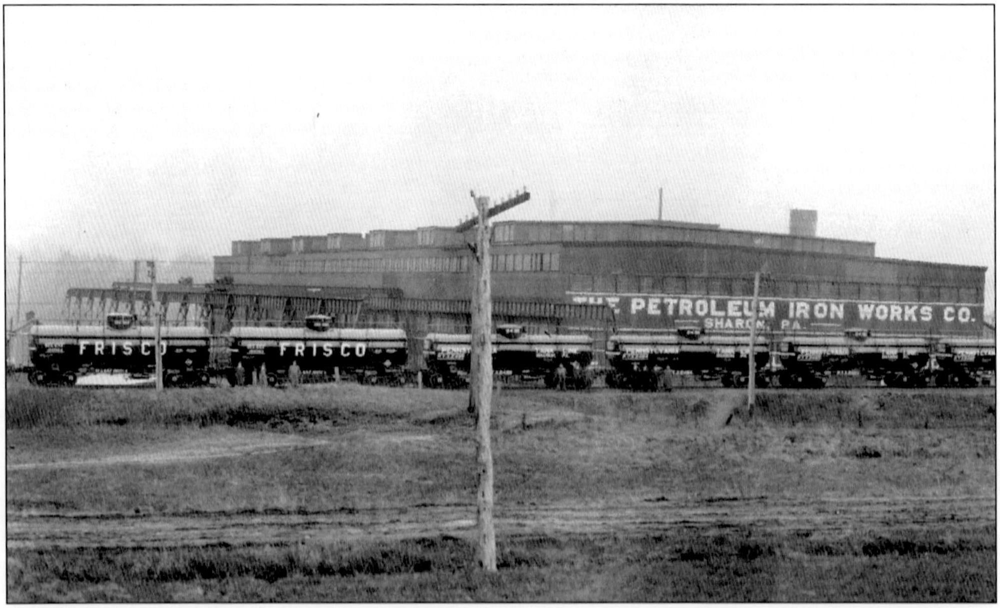

Petroleum Iron Works was built in 1907 on 40 acres of the old Mizner farm near Masury in Hubbard Township. They fabricated oil tank cars for the Standard Oil Company. (Photograph courtesy of John Schultz.)

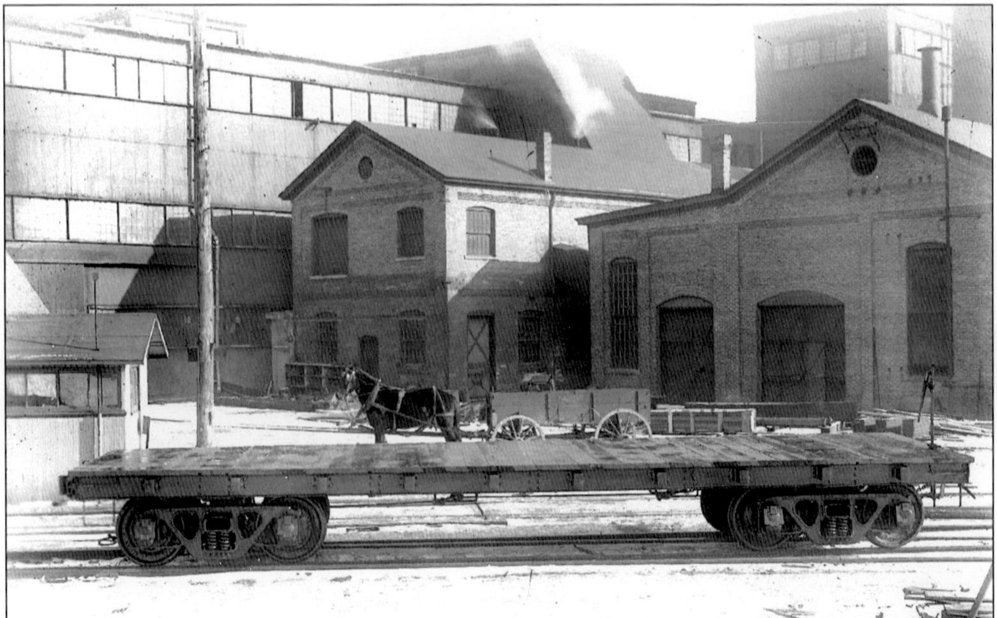
General American Transportation Corporation (GATX) purchased the Petroleum Iron Works. When GATX closed in 1984, Lee Industrial Properties bought the northern buildings. Warren Fabricating and Machining (WARFAB) bought the southern buildings. WARFAB does large fabrications and machining. (Photograph courtesy of Carol Palumbo Williams.)

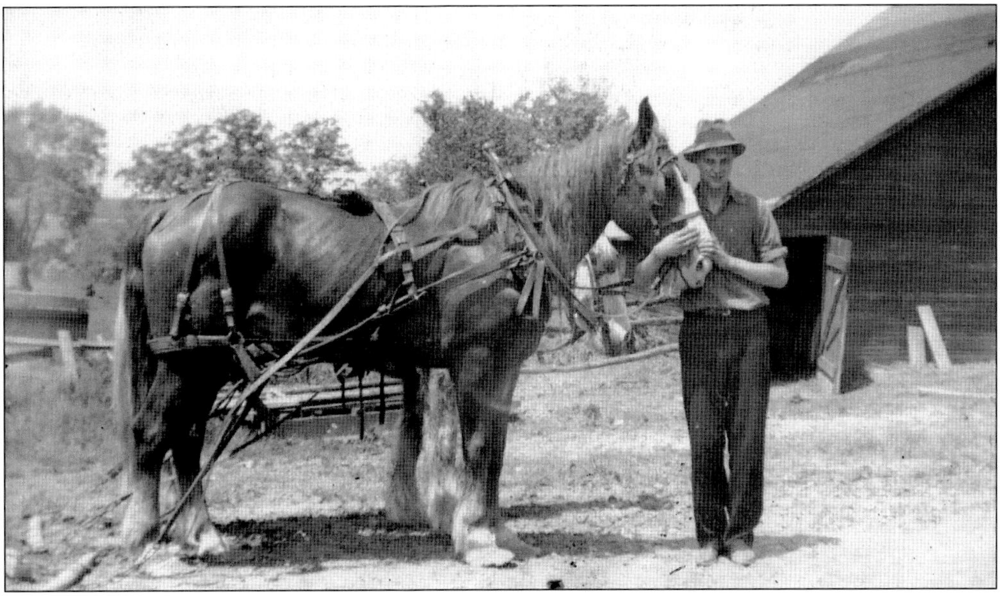

Art Weiser is shown with his horse in this 1937 photograph at his farm near Chestnut Ridge Road. He worked at General American (GATX) for 10 years as welding foreman on night turn. He left because he tired of breathing welding smoke. He made more money at Hubbard Coal and Supply, plus it was a cleaner place to work. He hauled a lot of coal in those days, as most people had coal furnaces. (Photograph courtesy of Violet and Art Weiser.)

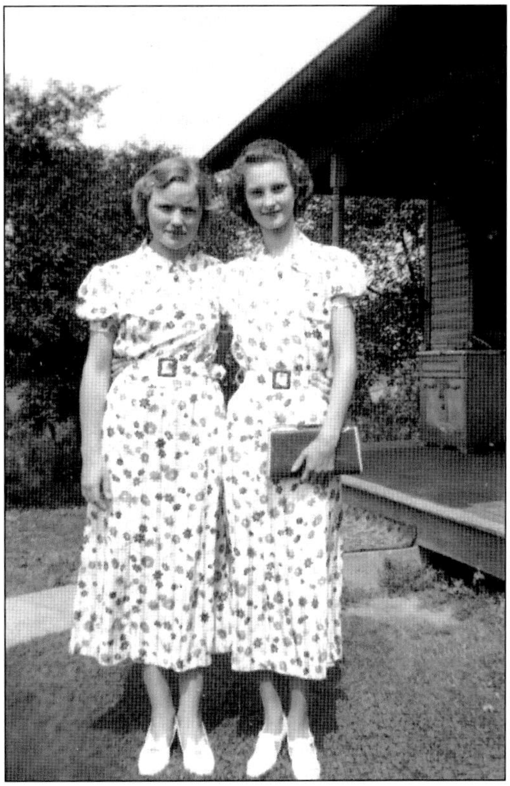

Violet King Weiser, left, and her sister-in-law, Mary Weiser Mauer, are seen in this 1938 photograph at Violet and Art Weiser's farm located near Chestnut Ridge Road. Violet remembered running down the hill on Chestnut Ridge Road with Mary to catch the streetcar at Stop 46 to go shopping in Sharon, Pennsylvania. One memorable shopping trip they bought fur coats. Art remembered movies at the Warner Theatre in Youngstown and streetcar rides were 10¢ each. (Photograph courtesy of Violet and Art Weiser.)

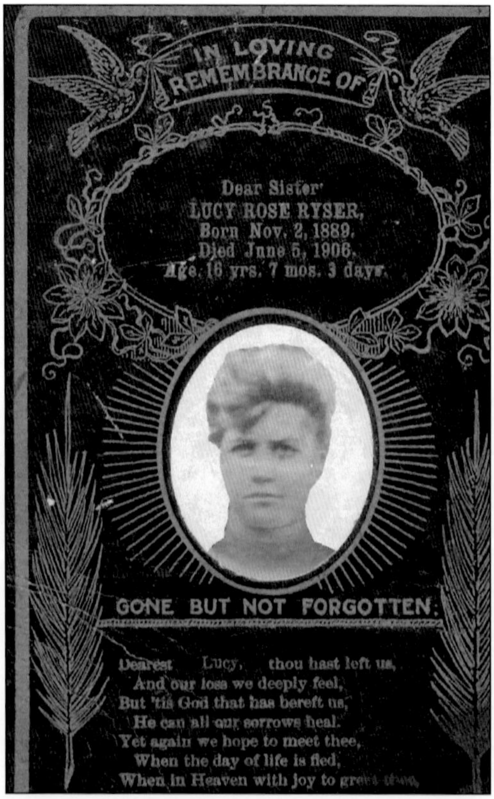

Lucy Ryser, daughter of Frederick and Elizabeth Ryser, worked at the Masurite Explosive Company, which was located on the east side of Hubbard Township. Masurite was used as an explosive in coalmines. It was supposed to be a safer than blasting powder. However, an accident resulted in Lucy's death and another worker was injured. Lucy was only 16 years old. At the time of the explosion the newspaper said that Lucy's arm was nearly blown off and she died shortly after being admitted to the hospital. (Photograph courtesy of Susan Corll Parkany.)

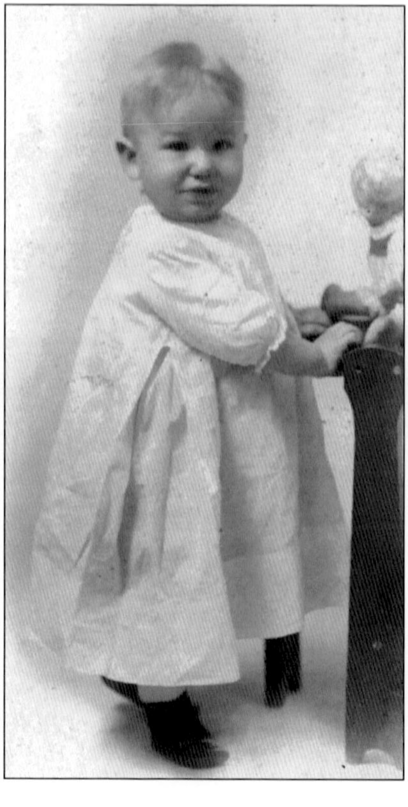

In the early 1900s, it was typical for boys under the age of four years to wear dresses. Edward Wilson Corll is three years old in this photograph. He rode a motorcycle as a young man and lost his leg in a tragic accident with a motor vehicle. It was after this accident that he opened Corll's Tractor Parts, Inc. on State Line Road in 1948, selling Ferguson tractors and equipment. Today his daughter, Cathy Corll Nickleson, operates the business. (Photograph courtesy of Susan Corll Parkany.)

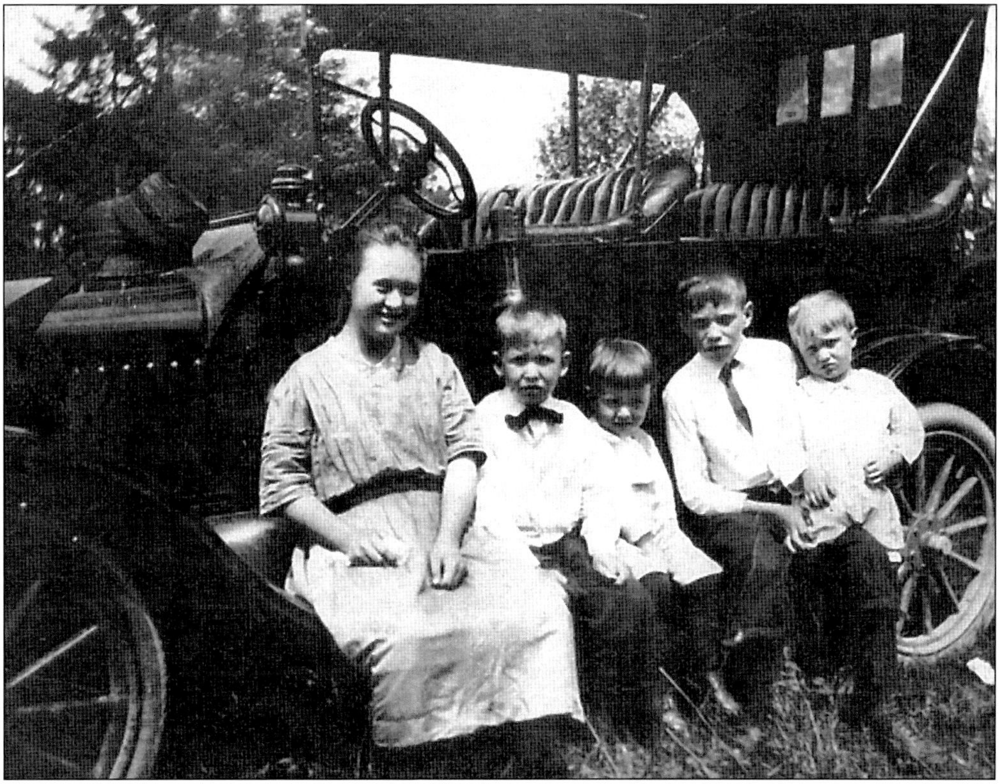

Pictured here, from left to right, are Esther Corll, Edward Corll, Leonard Stevenson, Oscar Corll, and Lewis Corll. Their grandfather, Frederick Ryser, and his aunt, Florence Ryser, died in a streetcar accident at stop 46 on the Youngstown-Sharon streetcar line on July 6, 1919. Two uncles were injured in the same accident. The streetcar was not able to stop in time and crashed into the Ryser family's stalled automobile. (Photograph courtesy of Susan Corll Parkany.)

Pictured here, from left to right, are Edward Corll, Leonard Stevenson, and Lewis Corll. Edward and Lewis were brothers and Leonard Stevenson was a cousin. Leonard's family owned Hubbard Coal and Supply Company and his parents were Mary Ryser and George Stevenson. (Photograph courtesy of Susan Corll Parkany.)

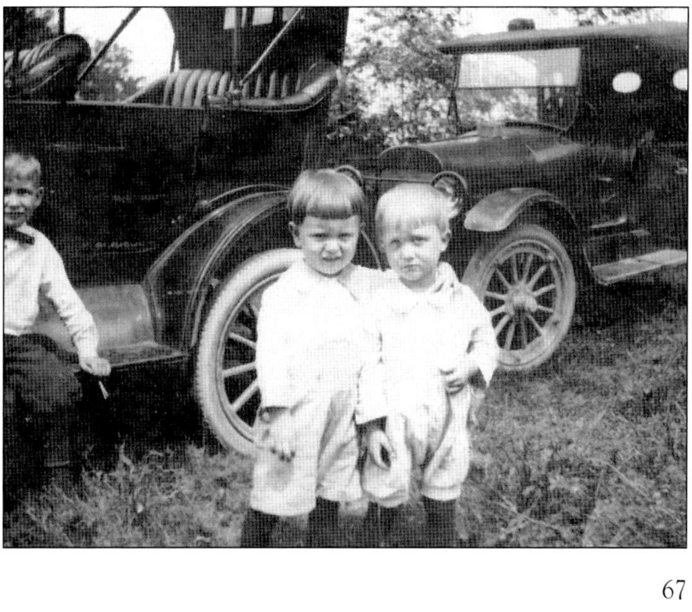

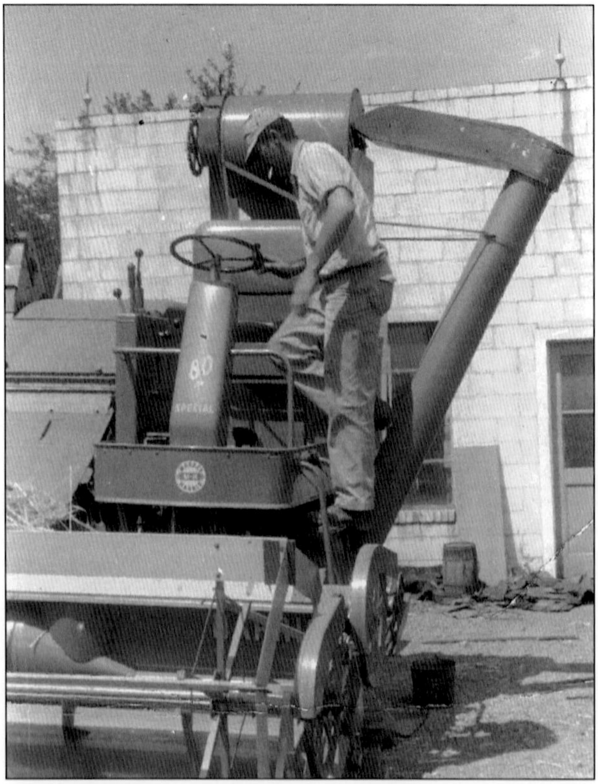

Lewis Corll is shown with his combine at his farm on State Line Road in Hubbard Township. Lewis was born on September 2, 1918, in the old farmhouse that was located at the present site of the Flying J Truck Plaza. His family moved to State Line Road and he went to first grade at the old Chestnut Ridge School. It consisted of two wooden schools, one housed grades one through six, and the other grades seven through twelve. On his way to school, Lewis would check his animal traps that were set in Yankee Run. The pelts were sold to fur traders. (Photograph courtesy of Susan Corll Parkany.)

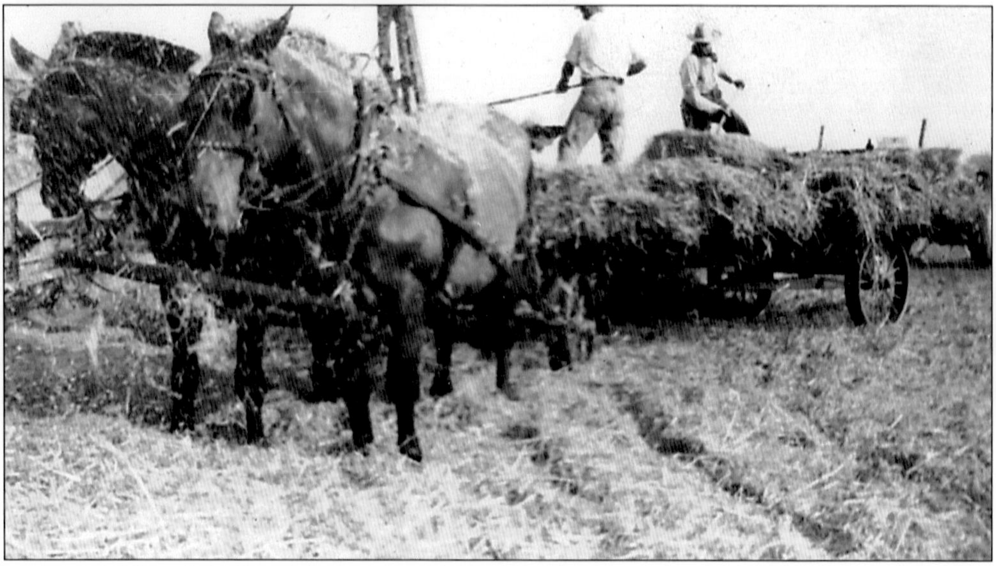

Lewis and Edward Corll are thrashing at the Miklos Farm on Chestnut Ridge Road. The Corll farm had dairy cattle and sold milk every day to local families. The milk was cooled in a springhouse and bottled in pints and quarts with paper caps. Customers would buy a pad of tickets for $5 and would tear them off according to how many bottles of milk they wanted. They would leave the tickets in the empty bottles to be picked up and refilled. (Photograph courtesy of Susan Corll Parkany.)

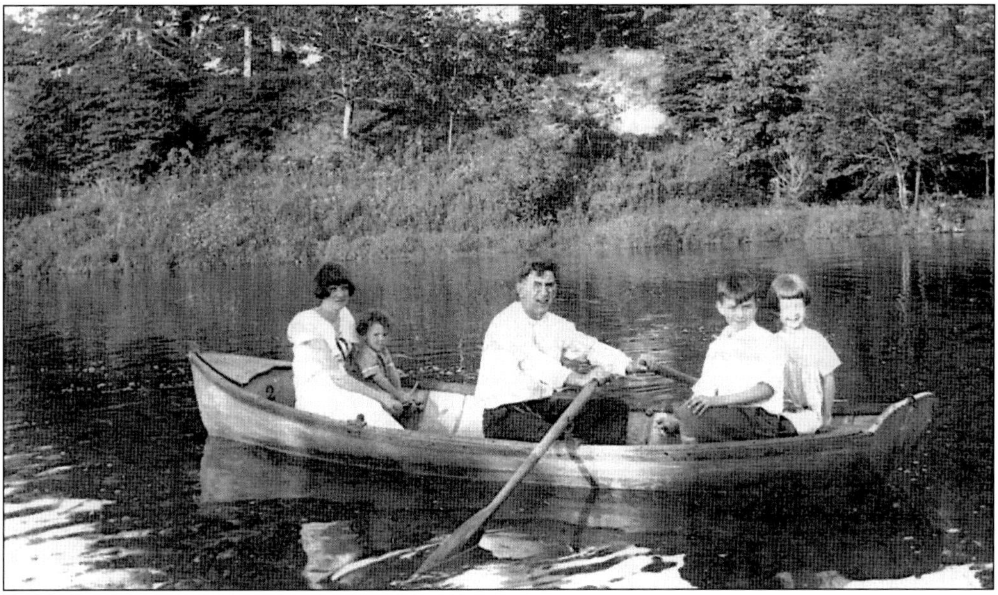

Laurice Neal, far right, is shown boating with her cousins and uncle on the lake at Harding Park in 1928. She was attending the Foreman family reunion (her mother's family). Pictured, from left to right, are Twila Marcella Braine, Velma Gibson, and her father George Gibson, and Phil Foreman. Laurice's father owned Neal's Cash Grocery which was located on North Main Street in the Murphy building (now the location of Golden Glow Tanning). (Photograph courtesy of Laurice Neal.)

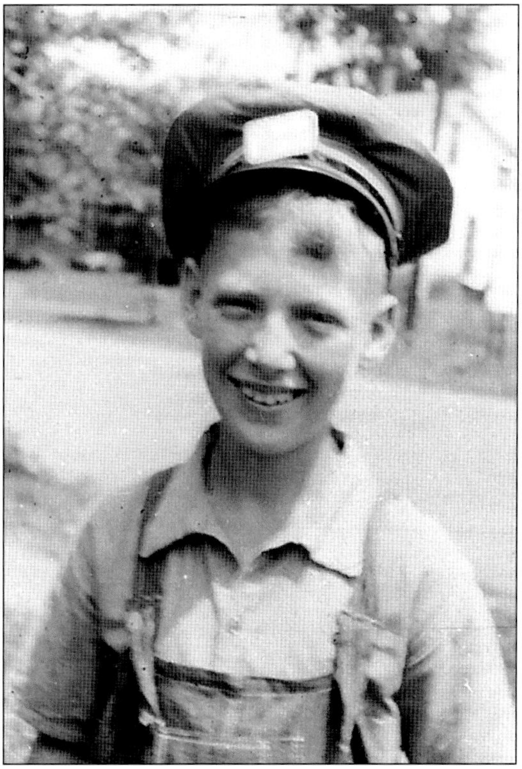

Jim Thompson was 11 years old in this photograph from August of 1942. He grew up in Hubbard, joined the U.S. Navy in 1948. Afterwards, he worked at the Air Force Base in Vienna as an Air Reserve technician and supervisor of avionics, retiring in 1987. He has been a member of the Hubbard Historical Society for 11 years, and was president in 2000 and 2001. He was instrumental in the renovation of the McBride House, the society's home. (Photograph courtesy of Jim and Betsy Thompson.)

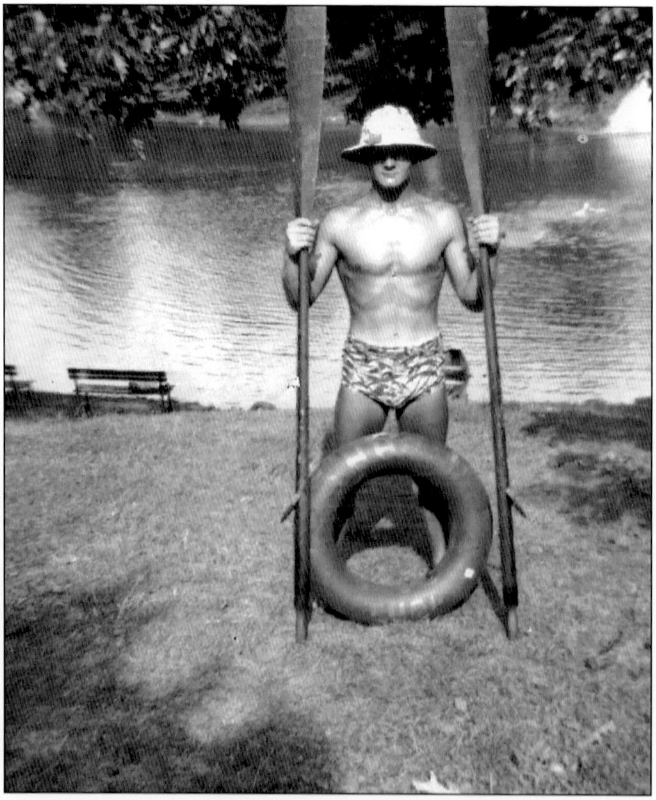

At 16 years of age Frank J. "Turk" Isabella was a lifeguard at Harding Park Lake. The bathhouse near the lake, now Pavilion No. 1, was where you could change to go swimming or rent a rowboat. The lake froze in the winter and kids from town would ice skate and gather around a fire to keep warm. Frank worked every day from 9AM until 9PM and was lucky to collect 50¢ a day. He was a Hubbard football star and later became a pilot. (Photograph courtesy of Betty Isabella.)

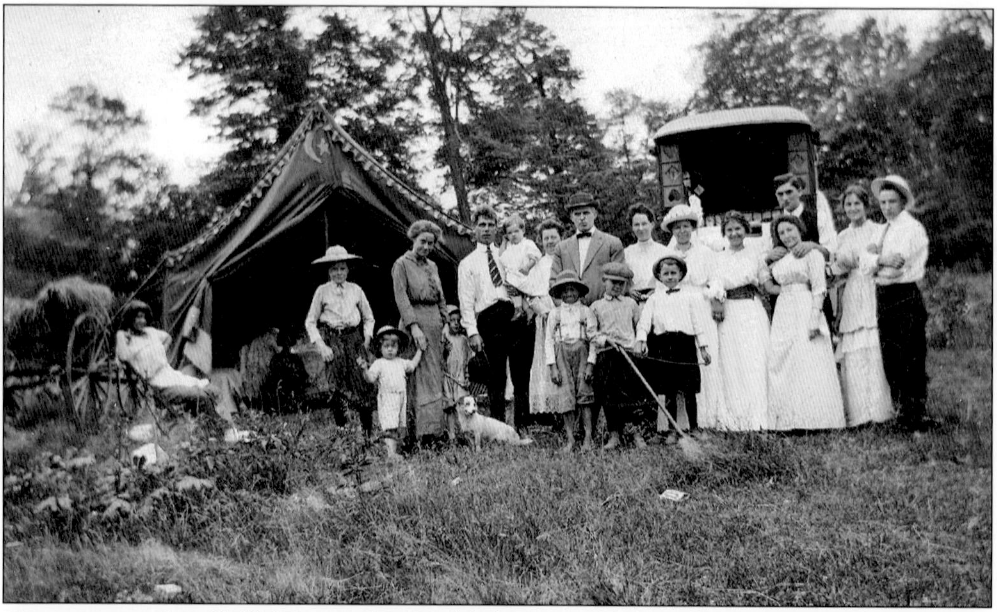

Gypsies camped in Hubbard near the Veach's farm, on the east side of Hubbard, in the early 1900s. Eva Allsop Jones is in the dark sash, fourth from the right. (Photograph courtesy of Nancy Gray Silvashy.)

Lulu Ann Baird Pettitt (1870–1906) and Dennick Wick "D.W." Pettitt (1854–1948) lived on the family farm on South Main Street, which was on Lot 76 in Hubbard Township. Earl J. Pettitt was born on May 1, 1902 and four years later, on November 6, 1906, a second son, Henry Baird Pettitt, was born. Lulu died of septicemia when Henry was six weeks old. He was sent to live with his Aunt Emma Hall in New Bedford, Pennsylvania. (Photograph courtesy of Henry Pettitt.)

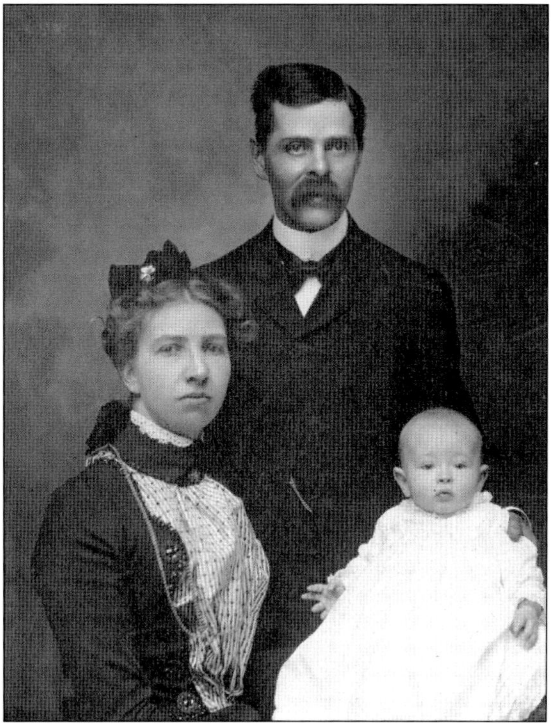

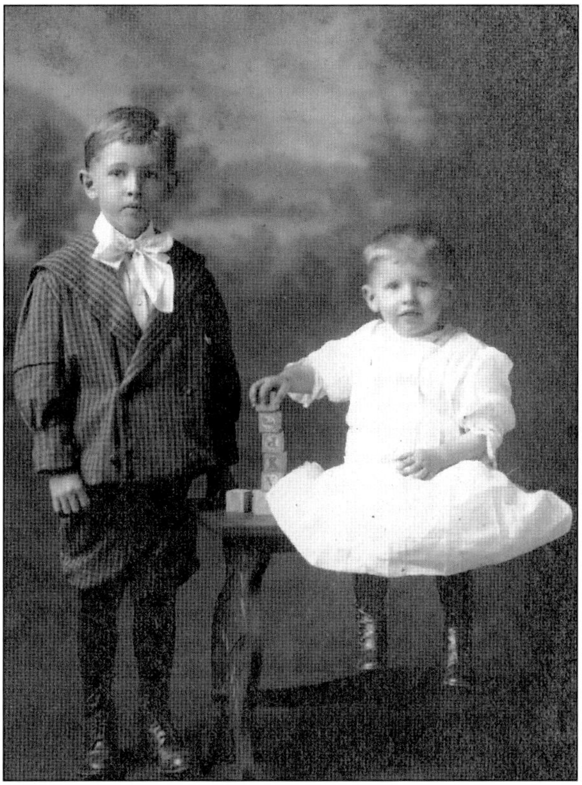

Earl and Henry Pettitt are shown in this photograph from approximately 1909. When Henry was five years old his father brought him back to the farm so he could go to Hubbard schools. Henry remembers his first day of school as Miss Myrta Bailey, his teacher who lived nearby, picked Henry up in a horse and buggy and drove him to the old red brick school. At Christmas time he got to play Tiny Tim in the Christmas play, *A Christmas Carol*. Sheldon Mathews from the high school played Scrooge. (Photograph courtesy of Henry Pettitt.)

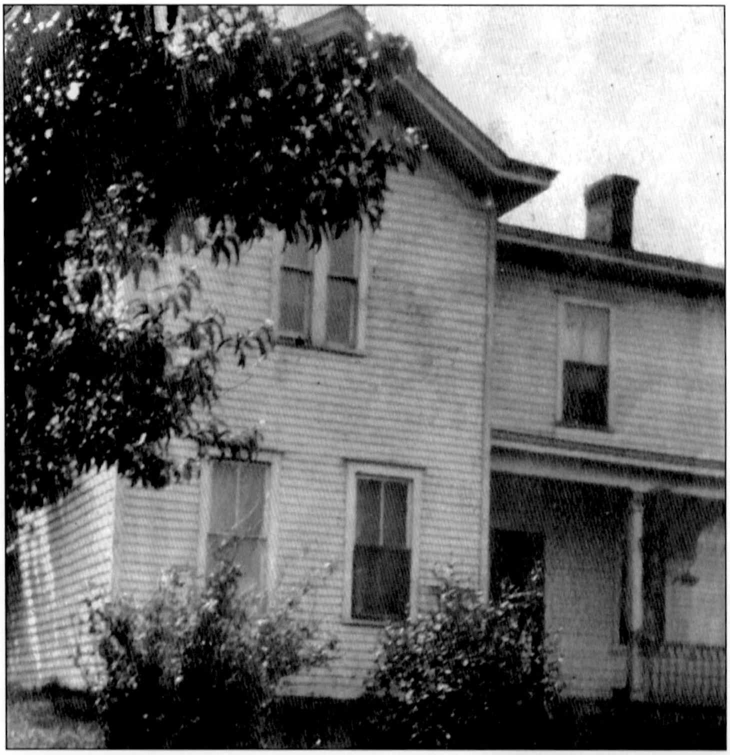

Samuel Pettitt, Henry Pettitt's grandfather, built the original Pettitt homestead in the 1840s. The farm was originally 75 acres, but today is only three acres as acreage has been sold over the years. Henry's father, Dennick was born there in 1854. The house is still standing and Henry continues to live there at the age of 98. (Photograph courtesy of Henry Pettitt.)

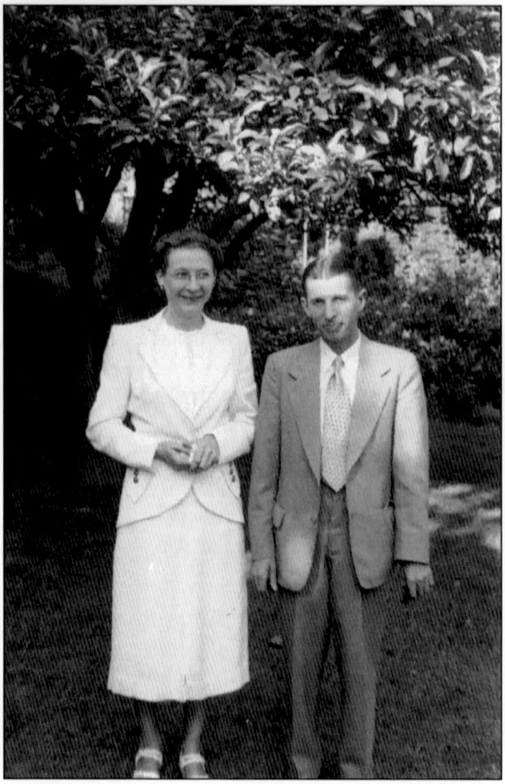

Henry Pettitt married Clara Clemens on June 19, 1937. After graduating from high school in 1924, he worked at the Hubbard Furnace for two years. He eventually ended up working at Youngstown Sheet and Tube in Campbell for 36 years. Henry and Clara came back to the farm in 1939 and Clara cared for Henry's father, Dennick, in his later years. Clara loved gardening, collecting owls, making quilts, hooked rugs, and needlepoint. She passed away on August 13, 2000 after 63 years of marriage. (Photograph courtesy of Henry Pettitt.)

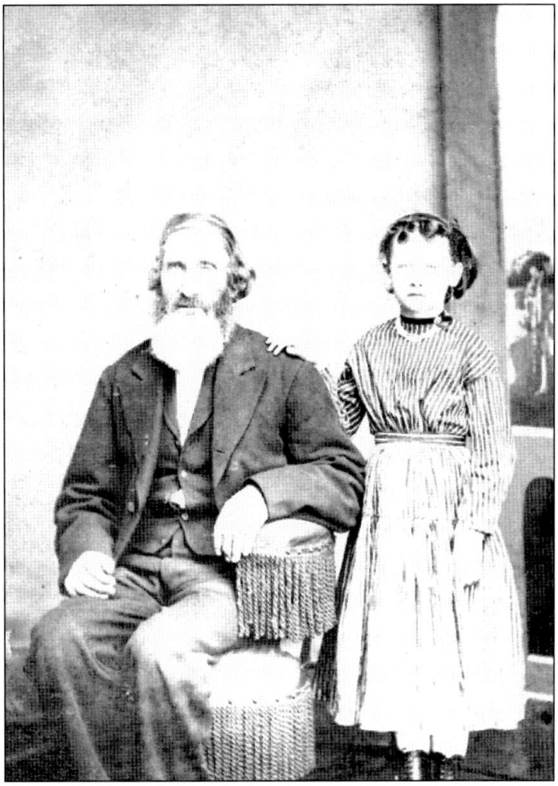

Elisha Snider, sitting with a grandchild, settled on Lot No. 69 in the southeast corner of Hubbard Township. The house was located at the end of a long lane on Bedford Road, which in the past, went through to John White Road. He was German and his wife, Sarah Huff Snider, was Scotch-Irish. He was a farmer and had three sons, Amos, Thomas, Joshua, and two daughters, Sarah (who married a Marstellar) and Nancy. (Photograph courtesy of Doris Burrows Valley.)

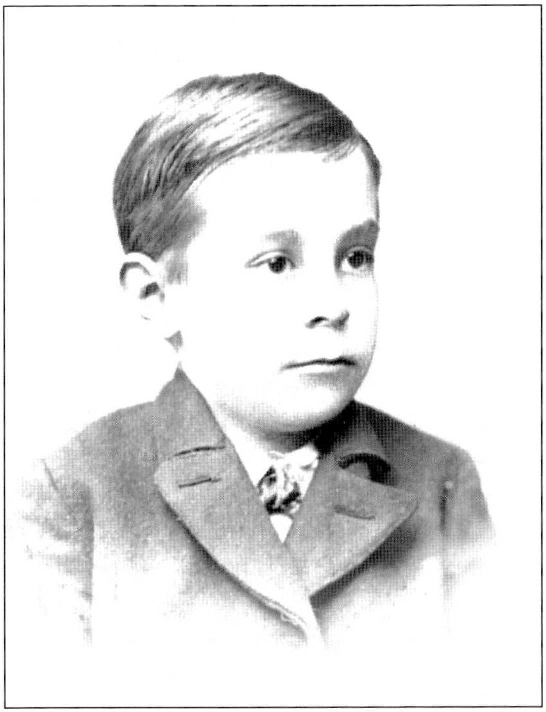

John Elisha "Lish" Snyder is shown in this picture from the early 1900s. His father was Joshua Snyder (whose family name was originally spelled Snider) and Doris Burrows Valley was his granddaughter. He was a dairy farmer and sold milk. (Photograph courtesy of Doris Burrows Valley.)

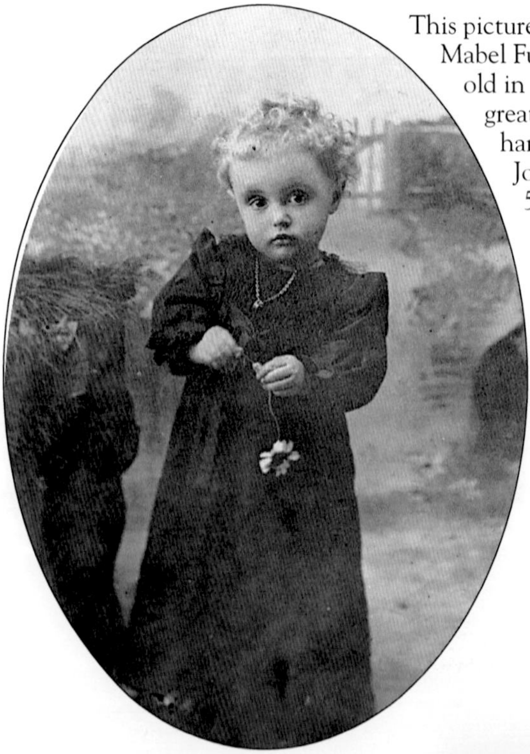

This picture, taken in the late 1890s, shows Mabel Furney Snyder at the age of two years old in her best grown-up dress. Mabel was a great seamstress and sewed clothing and handmade quilts. When her husband, John Elisha "Lish" Snyder, died at the age of 55 years, she was able to support herself by renting one of the properties that she had inherited. She later sold both properties and lived with her family. (Photograph courtesy of Doris Burrows Valley.)

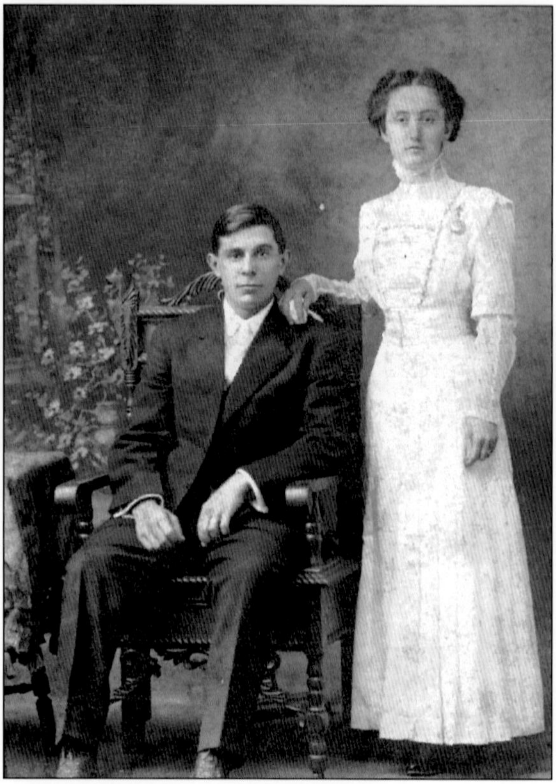

John Elisha "Lish" Snyder and his wife, Mabel Furney Snyder, are shown in this picture from the early 1900s. They lived at 8185 Bedford Road in Hubbard Township. They had four children—Sarah Elizabeth ("Betty"), Olive, Helen, and Robert (who passed away as an infant). Helen married Milo Burrows, and they had four children. (Photograph courtesy of Doris Burrows Valley.)

Three-year-old Doris Burrows is playing with her doll carriage in front of her grandparents' house that was located at 8185 Bedford Road in Hubbard Township. The house was built in the late 1800s. The original house was enlarged with an addition (on the left) that was part of the old family house, where Doris' great grandparents, Joshua Snyder and Carrie King Snyder lived. (Photograph courtesy of Doris Burrows Valley.)

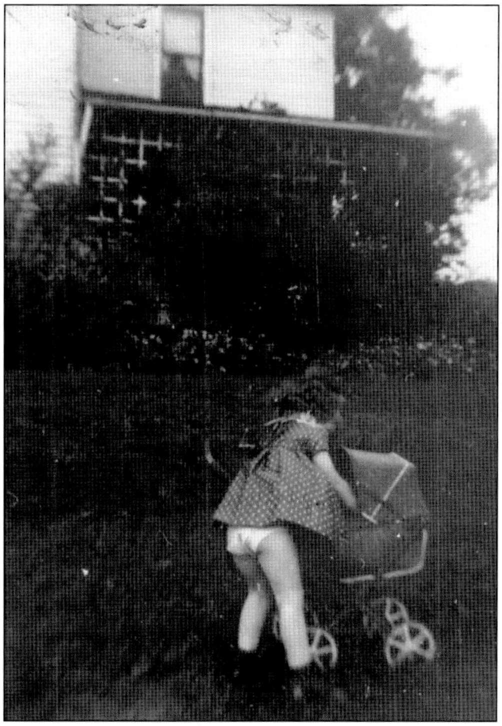

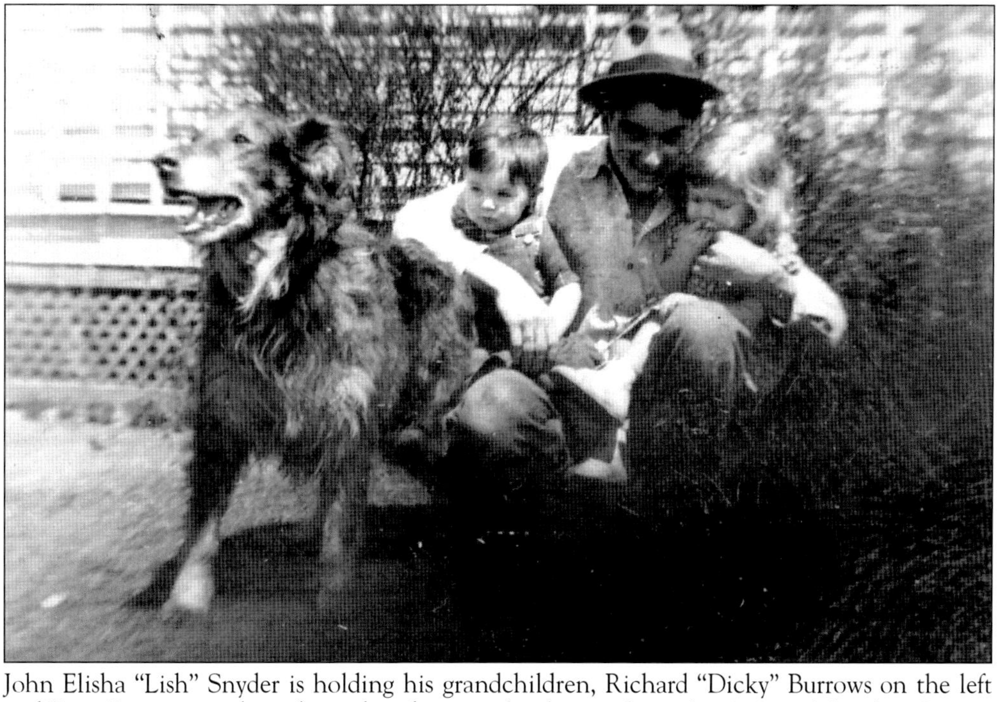

John Elisha "Lish" Snyder is holding his grandchildren, Richard "Dicky" Burrows on the left and Doris Burrows on the right in this photograph taken in the early 1940s with his dog, Ginger. "Lish" died soon after this picture was taken at the age of 55 years of a heart attack. He had a dairy farm, delivered milk to area families, and raised honeybees. (Photograph courtesy of Doris Burrows Valley.)

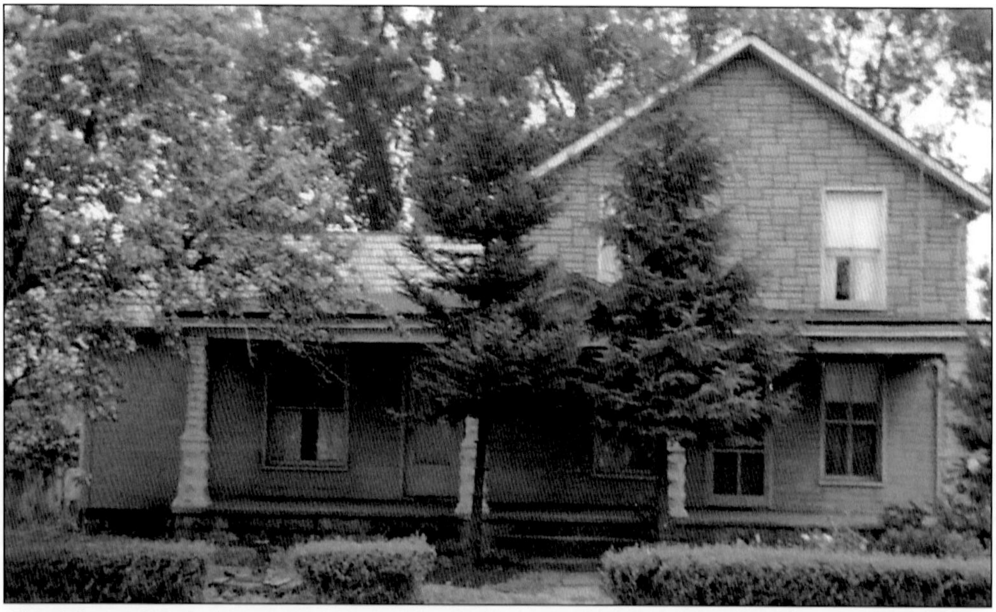

The Julia and Joseph Kuty homestead located at 3597 Pothour-Wheeler Road was used as a two-family home. The Kuty's resided on the left side of the house and they had a separate entrance. Their daughter, Anna Kuty Halicki, her husband, Anthony, and four children resided on the right side. It was larger, consisting of a living room in front, kitchen at the back and upstairs a large bedroom, a smaller bedroom, and a large hall. (Photograph courtesy of Ruth Halicki Means.)

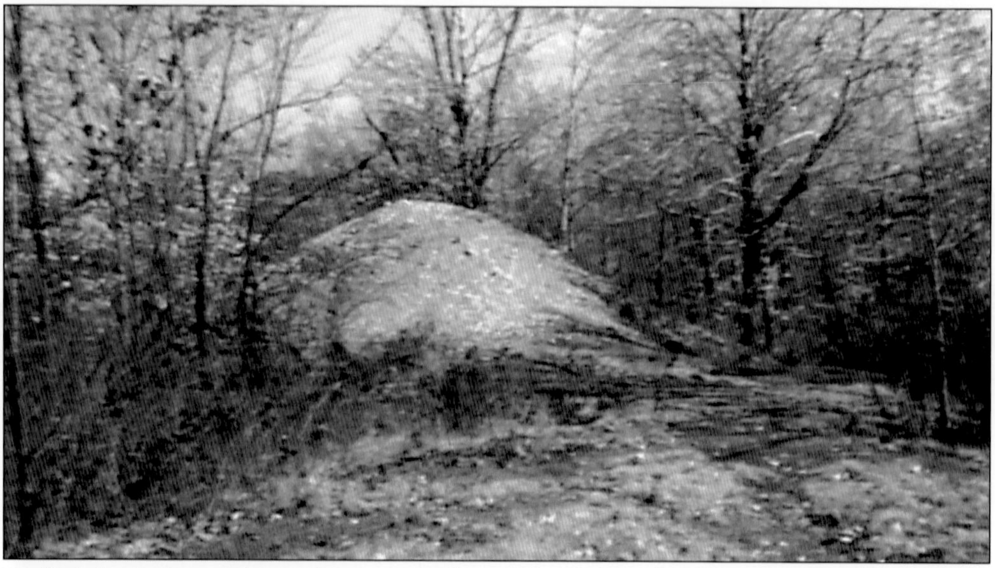

Dr. Dale Jacobs leased this coalmine on Pothour-Wheeler Road for 99 years even though it was only in operation until 1919. By the time this picture was taken in the 1960s the square shaft opening to the mine had filled in with water. The hill that can be seen in the picture consisted of slag and rocks that had been dug out of the mine. In the early 1990s, the mine was capped and filled in with dirt and the only evidence remaining is a ventilation pipe that was installed to vent gases. (Photograph courtesy of Ruth Halicki Means.)

Three

Coalburg and West Hubbard Township

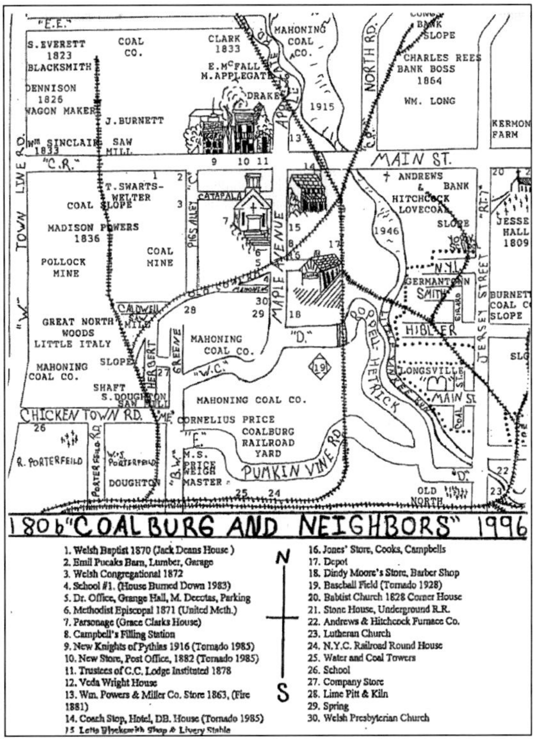

A map drawn by Jackie Miller with the help of long-time Coalburg residents, Grace Clark and Mildred DeCoda, shows Coalburg in the past. At one time Coalburg was larger than Hubbard because of all the coalmines. Jesse Hall, owner of one of the first coalmines, leased it to Powers and Arms, and later to the Mahoning Coal Company, who built railroad tracks to transport the coal. E.P. Burnett owned one of the most valuable mines and it was leased to Andrews and Hitchcock. By the 1880s most of the mines were mined out. The roads in Coalburg all had different names in the past. Chestnut Ridge Road was called Main Street; the west portion of Mount Everett Road was called Chicken Town Road; the east portion of Mount Everett Road was called Pumpkin Vine Road; Wick-Campbell Road was called Maple Avenue; Drummond Avenue Extension was called Ropell-Hetrick Road; and Collar-Price Road was called North Road. The Coalburg Train Depot was located at the east end of Old Station Road. Passengers could ride the train to Youngstown, Cleveland, Pittsburgh, or Erie. Italian immigrants settled at the intersection of Wick-Campbell Road and Bell-Wick Roads, so it was known as "Little Italy." The Coalburg railroad workers had a very good baseball team and their ballpark was located south and east of where Wick-Campbell Road and Drummond Avenue Extended intersect. They won the Vanderbilt Cup in 1924 and were honored with a dinner at the McKelvey's Tea Room. A tornado in 1928 damaged the fence and grandstand and it was never rebuilt because of the Depression. Coalburg had three churches at one time including the Welsh Baptist Church built in 1870, the Methodist Episcopal Church built in 1871, and the Welsh Congregational Church built in 1872. Only the Methodist Episcopal Church remains, and it is now called the United Methodist Church and is located on Wick-Campbell Road. (Map courtesy of Jackie Miller.)

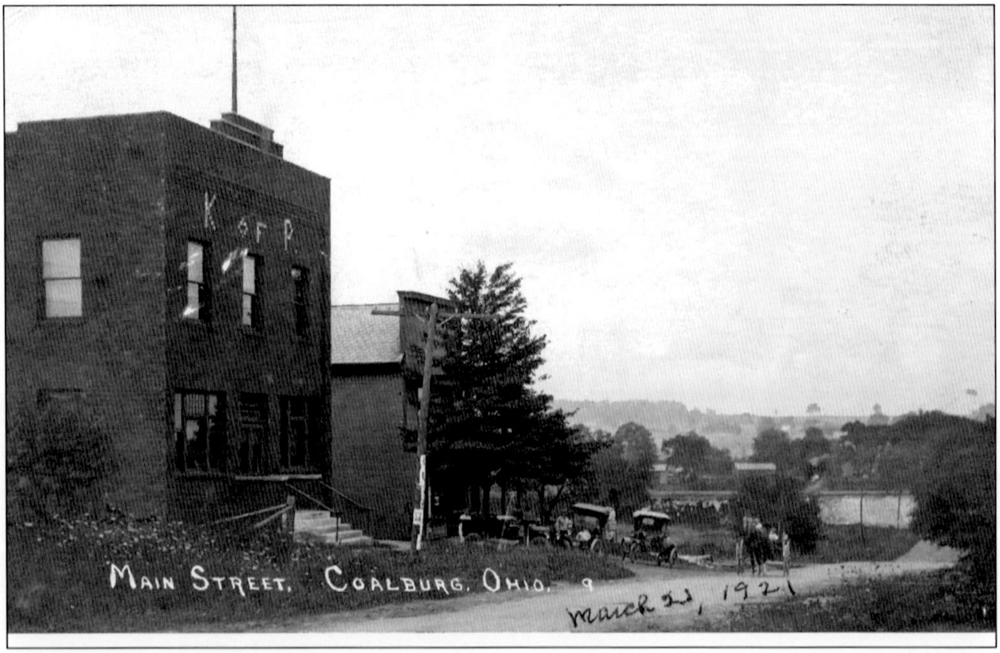

The Knights of Pythias Building, left, was built in 1914 and was located on Main Street (now Chestnut Ridge Road) in Coalburg. The old store was built in 1882. The picture is dated March 21, 1921. Both buildings were leveled by the 1985 tornado. (Photograph courtesy of Hubbard Historical Society from a collection of Mildred DeCoda.)

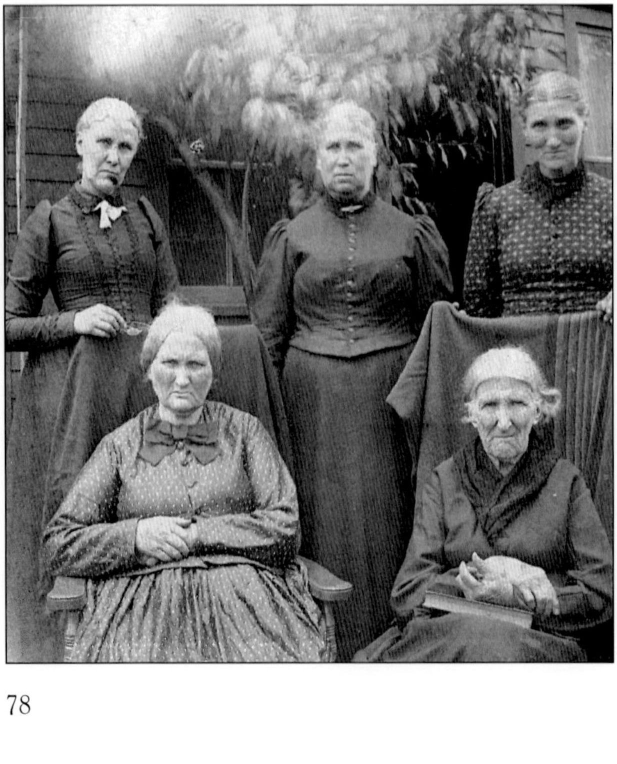

Julia Applegate McFall, is pictured at the bottom left with her mother, Mrs. Applegate, and her three sisters, Mrs. Hirst, Mrs. Demming, and Mrs. Augustine. Julia Applegate married Eli McFall on March 1, 1918. She was born in 1838 and died in 1908. Eli McFall was born on April 20, 1834 about one half mile west of Geography Hall in Coitsville Township. He died on June 7, 1904. Their children were Odisie, who died during childbirth, Ollie, Ellie, Harmon R., William A., and Ellis E. (Photograph courtesy of Harry McFall.)

Eli McFall joined the Ohio Volunteer Infantry on April 27, 1864, when he was 30 years old. He was stationed at Sandusky Trap, Kentucky. At Keller's Bridge, Kentucky Morgan's Cavalry attacked his unit on June 11, 1864. Thirteen men were killed, 54 were wounded, and many were taken prisoner, including Eli. He was later paroled and served at Johnson's Island as a guard. He was so sick with fever when he was discharged on August 20, 1864, that he was carried to the boat on a stretcher. (Photograph courtesy of Harry McFall.)

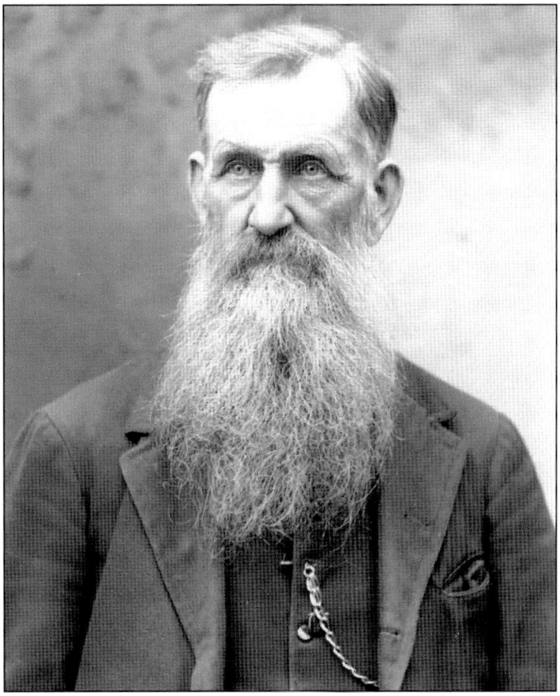

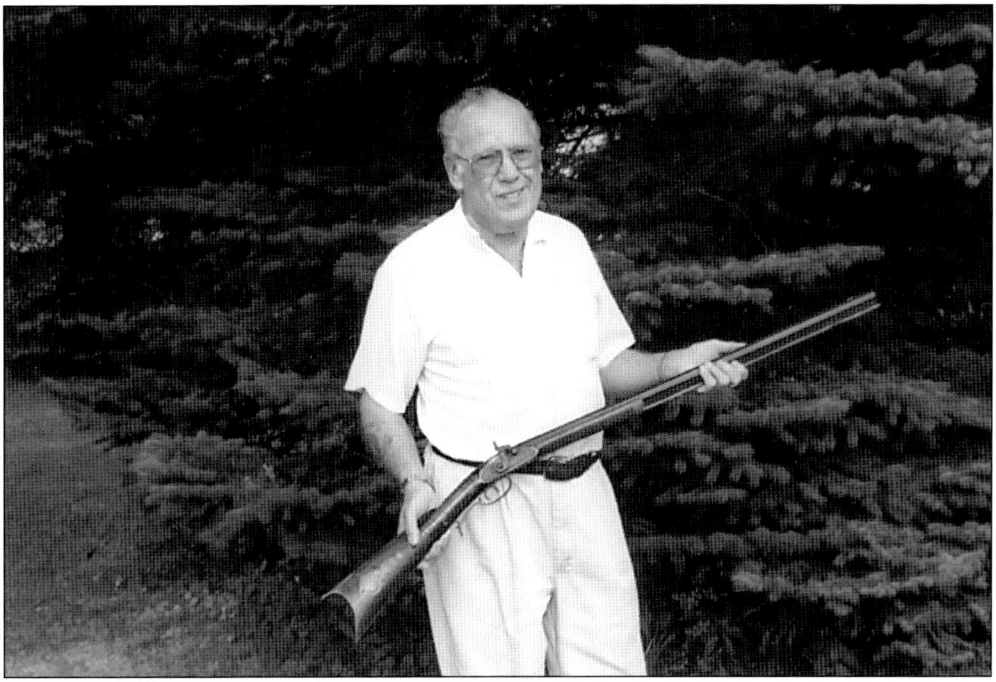

Harry McFall is holding his great grandfather, Eli McFall's, muzzleloader gun, which he used during his 100 day Civil War service. The gun has names and initials marked on its steel hex barrel: C. Kohl, J.H. Kein, and T.M. It used caps to set off the gunpowder, which would discharge the lead pellet. The gunpowder would be tamped down with a hickory rod stored under the muzzle. (Photograph courtesy of Harry McFall.)

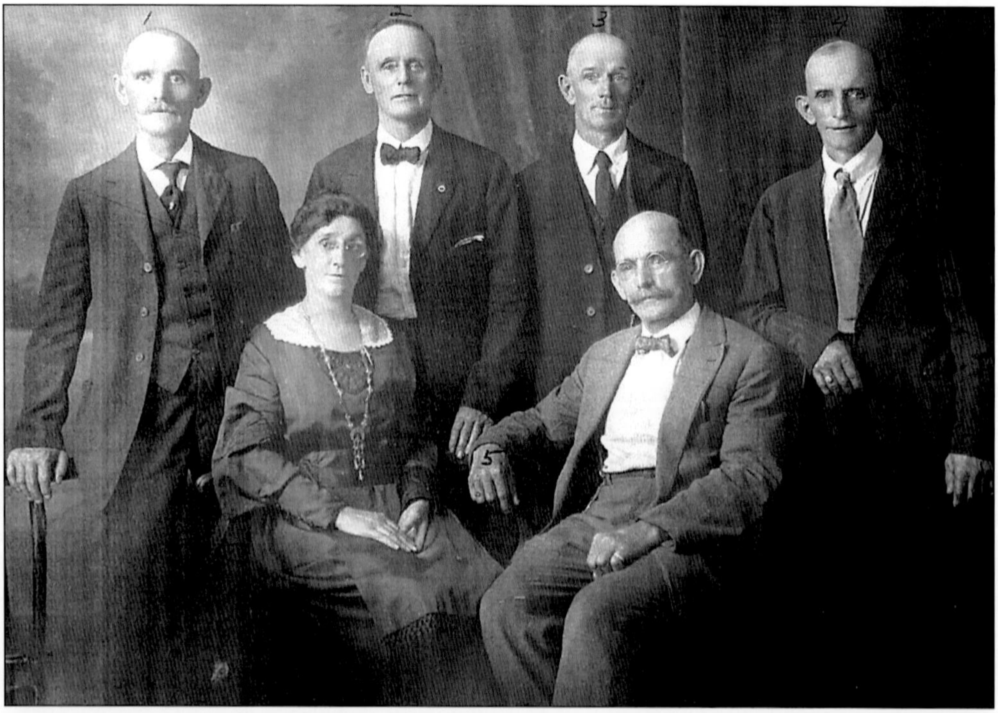

The children of Theobald Schilling, from left to right, are: (front row) Margaret and George; (second row) Theobald II, Frank, Daniel, and Lewis. Theobald emigrated from Germany in 1853 and came to Hubbard in 1865 to work in the Coalburg mines. On July 5, 1901, while riding an excursion train traveling through Sharon, he died while jumping off the train, as he wanted to visit his daughter. (Photograph courtesy of Edward F. Burns and Marian Harris.)

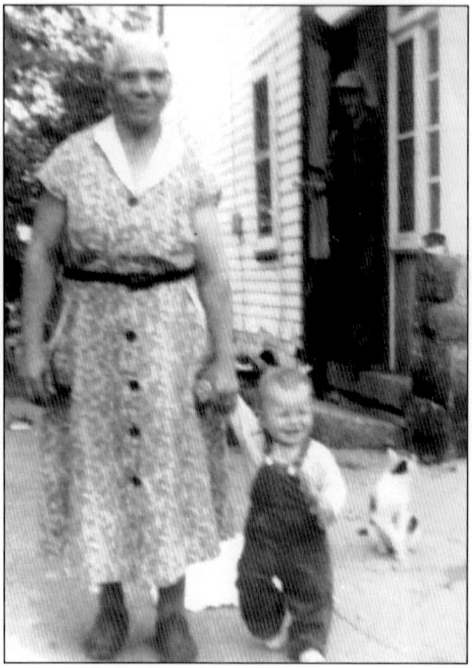

Mary Petrella is shown with her grandson, Salvatore (Sal) Halicki, who was around one-year old in this photograph from 1955. Sal's dad, Anthony, is in the doorway. Mary came from Italy in 1915 arriving in America through Ellis Island. She and her second husband, Salvatore Petrella, came to Coalburg to a 15-acre farm on Wick-Campbell Road. Many Italian immigrants lived on the northern part of Bell-Wick Road so it was known as "Little Italy." Their farms were small but self-supporting. At harvest time, the neighboring farmers would help each other, and their wives would cook. (Photograph courtesy of Cecelia and Sal Halicki.)

On the right is Ambrose "Ham" Zileski with an unknown individual on the left. "Ham" was a pitcher on the New York Central Railroad's Coalburg baseball team, which was started by Joe Murphy and "Ham" in 1906. The team won the Vanderbilt Cup in 1924 and was honored with a dinner at the McKelvey's Tea Room. Their field was located in Coalburg and was destroyed by a tornado and never rebuilt. (Photograph courtesy of Gerald and Mala Smith.)

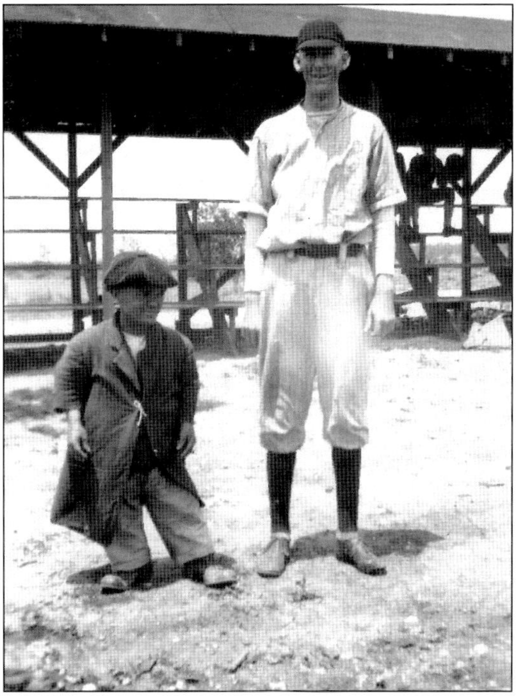

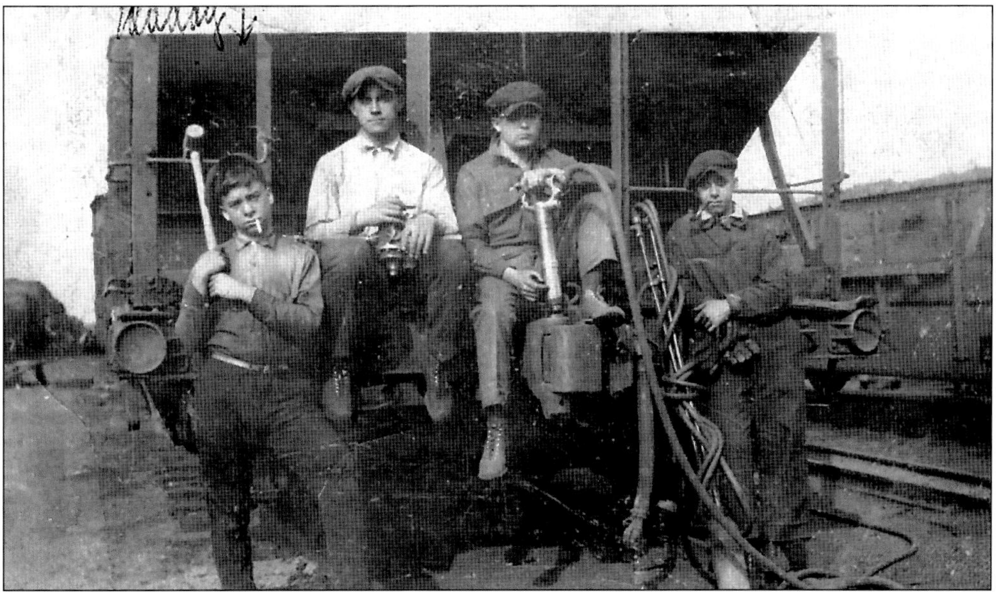

William "Butch" Ellsworth Arnold is shown on the left with three of his fellow railroad workers. "Butch" worked for the Pennsylvania and Lake Erie Railroad. He grew up in Hubbard on South Main Street, married Maryland Worley, and then moved to Youngstown when he was 23. He worked for Budno's Meat Market as a teenager, delivering meat to customers. Budno's was located on West Liberty Street in the IOOF building next to the Liberty Confectionery. (Photograph courtesy of Betty Arnold Linebaugh.)

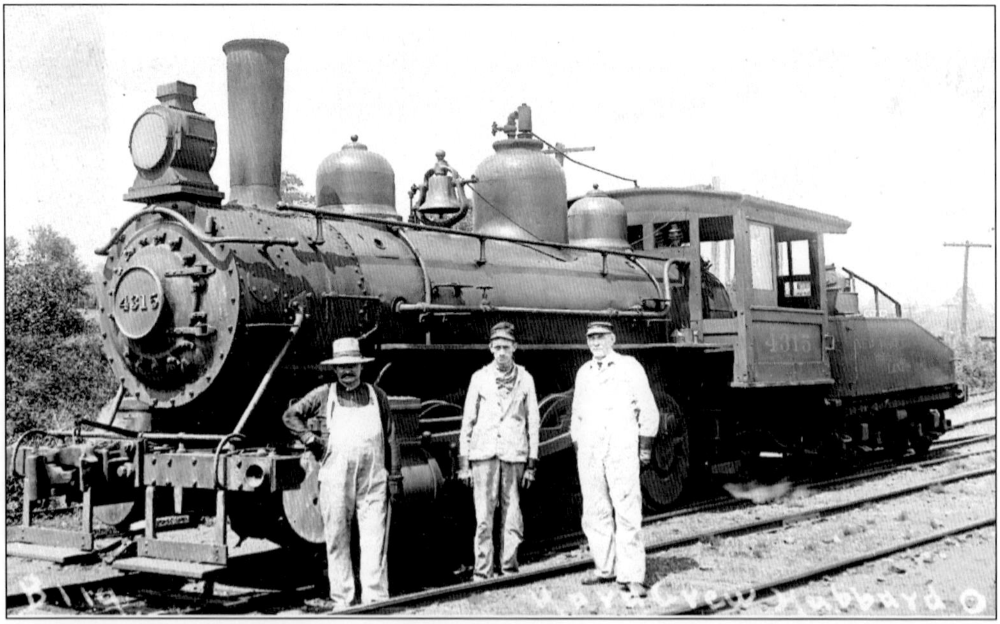

A yard crew is standing in front of their steam locomotive at the LS&MS (Lake Shore and Michigan Southern) rail yard in Coalburg. The fireman's most important jobs were keeping water in the boiler, and coal in the firebox. Water from the tender was pumped to the boiler where it turned into steam. Coal was loaded into the front part of the tender. The fireman shoveled coal into the firebox after stepping on a pedal to open the doors. Diesel engines replaced steam locomotives in the Hubbard area in 1954. (Photograph courtesy of Harry McFall.)

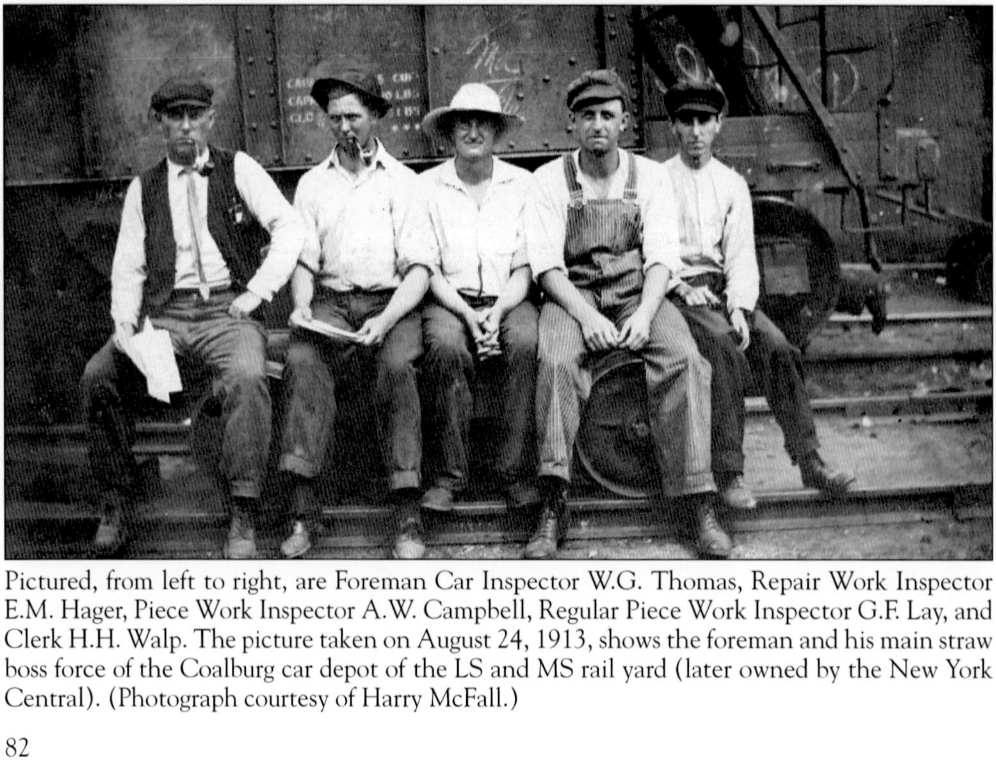

Pictured, from left to right, are Foreman Car Inspector W.G. Thomas, Repair Work Inspector E.M. Hager, Piece Work Inspector A.W. Campbell, Regular Piece Work Inspector G.F. Lay, and Clerk H.H. Walp. The picture taken on August 24, 1913, shows the foreman and his main straw boss force of the Coalburg car depot of the LS and MS rail yard (later owned by the New York Central). (Photograph courtesy of Harry McFall.)

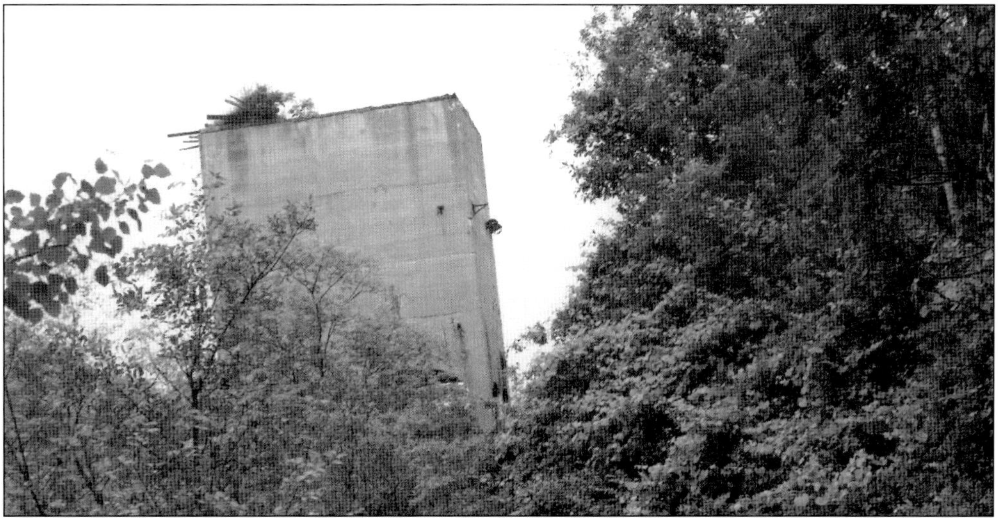

A water tower of the old New York Central Railroad Yard, located east of Bell Wick Road and south of Drummond Avenue, is shown in this photograph taken in 2004. After the coalmines were exhausted in Coalburg and Hubbard Township in the late 1880s, the opening of the New York Central Railroad Yard in the early 1900s revived the economy for a short while, as yard work was transferred here from Youngstown. The water was used for the steam engines.

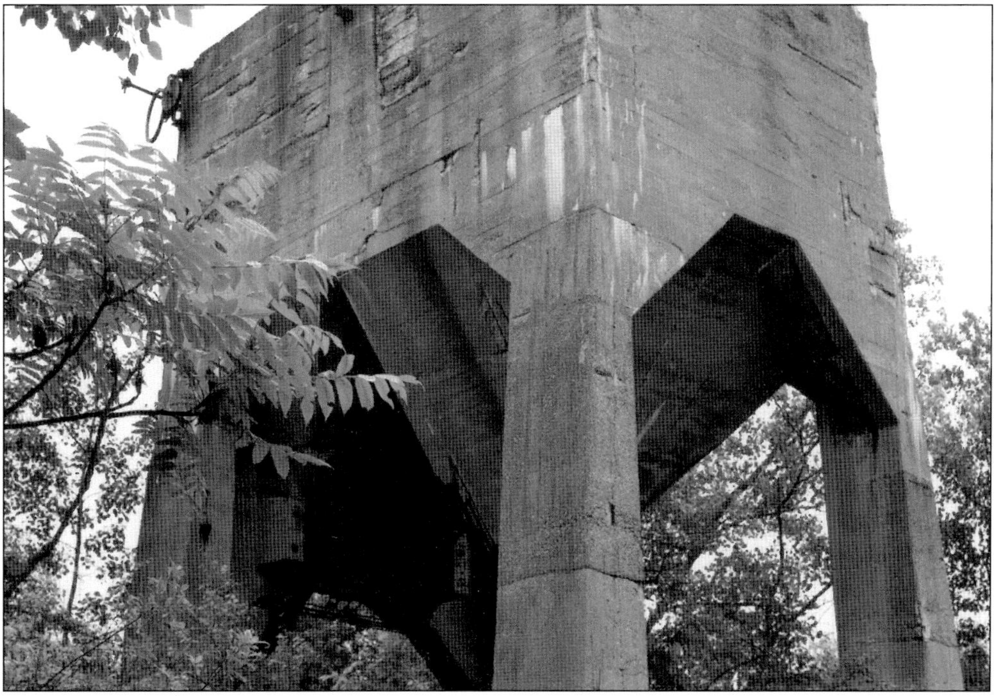

The coal tipple of the old New York Central Railroad Yard in Coalburg, located east of Bell Wick Road and south of Drummond Avenue, as pictured as it looked in 2004. The coal would be taken to the top of the tipple with a conveyor belt and would be loaded into the steam locomotive's tender underneath. All the metal structures that were at the top of the coal tower are gone and just the lower cement structure is left.

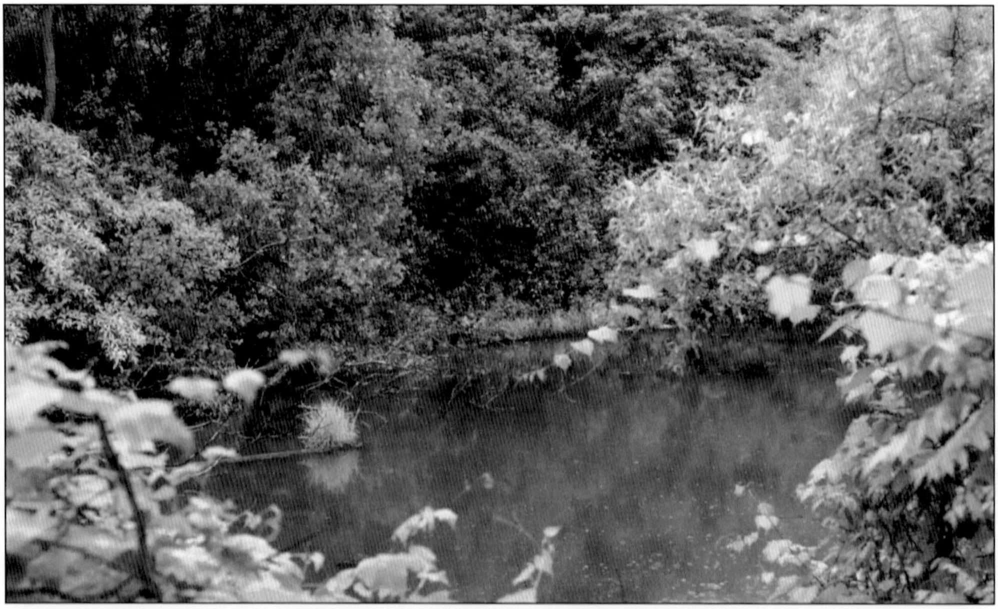

At the old New York Central Railroad Yard in Coalburg, a turntable and a roundhouse were used to repair locomotives. Today, where the turntable originally was located, is a small pond. When the railroad yard was operating, there was a small hotel to the north of the roundhouse. The roundhouse had a red brick chimney and after the yard closed in the mid 1920s, the bricks were used to make driveways.

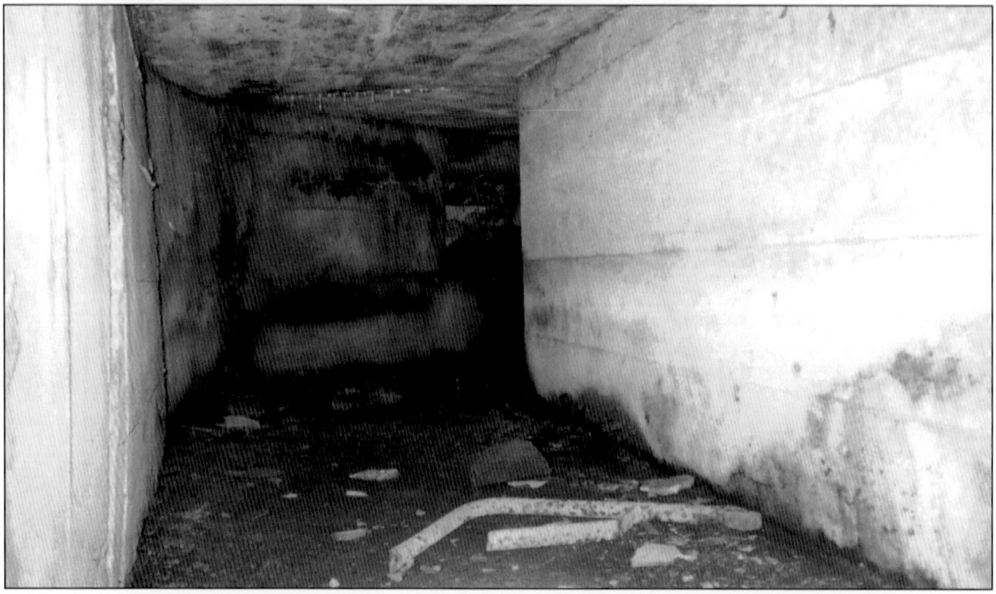

Tunnels were built under the roundhouse at the New York Central Railroad Yard in Coalburg to maintain the locomotives and provide electric and plumbing for the turntable and roundhouse. The electric cables that provided electricity for the turntable were made of copper, six inches in diameter. The main tunnel is in good condition, but stalactites are on the ceiling and the side tunnels have caved in. The tunnel curves to the right as it was built in a semicircle, with smaller tunnels radiating outward like the spokes of a wheel.

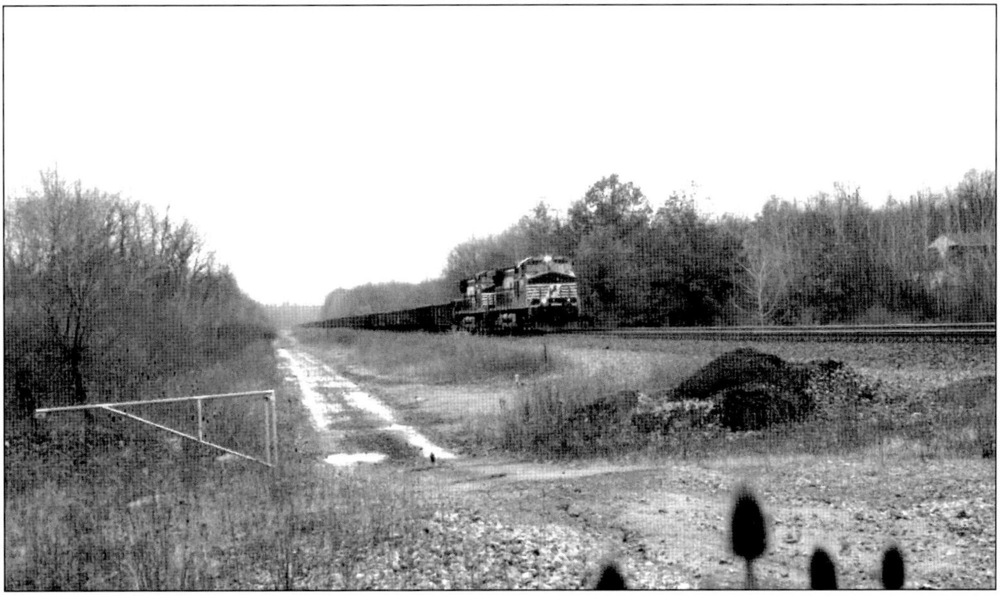

Familiar sights to everyone are the Norfolk Southern trains crossing Hubbard's roads. On the west side of Hubbard, especially at night, the train whistle can be heard at five crossings—Logangate Road, West Liberty Street, Lewis Seifert Road, Bell-Wick Road, and Mt. Everett Road. The whistle starts when the engineer sees the "W" sign on the side of the track. The whistle pattern is two long whistles, one short whistle, and one long whistle, which must be extended through the crossing. There is also a bell that the engineer rings.

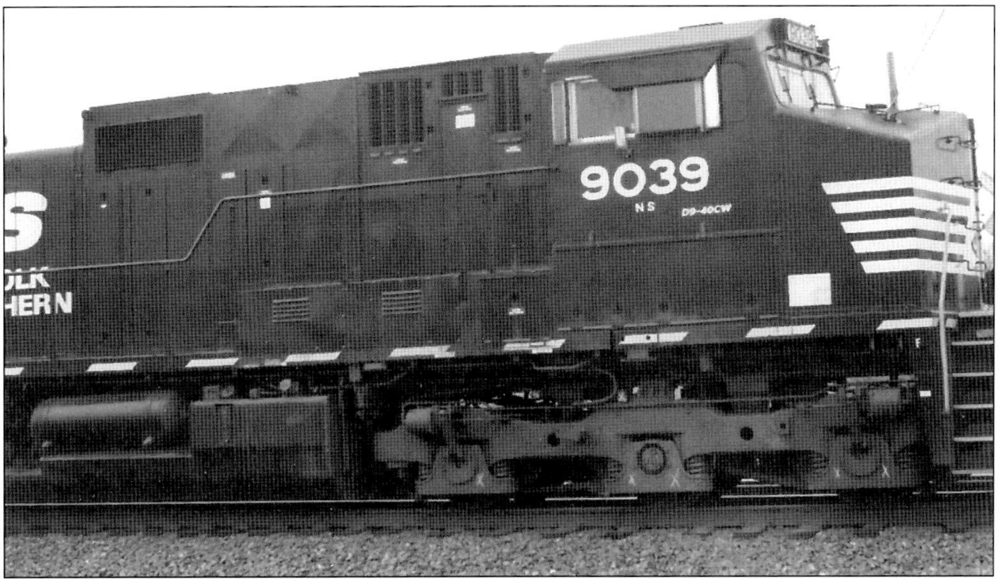

Trains that come from Valley Street in Youngstown have a five-mile gradual uphill climb that ends at Bell-Wick Road in Hubbard. After crossing Bell-Wick Road, the trains go east and north to Meadville, Pennsylvania or north to Ashtabula, Ohio. Coal and steel are the most common loads carried through Hubbard on their way to either power plants or steel companies. Occasionally, Norfolk Southern or CSX will lease other engines, such as Burlington Northern, Union Pacific, or Santa Fe.

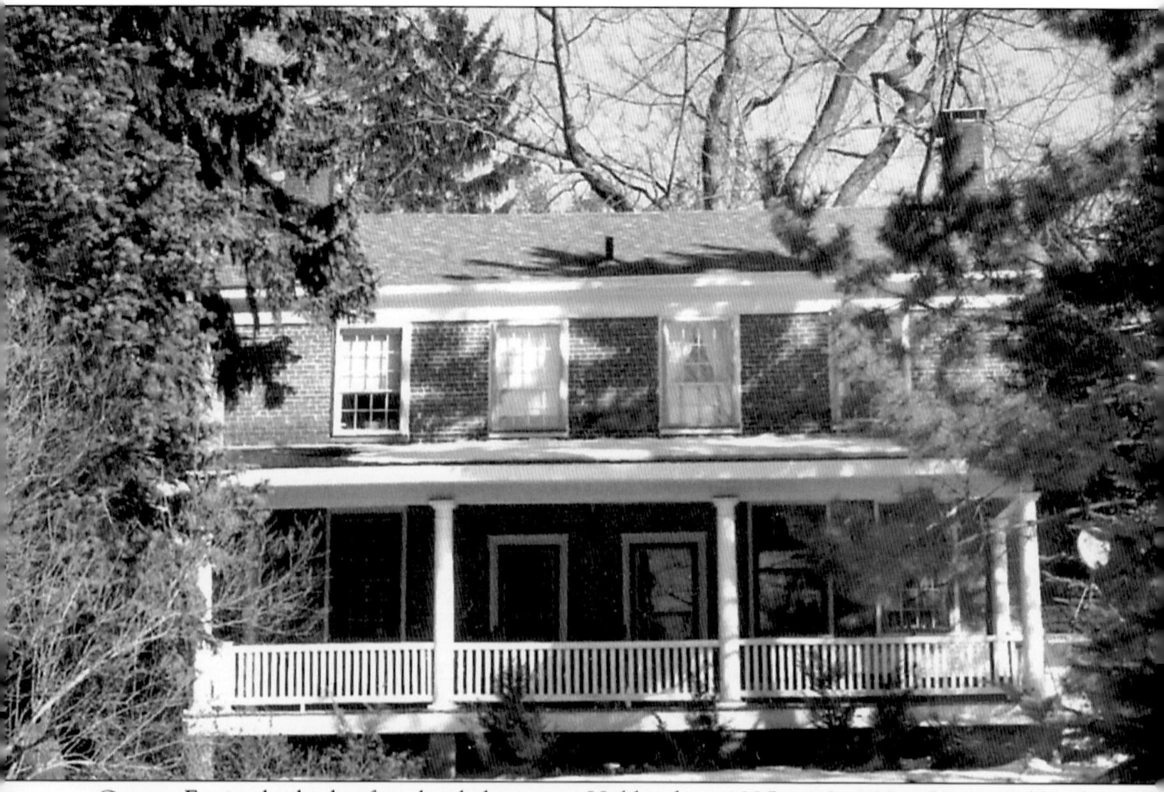

George Frazier built the first brick house in Hubbard in 1825 on Lot No. 58 in Hubbard Township. Oak trees were felled, trimmed of limbs, and left to lie where they fell to cure for three years. While curing, worms bored straight holes in the wood, one-sixteenth inch in diameter and two-inches deep where they made their home. We now call this lumber wormy oak. The holes are still visible in the ceiling beams of the basement. Also, while the wood was curing, George Frazier and David Doughton burned the bricks used to build the house. Brick was laid in a five-course common bond pattern which is weight bearing masonry. After the wood cured, the bark was removed. The trees were cut to 40-foot lengths. One-foot length of each end was placed on top of the large sandstone foundation on opposite ends, exposing 38 feet of beams on the ceiling in the basement, which is now a family room. The beams for the other two floors were made square with an adz. These are visible in the ceiling of the dining room. The age of the house was searched at the Trumbull County Records Archives in Warren by an abstract of the deeds and tax records from Frazier to Johnson. When taxes jumped from $1.17 in 1825 to $3.29 in 1826, this indicated a major improvement, most likely that a house had been built. Taxes were paid a year behind. Frazier owned a larger part of Lot No. 58 consisting of 117 acres. The house was built 100 feet from the existing spring, said to be built by the Indians using four huge sandstones, very neatly cut and butted tightly end to side on each corner, three feet deep with a sand bottom. It is still in existence with plenty of good water. The spring feeds Frazier's Creek, which eventually finds its way to Little Yankee Run. Bill and Dotty Johnson bought the house in August of 1966 and over a period of ten years restored the house beautifully. The front of the house faces west on Bell-Wick Road (formerly called Coalburg Road), however, Bill and Dotty use Shadyside Drive as their address. To the east of the house was a large deposit of sand, which was excavated and used in making concrete for Hubbard High School on Hall Avenue. The door on the right side of the front of the house is wider in order to allow the passage of a coffin when a family member died, because funerals were held in homes at this time. (Photograph courtesy of Bill and Dotty Johnson.)

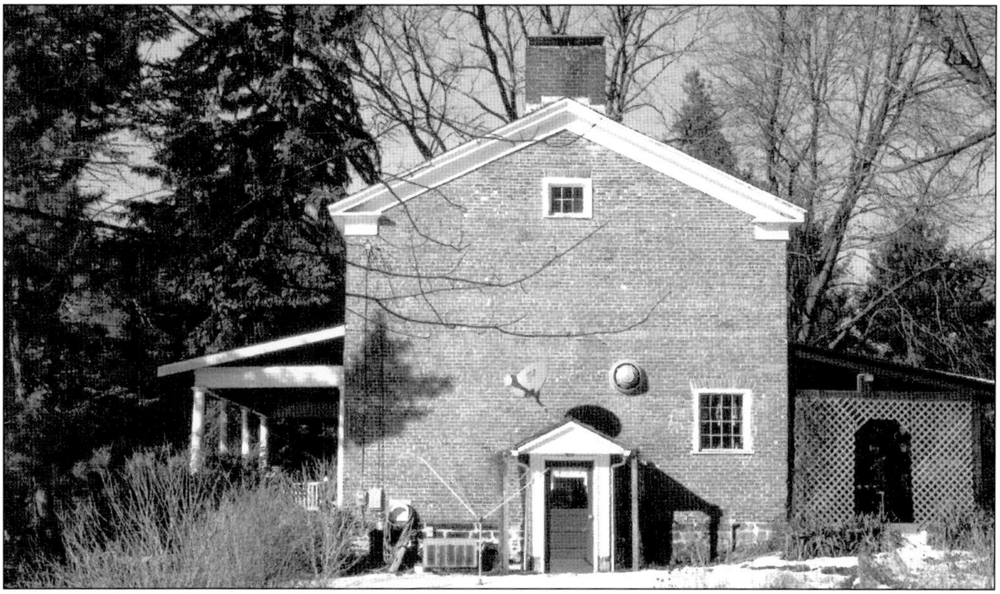

A porch (on the right side of the picture) was added onto the house and built of oak beams from an Amish barn that was torn down in Pennsylvania. Most of the windows in the house are original to the house, except one on the north side of the house and the kitchen window, which was too small and high so it was enlarged. It can be seen on the bottom right in the picture. The first floor consists of a kitchen and dining room on the south side, and a large living room, which extends the length of the house on the north side. There are four bedrooms, a large sitting room/hallway, and a bathroom on the second floor. (Photograph courtesy of Bill and Dotty Johnson.)

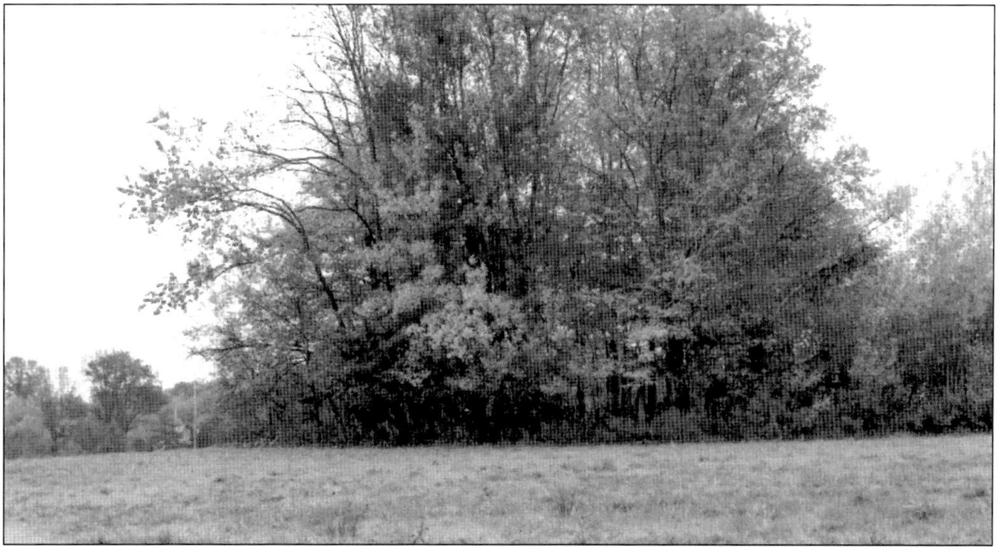

The Frazier family cemetery is located in a farm field, between Jacobs Road and the southern end of Roseview Drive. Today, only a small grove of trees with several cast iron fence posts remains of the cemetery. The headstones have either been taken or buried. An 1847 deed from John Frazier to Robert Stewart describes the property being sold, except for a small piece of land, 30 feet by 40 feet, which has been occupied as a burying ground. (From Trumbull County Deed Record 59, page 346.)

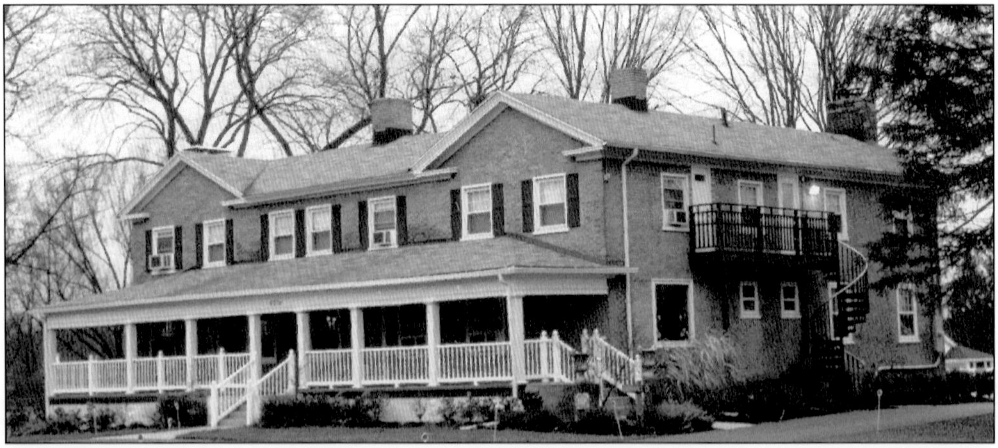

Julia's Bed and Breakfast, pictured in 2005, is located at the Pine Lakes Golf Club and Estates on West Liberty Street. Bradish Danforth most likely built the house in 1825. Other owners included: William Clingan Jr., 1850; Ohio Governor David Tod, 1906; and William J. Powell, 1927, owner of Powell Pressed Steel. J.V. Ferrara purchased the property in 1997, and after six years of renovation, opened the bed & breakfast for business. Future plans include the building of single-family homes, villas, and condominiums on the golf course.

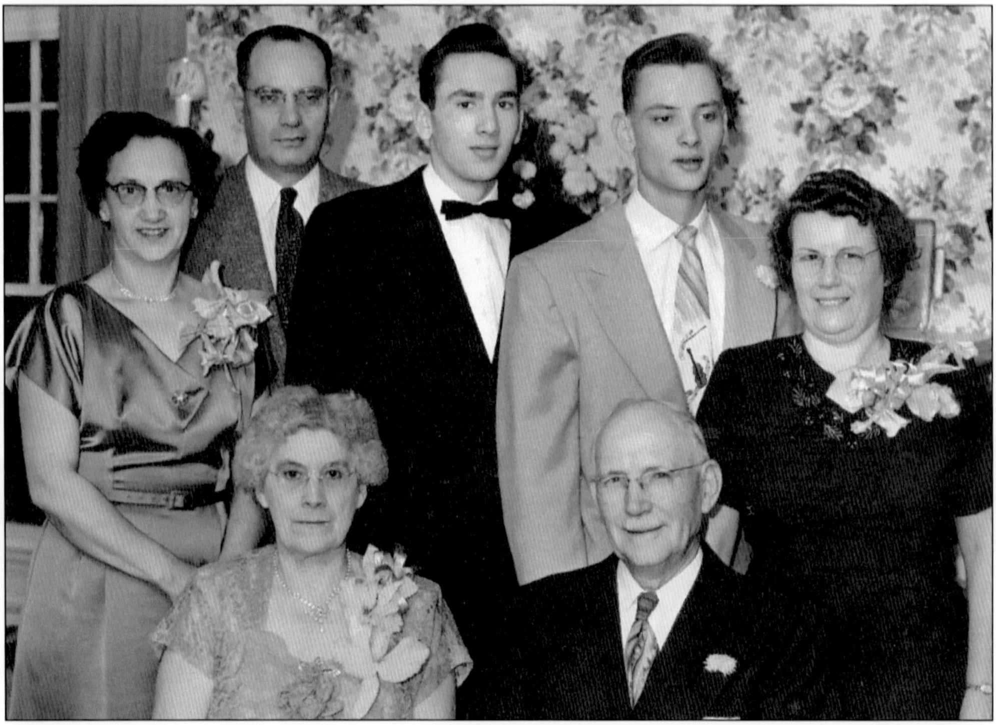

The William J. Powell family includes, pictured here from left to right: (front row) Mattie and William J. Powell; (back row) Marion Inglis Powell, Harold Powell, William R. Powell, Harold Powell Jr., and Mildred Powell. William J. Powell was the founder of Powell Pressed Steel and started the Powell public golf course on July 4, 1927 and operated it until 1956. It was later known as Hubbard Golf Course and now called Pine Lakes Golf Course. (Photograph courtesy of Hubbard Historical Society.)

Four

SCHOOLS

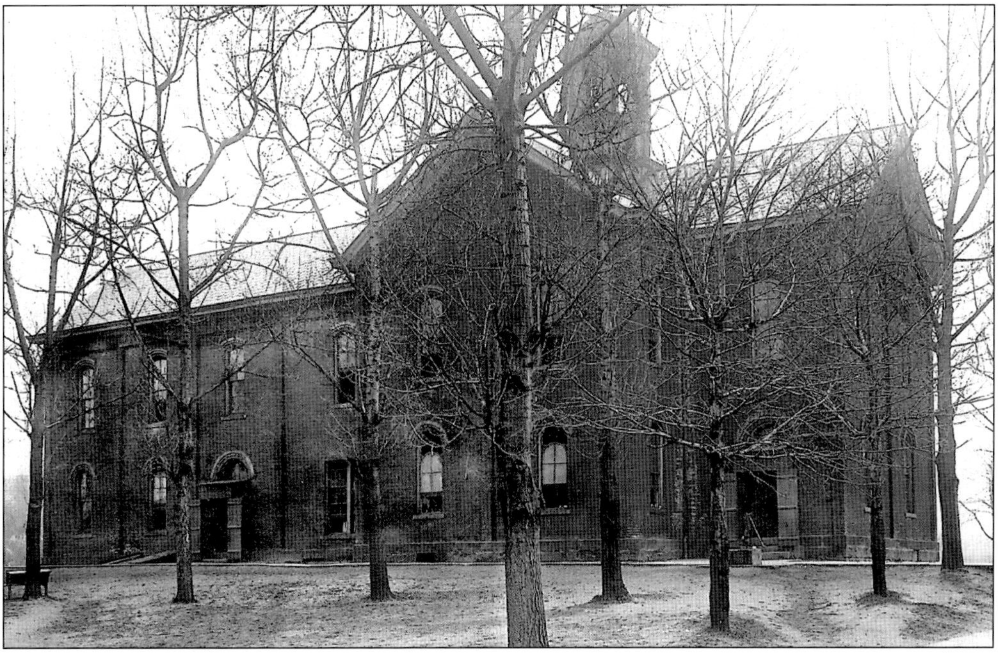

The old red brick school was built in 1870 and was the first free high school. It was located east of the present Roosevelt Elementary School and faced east. The township did not want to consolidate its schools with the village so a brick wall divided the school, with the village on the south side and the township on the north side. The grade schools for the village and the township were located on the first floor and the high schools for both were on the second floor. Later, Hubbard's population increased so rapidly that portable wooden buildings were used for the village fifth, sixth, seventh, and eighth grade students. (Photograph courtesy of Rich Stiver, history courtesy of Henry Pettitt.)

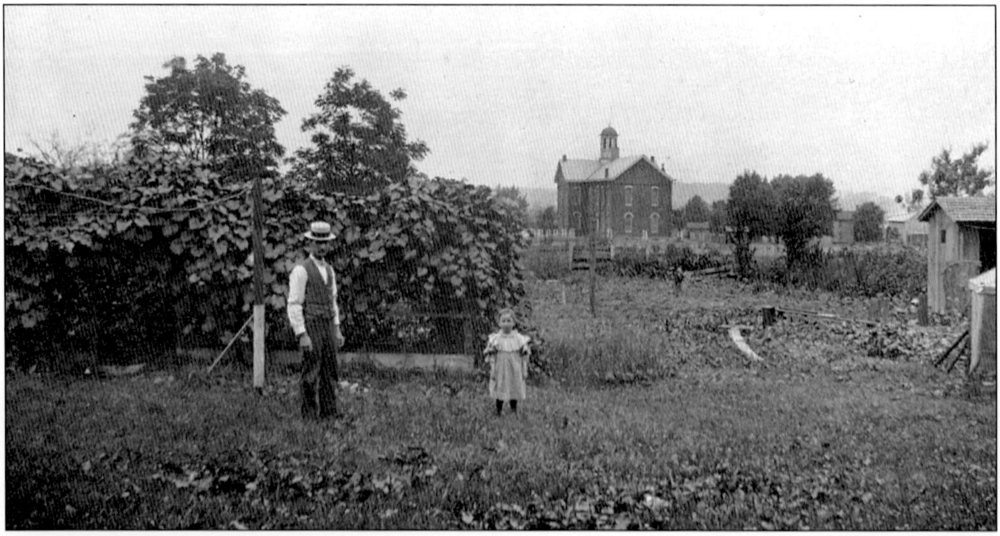

Vernell Brown Gray is pictured with her "Pa Pa," W.L. Brown, in 1895. The old red brick school is in the background facing east and the photographer was facing south to take this picture. This picture shows how rural Hubbard was in those days with farmland being the predominate feature. (Photograph courtesy of Nancy Gray Silvashy.)

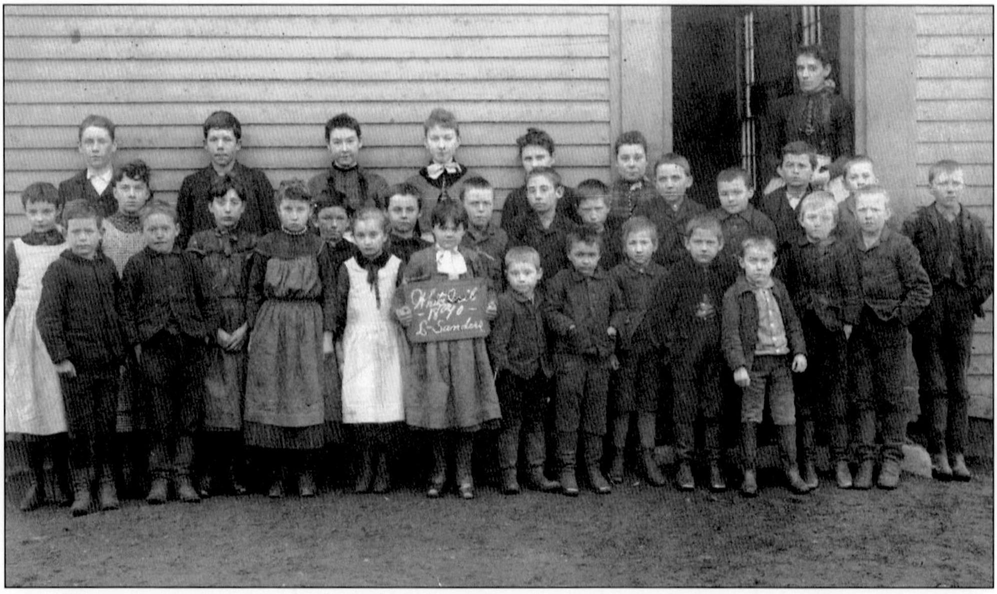

The White Jail School on Hubbard Bedford Road is now a residence. In 1890, the students were: (top row) Tom Mathews, Freeman Young, Flora Bentley Evans, Lois Pothour Brown, Carrie Mathews Bentley, Dora Marstellar Augustine; (the next two rows, up and down) include Alta Marstellar Anderson, Jay Mayers, Priscilla Curry, Arthur Williams, Elizabeth Williams, Myrtle Snyder Worley, Clate Bentley, Maude Randall Wise, Ray Mathews, Harriet Williams, George Snyder, Norman "Dick" Huff, Norman Marstellar, Lafe Williams, Cliff Brewer, Bernard Wittenauer, Morton Veach, Joy Marstellar, Ed Williams, Lawrence Snyder, Jim Williams, Bert Marstellar, Claude Randall, Jesse Marstellar, and Jim Huff. The teacher was Elizabeth Sanders Brown. (Photograph courtesy of Nancy Gray Silvashy.)

The eighth grade class of 1911 is pictured with their teacher, Hannah Gray Winkle, in front of the old red brick school. In the front row, from left to right, are Elizabeth Simeon Hoover, Elma Veach Malin, Lucille Farley, Lucille Lane Aiken, Lucille Quigley McDonald, Edna Quigley Becker, Marie Kimmell, Helen Ferguson, Wilda Davis, Mary Thomas Notman, and Hannah Gray Winkle. The boys in the back row are Ben Wolf, Carl Creed, Tom Mathews, Jessie Mitcheltree, William Paschki, Harold Hibler, Elmer Schottenberg, Harold Elliot, Lee Jackson, Frank Harris, and Harry Mathews. (Photograph courtesy of Nancy Gray Silvashy.)

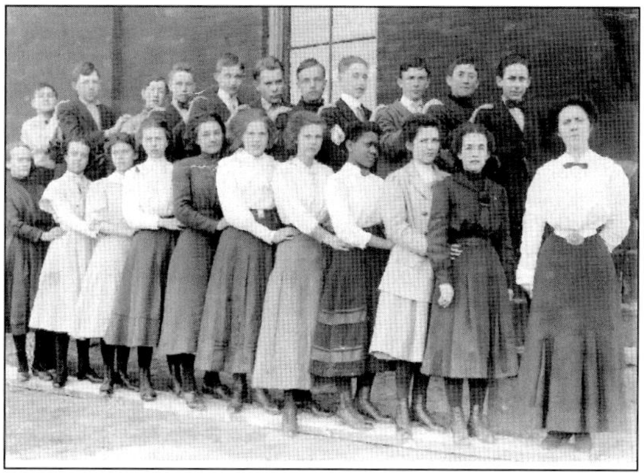

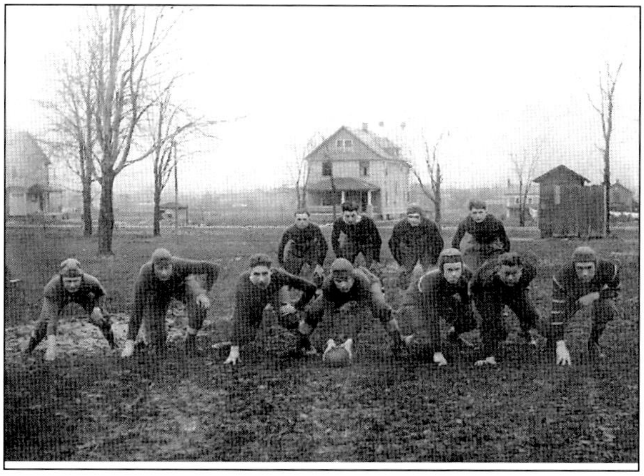

The football team at Hubbard High School in 1918 is in the muddy field, behind the old red brick school. The street in the background is School Street and all three houses look the same today. The muddy field is now the back parking lot for Roosevelt Elementary School (behind the gymnasium) and the outhouse is located near the driveway to the lot. The captain for the team was George Thomas and the manager was Frank Burr. (Photograph courtesy of Jerry and Cheryl Bell.)

Most of the members of the 1921 Hubbard High School's Girl's Basketball team had a nickname. From left to right the girls nicknames and real names (where known) are Olive "Shorty" Brown, "Curly" Davis, "Ruth," "Bill," Mariel "Jim" James Jenkins, Marybell "Skinny" Kerr, and teacher "Bob" Miss Forsythe. (Photograph courtesy of Nancy Gray Silvashy.)

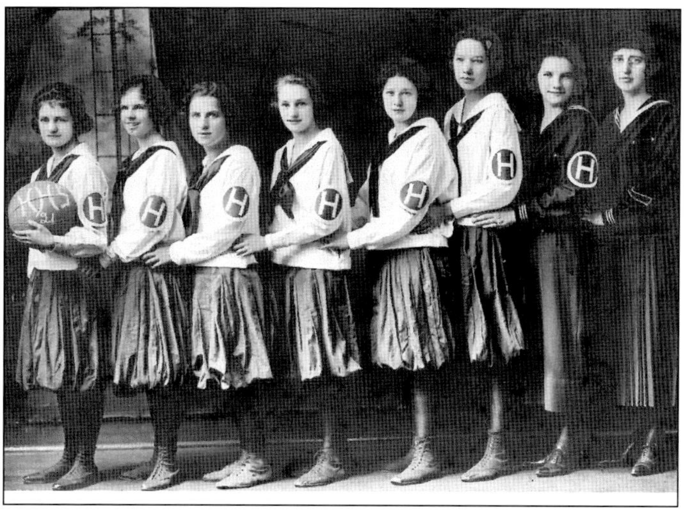

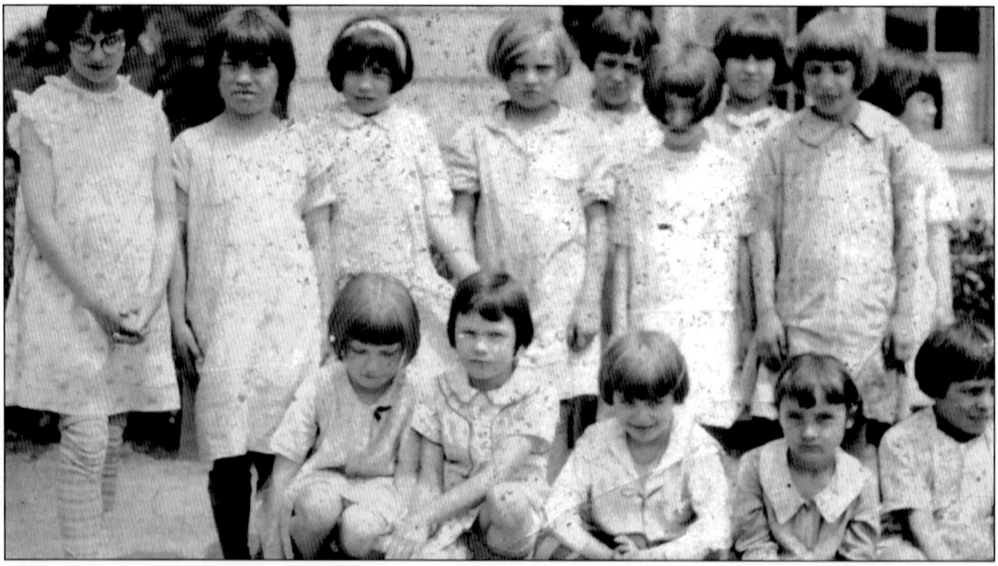

Miss Williams was the teacher of this second grade class in this picture from 1928. Pictured from left to right are: (first row) Betty Hammoc, Betty McMurray, Mary Pacura, Geri Springer, and Cecelia Petrella; (second row) unidentified, Grace Wilson, unidentified, unidentified, unidentified, Laurice Neal, unidentified, unidentified, and Isabelle Patton, Wilson Patton's sister. Cecelia Petrella, daughter of Mary and Salvatore Petrella, attended first grade at the Coalburg United Methodist Church in 1927. (Photograph courtesy of Cecelia Petrella Halicki and Sal Halicki.)

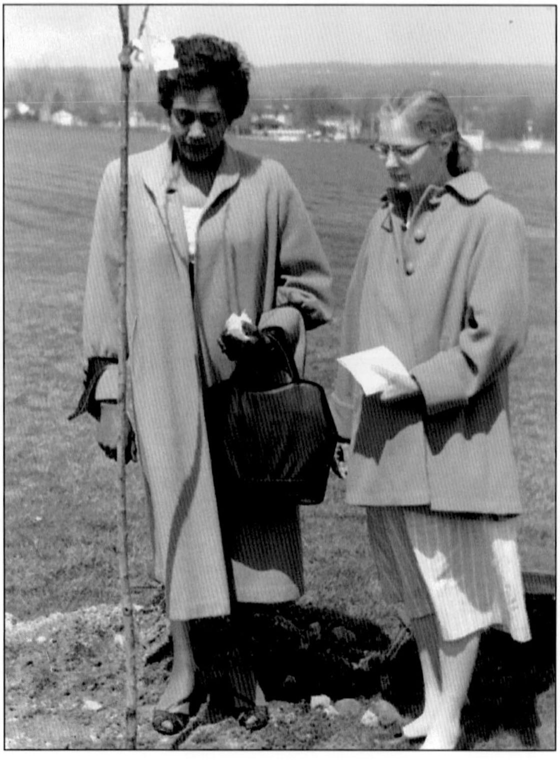

The semicircle of Hubbard High School on Hall Avenue is located to the left of this picture taken in 1958. Mrs. Holmes (on the left) and Mrs. Anna Kuty Halicki were dedicating a tree in honor of their deceased children. Anna lost her son, James Richard, on March 15, 1956 to rheumatic fever and leukemia when he was only 12 years old. (Photograph courtesy of Ruth Halicki Means.)

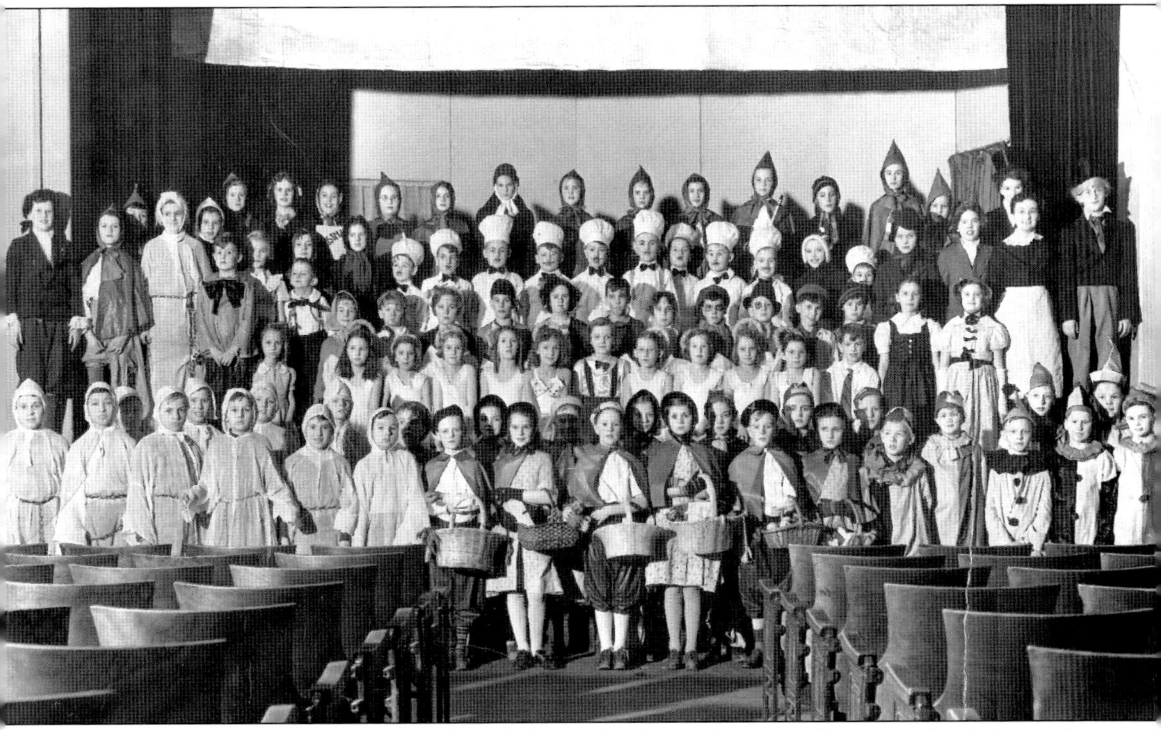

Scrooge's Christmas, an operetta adapted from Charles Dickens' A *Christmas Carol* featured students from Roosevelt Elementary School, mostly from the fourth, fifth, and sixth grades. Miss Gladys Harder directed this presentation in 1939. Pictured, from left to right, are: (front row) Bob "Pippy" Beaumire, Tom Angelo, Donald Klug, Harry Davis, Bob Gangloff, Bob Barhoover, Bill Mason, unidentified, Clayton Linsley, Barbara Reese, unidentified, Phyllis Balliet, unidentified, unidentified, unidentified, Clara Tribely, unidentified, Kenny Tufts, Don Tribely, Eldora Loy, Jim Thompson, unidentified, Wayne Allbright, unidentified, Danny Price, Bob Rieser, and Kenny Vasey; (second row) Ruthie Allen, unidentified, Barbara Reese, unidentified, unidentified, Cora Jean Jenny, Yvonne Yaley, unidentified, unidentified, Helen Reese, unidentified, unidentified; third row: Rose Marie Clark, unidentified, Adele Linsley, unidentified, ? Doyle, unidentified, unidentified, unidentified, unidentified, Jack Norton, unidentified, Delores Blose, and Suzanne Gangloff; (fourth row) Louis Patton, Eugene Letcher, Walter Moore, unidentified, ? Boothe, Danny Karnitski (Tiny Tim) behind Danny, unidentified, unidentified; the bakers starting with Billy Rolfe, Robert Fulton, Noel Hunsinger, Charles Thompson, Jack Wilson, Mike Faber, unidentified, Jack Mason, unidentified, unidentified, and Wayne Fry (last baker), Robert Legler, Bob Luce (Mr. Cratchit), Dolly Brownlee (Mrs. Cratchit), and John Horn (Scrooge); (fifth row) unidentified, unidentified, unidentified, Marjorie Marsteller, unidentified, Becky Gibson, Phyllis Mayers, Don Diroll, Margaret Layman, unidentified, unidentified, Mary Ellen Frye, unidentified, unidentified, and Mark "Ted" Franklin. (Photograph courtesy of Dolly Brownlee Hardin. Thanks to Dolly Brownlee Hardin and Jim Thompson for identifying students.)

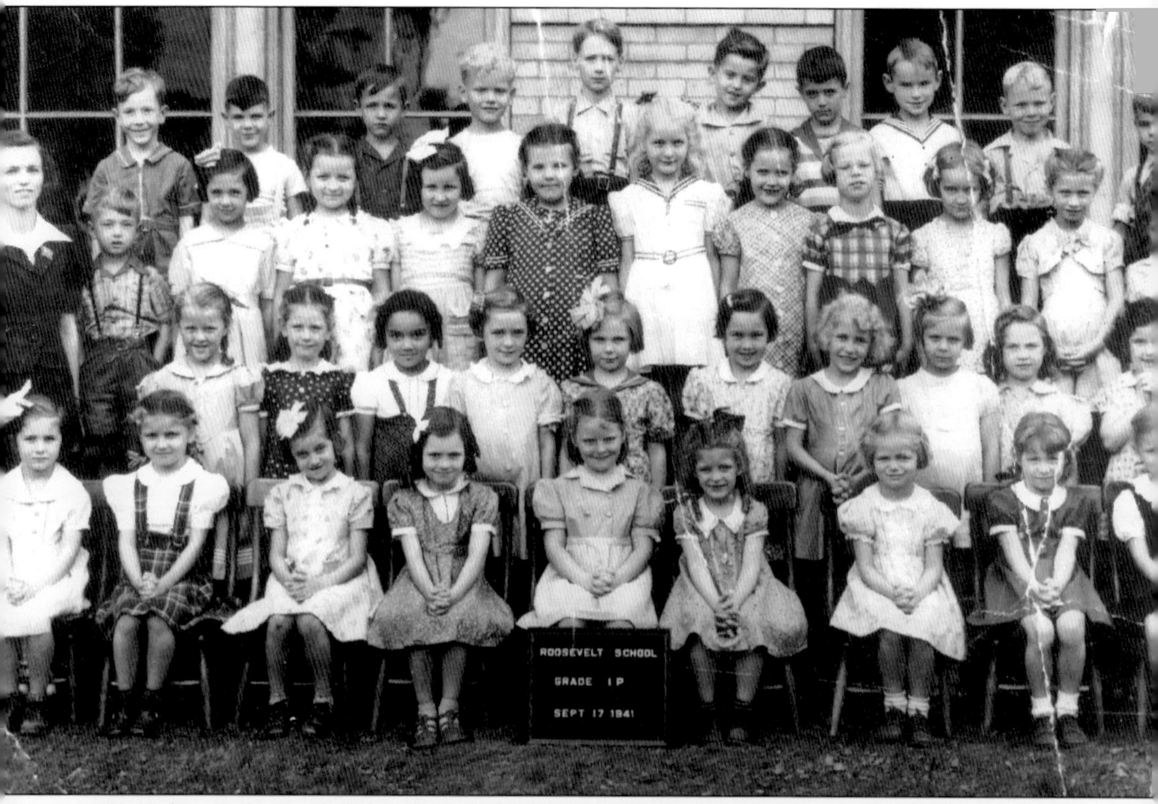

Mrs. Johns is shown with her first grade class from Roosevelt School on September 17, 1941. They belonged to the Hubbard High School Class of 1953 and would be the last class to graduate from Roosevelt High School on Orchard Avenue. Pictured from left to right are: (first row) Mary Margaret Weirick, Norma Jean Doyle, Beverly Hodgson, Betty Ours, Aileen Hinerman, Dorothy Cavanaugh, Carole Rae Farmer, Mary Joe McAlpin, and Iris Wolfgang; (second row) Jane Stewart, Nancy Koehli, Elva Faber, Shirley Mason, Shirley Tribley, Mary Jane Newell, Janet Ross, Judy Hamill, Alice Gardner, and Jackie Ritenour; (third row) Mrs. Johns, Donald Pettit, Marie Felca, Lillian Dudarewicz, Doris Jean McClelland, Shirley Bowers, Joyce Hunsinger, Beverly Wills, Joey Phillips, Veda Clark, Margaret Maines, and Tom Nutter; (fourth row) John Curry, Russ Webb, James Fedorchak, Tom Johnson, Bill Waltman, Don Fedor, John Rosile, Alan Gunner, Bob Wolford, and Bob Castner. (Photograph courtesy of Carol Rae Farmer Hurl. Thanks to Judy Hammill Ruby and Bev Wills Creed for identifying students.)

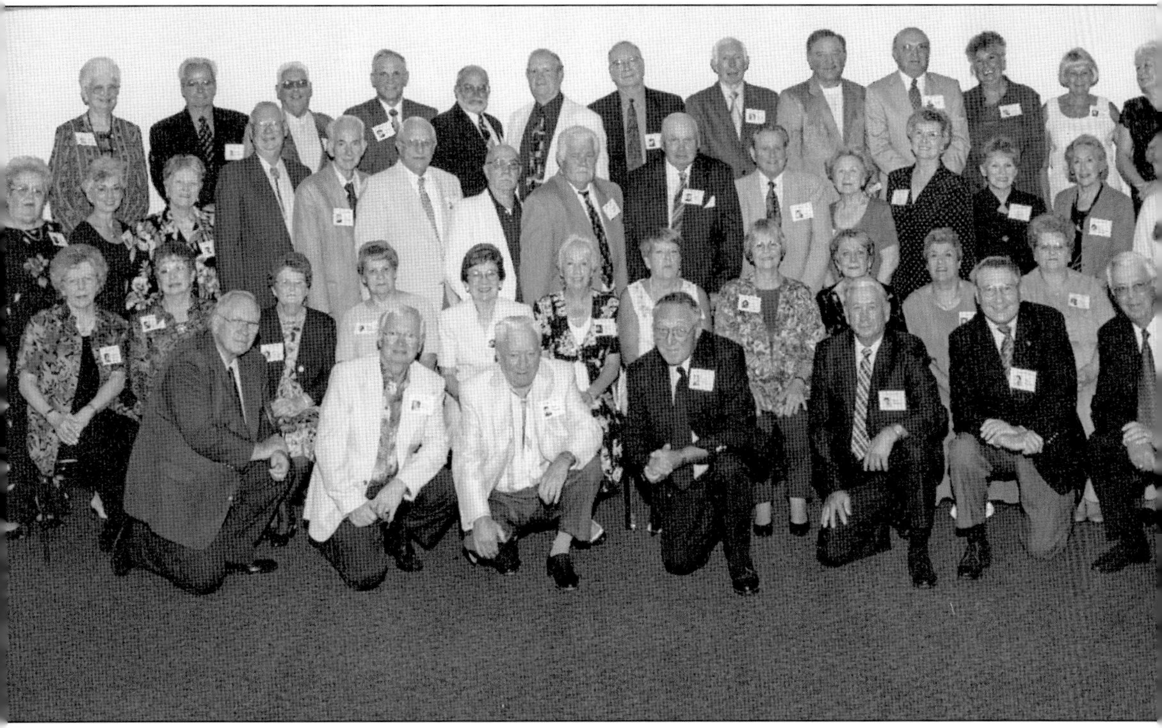

The last class to graduate from Roosevelt High School on Orchard Avenue was the class of 1953. Their 50th class reunion was held at The Gentry in August of 2003. Pictured here from left to right, are: (kneeling in the first row) Tom Plumeret, George Whittle, Bob Walker, Jack Houy, Bob Smelko, Bill Klucher, and John Rosile; (second row) Shirley Bowers Kulig, Mary Ann Wadjun Marciano, Aileen Hinerman Wayland, Doris Neider Anderson, Shirley Mason Baldine, Madelyn Jameson Tuck, Jane Stewart Warner, Eva Troyer Knab, Mina Jean Lesh Price, Theresa Choppa Benden, Shirley Tickey LaCivita, and Pauline Patton Darko; (third row) Beverly Wills Creed, Mary Jane Lehn Collins, Joan Hettrick Gibson, Bill Waltman, Ron Schmidt, Jim Fedorchak, Vince Rosile, Ronald Rowe, Dale May, Bob Leone, Rosemary Hines Hollenbank, Joyce Hunsinger Pogany, Shirley Higgins Rosine, Betty Pannunzio Martin, and Delaine Fricker Koelliker; (fourth row) Veda Clark Wright, Bob Castner, Jim Castner, Richard Horvath, Tom Nutter, Russ Webb, John Curry, Ron Ensley, Pat Camuso, George Praznik, Virginia May Nicholas, Judy Hammill Ruby, and Betty Hetrick DeMaiolo. (Photograph courtesy of Carol Rae Farmer Hurl. Thanks to Judy Hammill Ruby and Bev Wills Creed for identifying students.)

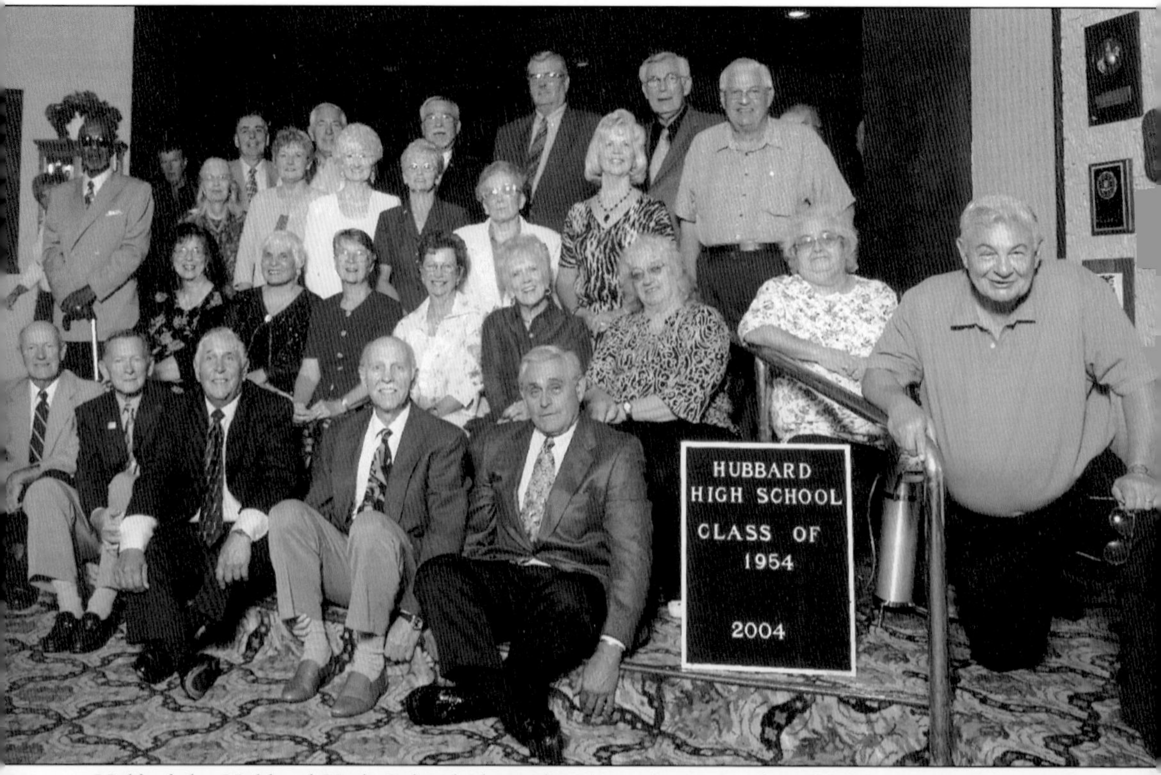

Half of the Hubbard High School class of 1954 is shown in their 50th reunion photograph taken on August 7, 2004. Their class was the first class to graduate from the new Hubbard High School at 150 Hall Avenue. Pictured from left to right are: (first row) Bob Welton, Pete Snyder, Tom Madeline, Jack Knirk, and Ed Fabian; (second row) Andy Hill, Rita Phillips Hetson, Jean Scimone Carabelos, Judy Doughton Ours, Mary Ruth Cooksey Williams, Joan Kriech Stranix, Ruth Davis Duvich, Patricia Walts Graban, and Joe Karcher; (third row) Judy Hollenbank Miller, Betty Brownlee Pipic, Grace Crytzer Castilla, June Himes Osiniak, Sophia Glus Misinay, Mary Foraker Amatore, and James King; (fourth row) Louis Cassimatis, Leonard Carabelos, Ronald Gergel, Frank Crea, and Howard Andrews. (Photograph courtesy of Prosser Yosay Photography. Thanks to Ruth Halicki Means for identifying class members.)

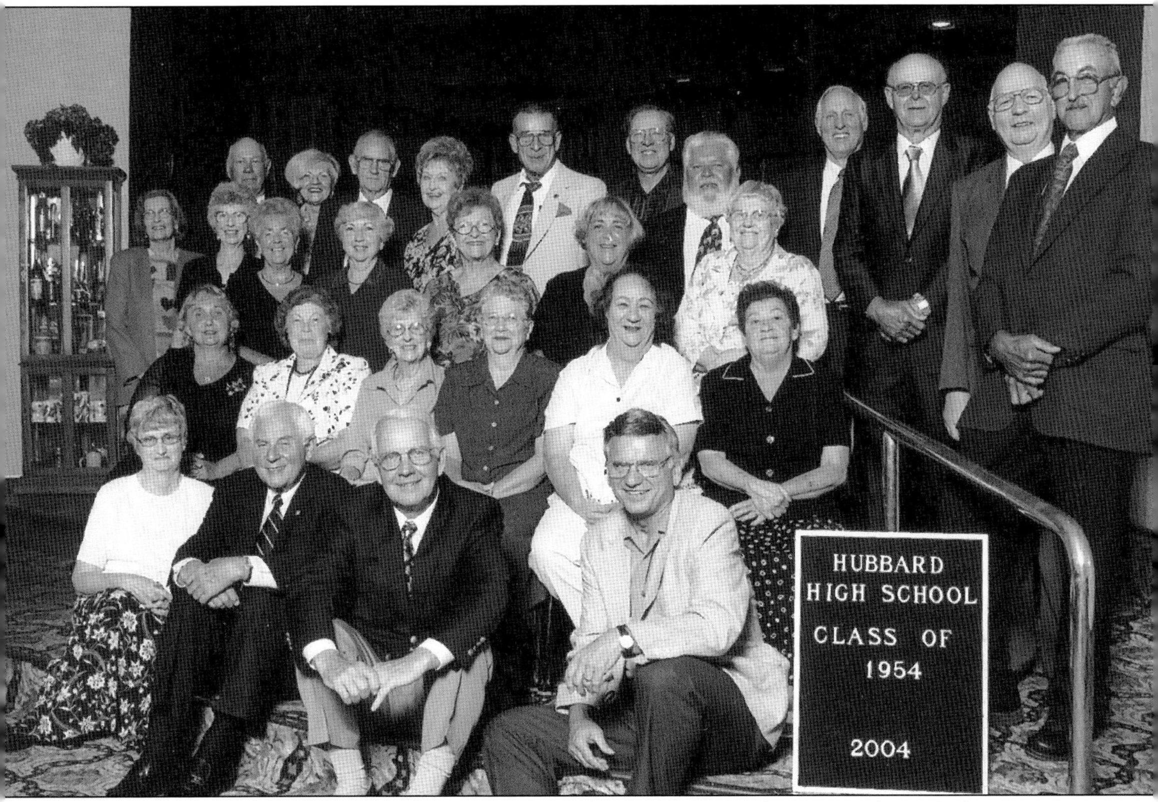

The other half of the Hubbard High School class of 1954 is shown in their 50th reunion photograph taken on August 7, 2004. Pictured from left to right are: (first row) Ruth Halicki Means, Ron Zetterquist, Harold Moyers, and Joe Pasquarella; (second row) Eileen Kougher Spadford, Nancy Nadeja Melanson, Shirley Deal Clark, Nancy Roose Houy, Lorena Rummell Latham, and Mary Jane VonKennen Toda; (third row) Paula Kirkwood Martinec, Jacque St. John Setny, Betty Yeager Colapret, Pat Pritchard Wayland, Alberta "Jeanie" Pedigo Slenker, Patricia Pascarella Carsone, and Pat Duke Osberg; (fourth row) John Faber, Patricia Pushkar Badaluc, Roger Paroz, Doris Polochak Ensley, Dave Kulow, Jack Glod, Jack Reese, Thomas Orr, Frank Petrek, Roger Mott, and James Vernell. (Photograph courtesy of Prosser Yosay Photography. Thanks to Ruth Halicki Means for identifying class members.)

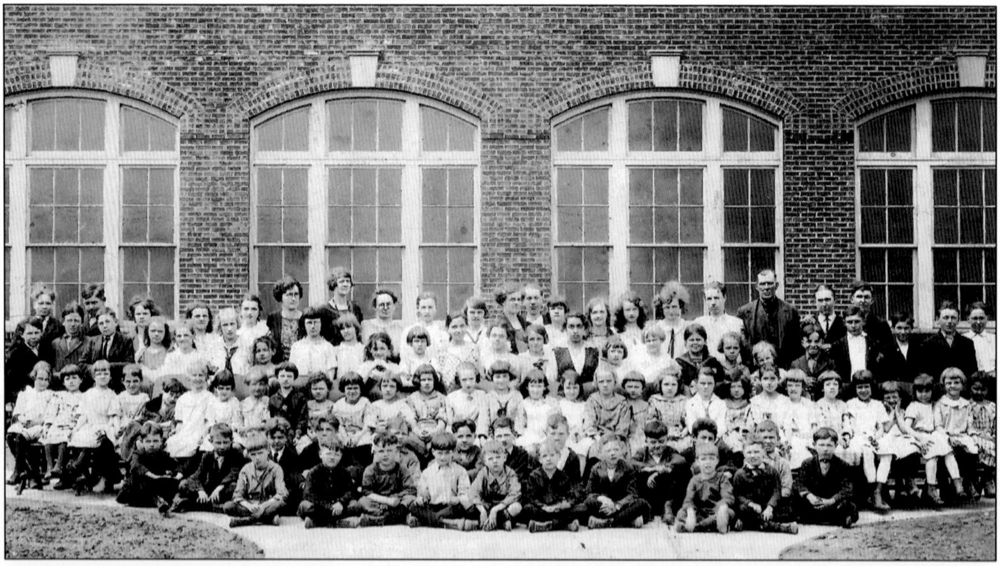

The front of Chestnut Ridge School in the early 1920s shows all the students from grades one through eight and their teachers. Miss Maude Reed is the third teacher from the left in the top row (in the middle of the second window). Miss Reed taught at No. 8 School, Coalburg School, Chestnut Ridge School for three years, and retired in 1962 after 57 years of teaching in Hubbard Schools. Reed Middle School, built in 1960, was named in her honor. (Photograph courtesy of Doris Corll Evans.)

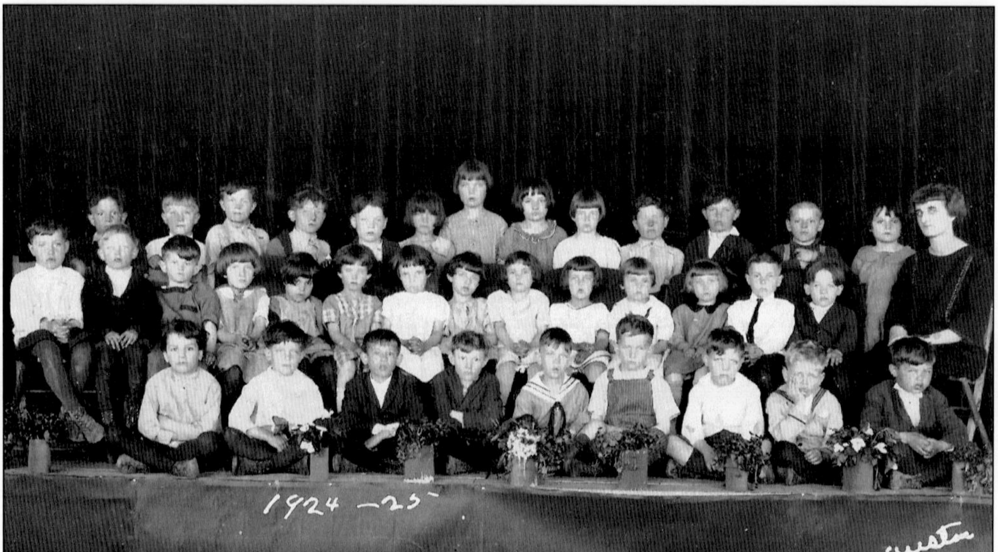

Chestnut Ridge School's first grade class in 1924 included Doris Corll, pictured here in the second row, tenth from left. The school was built on land that was offered to the Board of Education for $1 on January 3, 1921, by owners George and Evan Evans, with the stipulation that if the school closed it would revert back to the Evans family. The school opened in 1923 and housed grades one through eight, until the 1960s when it housed grades one through six. In 1960, the building had six classrooms, 182 students, and six certified personnel. (Photograph courtesy of Doris Corll Evans.)

Chestnut Ridge School from 1923 until the 1960s included grades one through eight. The basketball team from 1927 includes ball boy Evan Evans. Pictured from left to right are: (first row) John Robert Evans, unidentified, and unidentified; (second row) Coach Metzger, George Loveless, David Coxson, John Paisley, Mark Marshall, and unidentified. (Photograph courtesy of Jerry Coxson.)

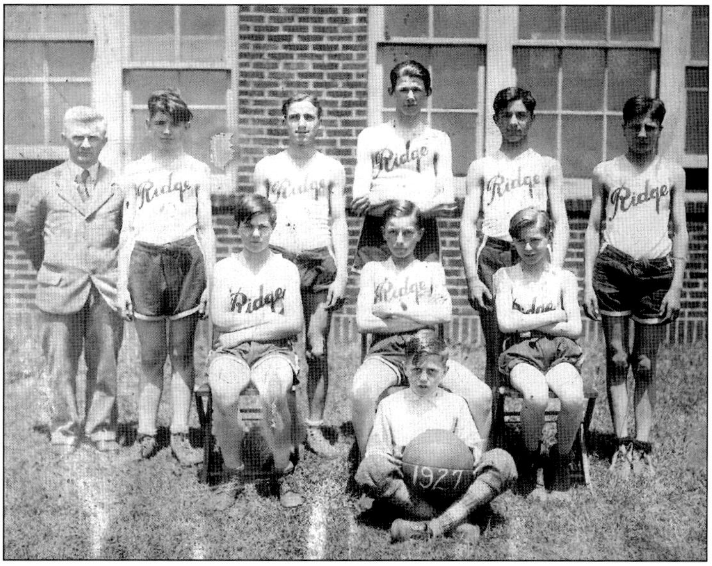

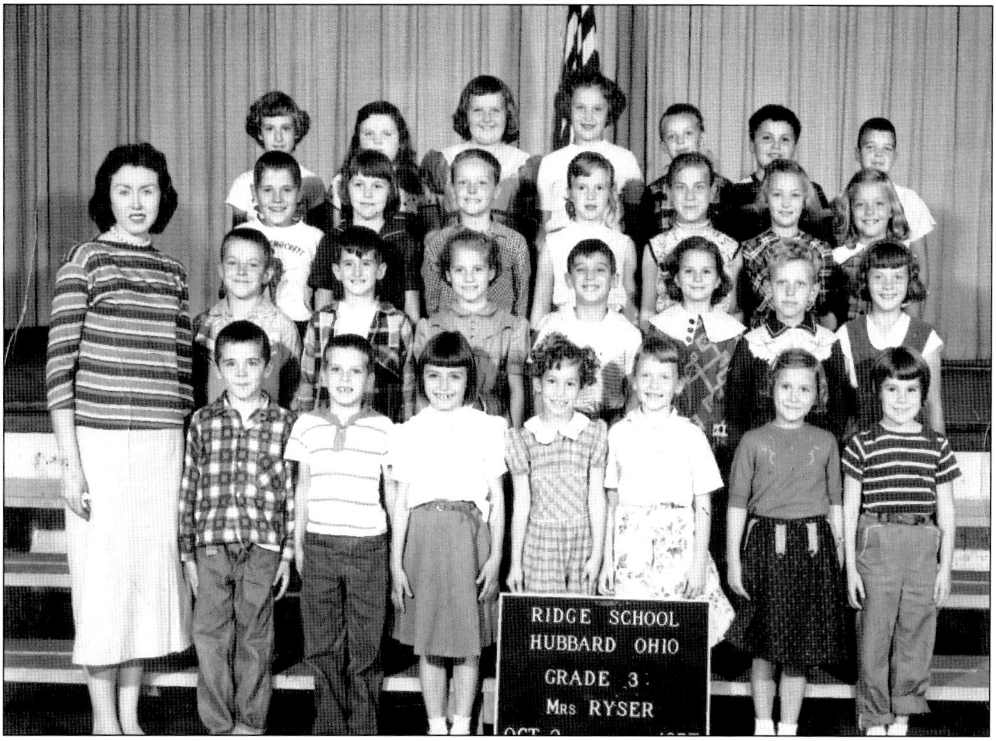

Third grade students and teacher Mrs. Ryser are pictured here at Chestnut Ridge School on October 2, 1957. Included from left to right are: (first row) Terry Crea, Kenny Yoman, Carol Hunt, Valerie ?, Linda Wilkinson, Kathy Horvath, and Jackie Cupp; (second row) Fred Thompson, Dean Evans, Sandy Crawford, Gary Gazzoni, Janice Swogger, Bud ?, and Sharon Ducaster; (third row) Kenny Tucker, Vivien Miller, Wade Foltz, Bonnie Blair, Susan ?, Linda Evans, and Mary Atkins; (fourth row) Kathy Rosetta, Sally Coxson, Cathy Corll, Judy Corll, David Ondich, Tommy Miller, and Johnny Martin. (Photograph courtesy of Judy Corll Lutz.)

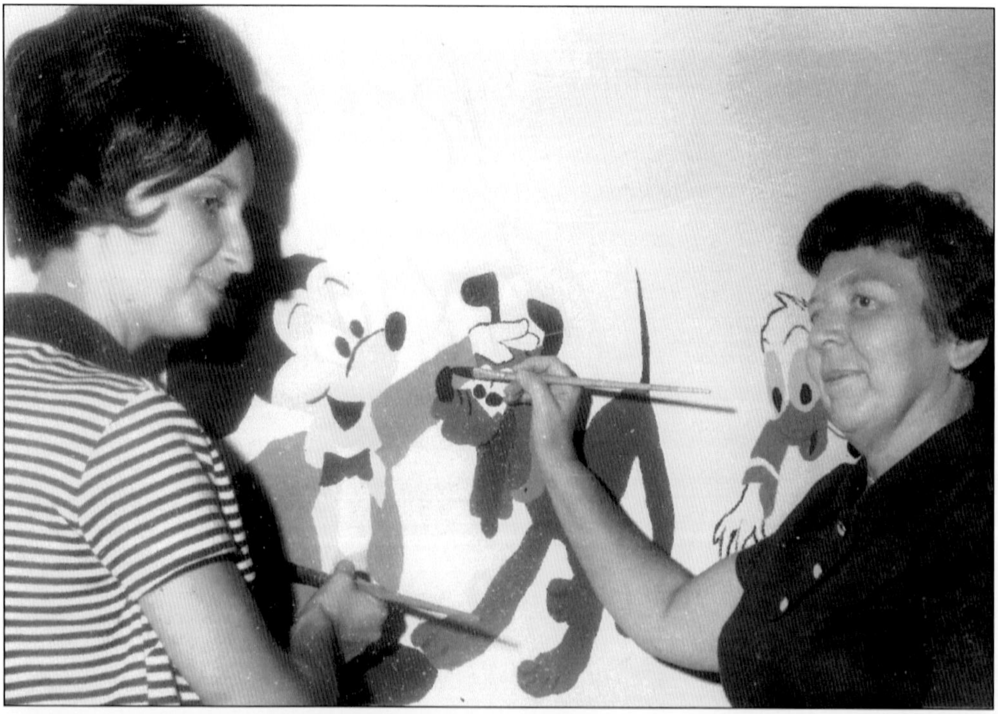

In 1970, teachers Barbara Kindler, left, and Evelyn Schafer, right, painted nursery characters on the hallways at Chestnut Ridge School when the kindergarten moved there. Mrs. Schafer's first year of teaching in 1938 was in a one-room school located on the east side of Jacobs Road. She taught grades one through four and rode the streetcar from her home on Drummond Avenue, Stop 39, to the school, Stop 28, until the streetcar service ended in January of 1939. (Photograph courtesy of Kathy Skarote, Marianne Modarelli, and Barbara Kindler.)

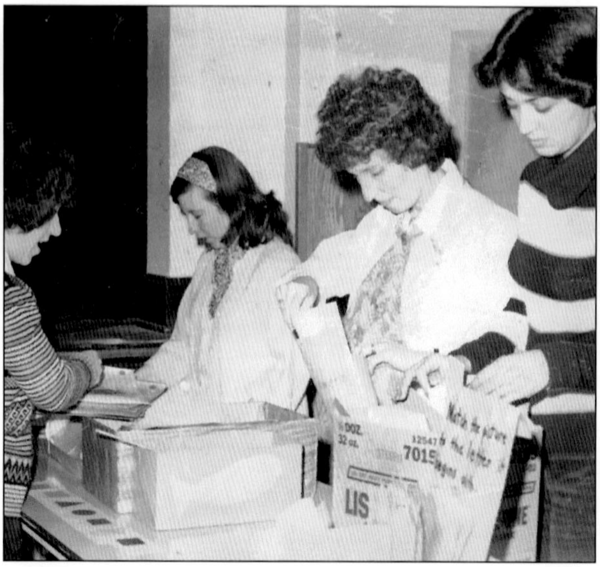

In the late 1970s, kindergarten teachers at Chestnut Ridge School, Kathy Skarote, Claudia Lang, Barbara Kindler, and Marianne Modarelli pack "Make and Take" games for parents to take home to their children. Mrs. Kindler remembers the school fondly. If a rainy day produced puddles, the children made boats to float in miniature lakes. The children planted flowers in tire planters, and bird's nests were made of clay and the children collected sticks, moss, and leaves to finish the nests. It was a magical place for children to learn. (Photograph courtesy of Kathy Skarote, Marianne Modarelli, and Barbara Kindler.)

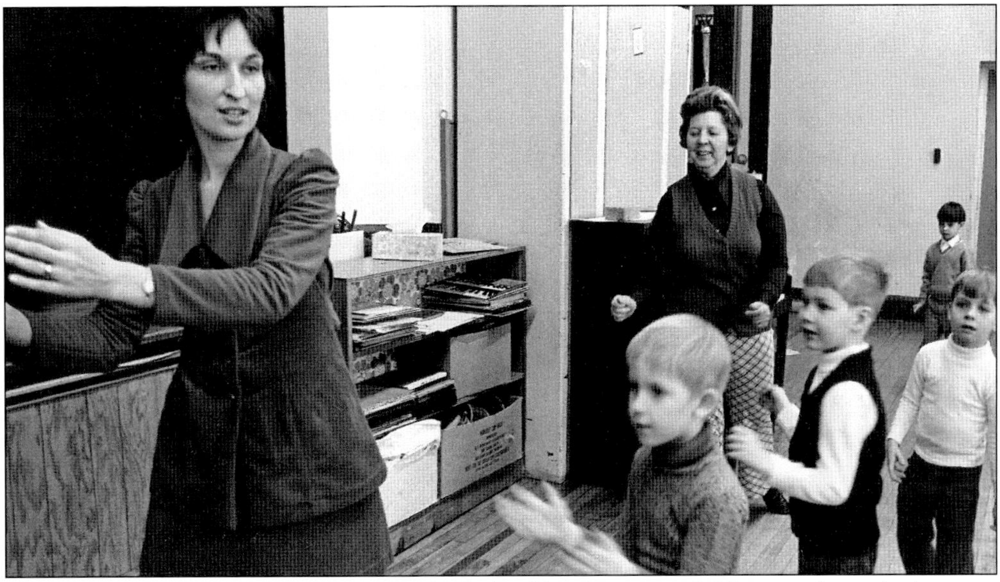

Mrs. Barbara Kindler and Mrs. Evelyn Schafer lead kindergarten children in physical education at Chestnut Ridge School's gymnasium in the late 1970s. Behind Mrs. Kindler is the stage area of the combination gymnasium/auditorium/cafeteria where the children could perform for parents. To the right of the stage are tables and benches that could be folded down for the cafeteria. (Photograph courtesy of Kathy Skarote, Marianne Modarelli, and Barbara Kindler.)

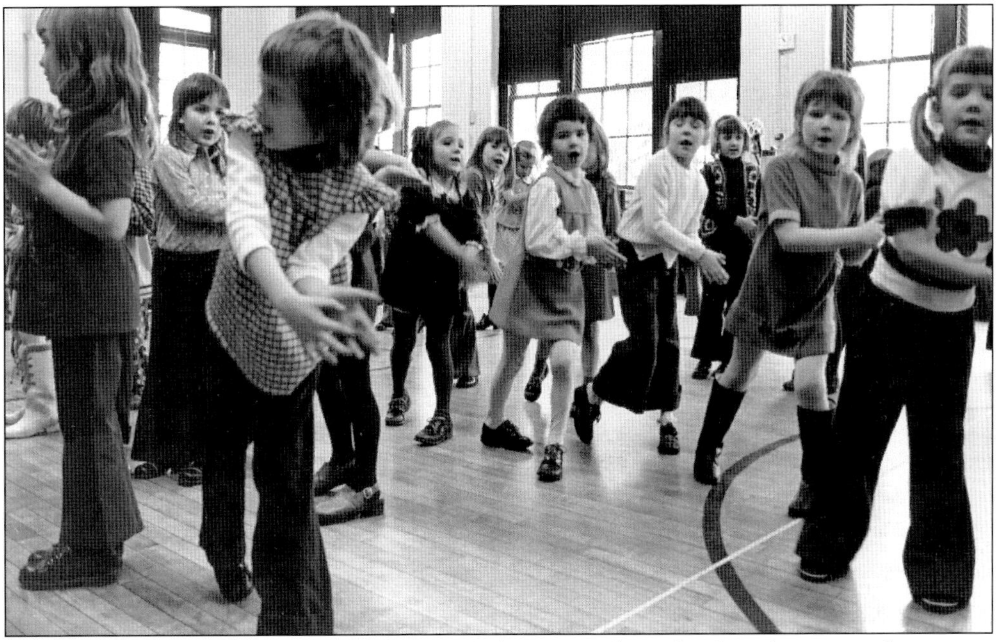

The gymnasium windows on the south side of Chestnut Ridge School can be seen in this picture of kindergarten children in a physical education class in the late 1970s. Previously, Mrs. South and Mrs. Schafer, Mrs. Kindler and Mrs. Skarote, team-taught at Reed Middle School in rooms that had no windows and were not very well suited for teaching kindergartners. (Photograph courtesy of Kathy Skarote, Marianne Modarelli, and Barbara Kindler.)

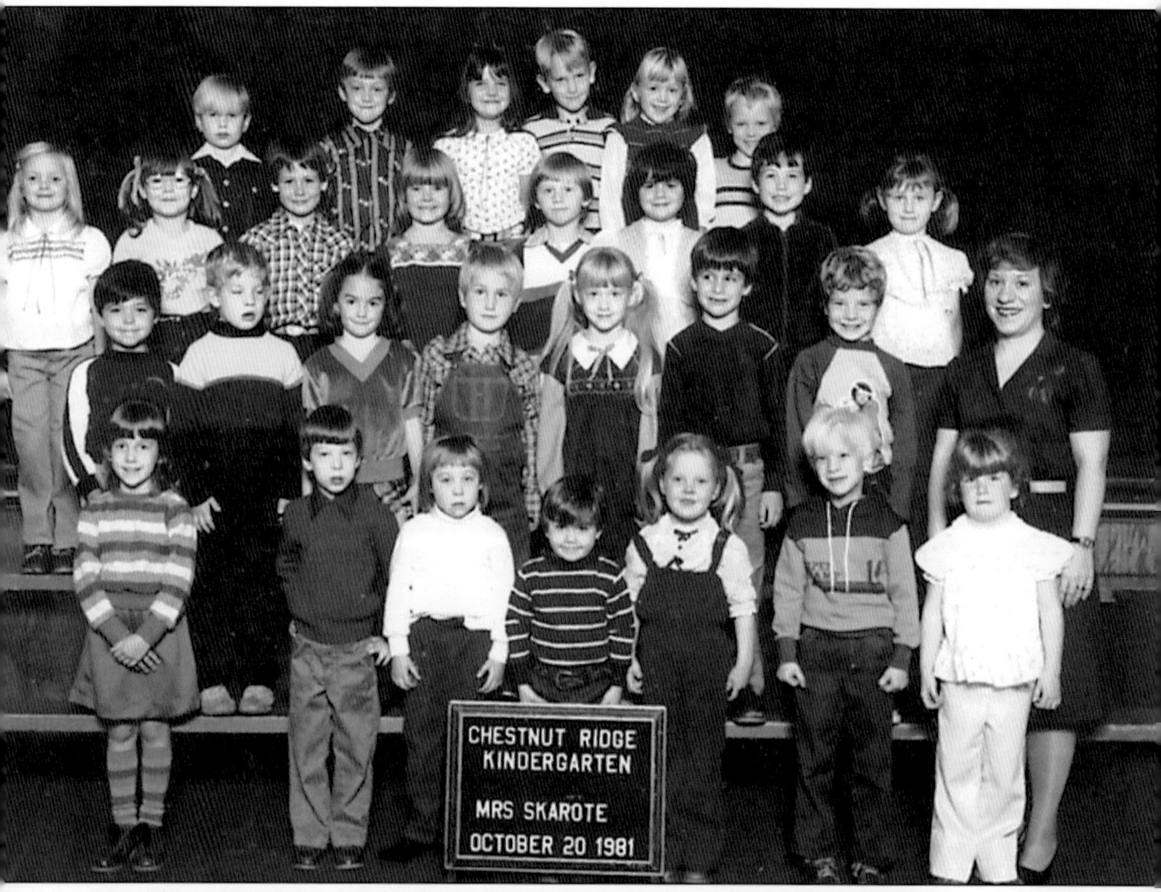

Mrs. Skarote's morning kindergarten class is shown in this picture from October 20, 1981. The children in kindergarten during the school year 1981–1982 (the class of 1994) were the last children to go to kindergarten at Chestnut Ridge School. The children performed for their parents for the last time in June of 1982 and sang "Goodbye, Farewell," from the Sound of Music. A big "Goodbye" sign was behind the children and the performance brought tears to everyone's eyes. From left to right are: (row one) Dawn Petro, unidentified, Deanna Orr, Richard Susak, Michelle Medvec, unidentified, and unidentified; (row two) Michael Clark, Bradley Biro, Rachel Faringer, unidentified, unidentified, Michael Christoff, unidentified, and Mrs. Kathy Skarote; (row three) Connie Miklos, Karen Joy, Gregory Hess, Kelly McNeely, unidentified, Carla Biastro, Todd Emch, and Vickie Cataline; (row four) Gregory Bresnahan, Ernest Cornwell, Jennifer Myers, Michael Benton, unidentified, and Carl Brown. Thanks to Mrs. Kathy Skarote, Todd Emch, Kendall and Michael Christoff, Erin Hacker, Jennifer Myers Cooley, Vickie Cataline, Deanna Orr, Kelly McNeeley Flowers, and Geri Bray for identifying students.

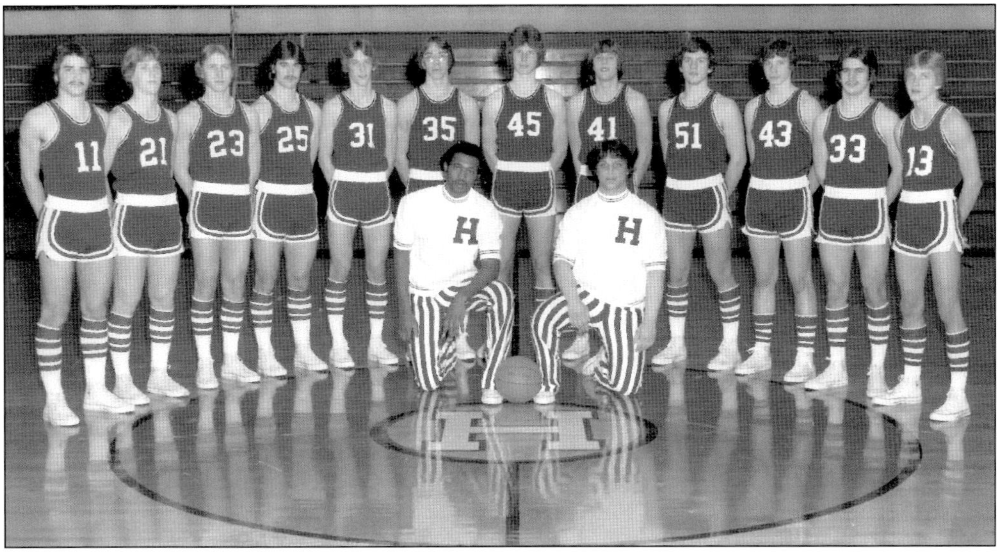

The Hubbard Varsity Basketball Team in 1977 was the Steel Valley Co-Champs with Austintown Fitch High School. Pictured in front are coaches Claude Fisher (left) and Anthony Carsone. Players, from left to right, are James LaCivita (11), Don Fusselman (21), Brian Piskur (23), Andy Gonci (25), Howard Slemons (31), John Kosar (35), Kevin Franczkowski (45), Rick Pucak (41), Dan Camuso (51), David Kyle (43), Chris Romano (31), and David Kuzniar (13). (Photograph courtesy of Dr. Howard Slemons.)

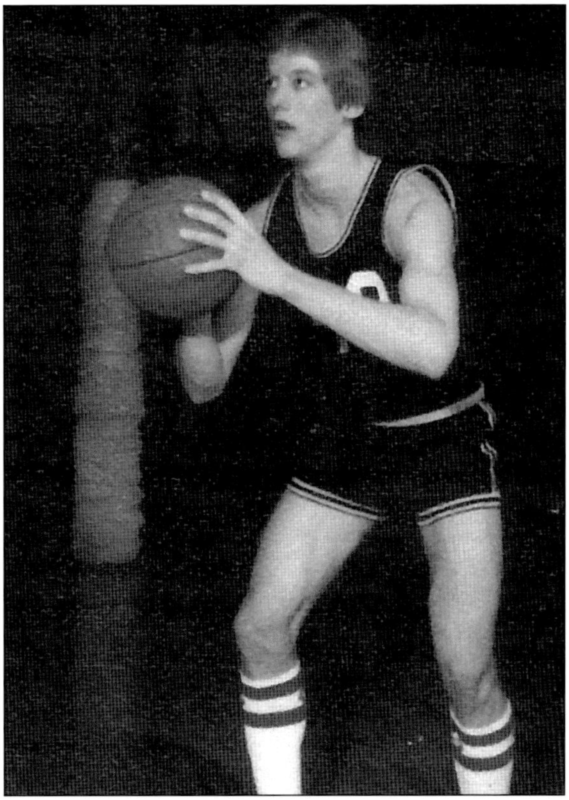

Howard Slemons is pictured at the April 7, 1979 North-South Cage Classic in Canton, Ohio. He is remembered as the basketball player who scored over 840 career points, a record up to that time for boys at Hubbard High School. He received his doctor of osteopathic medicine degree in 1987, was chief resident at North Side Hospital in Youngstown and started his practice in Hubbard in 1990. His office is currently located at 55 Hall Avenue in Hubbard. (Photograph courtesy of Dr. Howard Slemons.)

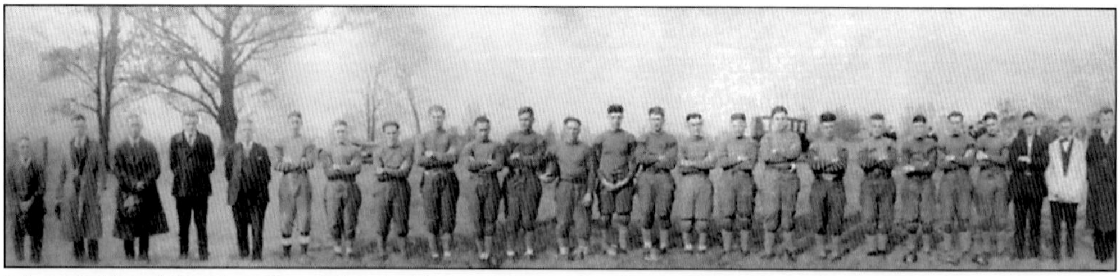

The Hubbard High School football team from the late 1910s or early 1920s is shown in this panoramic photograph. In the white jacket, third from the right, is James Roland Mitchell, seventh from the right is George Bennett Mitchell, and fourteenth from the right is Lester Mitchell. The three Mitchell boys were brothers and their other siblings were Oscar, Florence, and Bertha. George Bennett Mitchell was Kathy Mitchell Esbenshade's grandfather. Kathy grew up in Hubbard and now lives in Ashland, Ohio. (Photograph courtesy of Kathy Mitchell Esbenshade.)

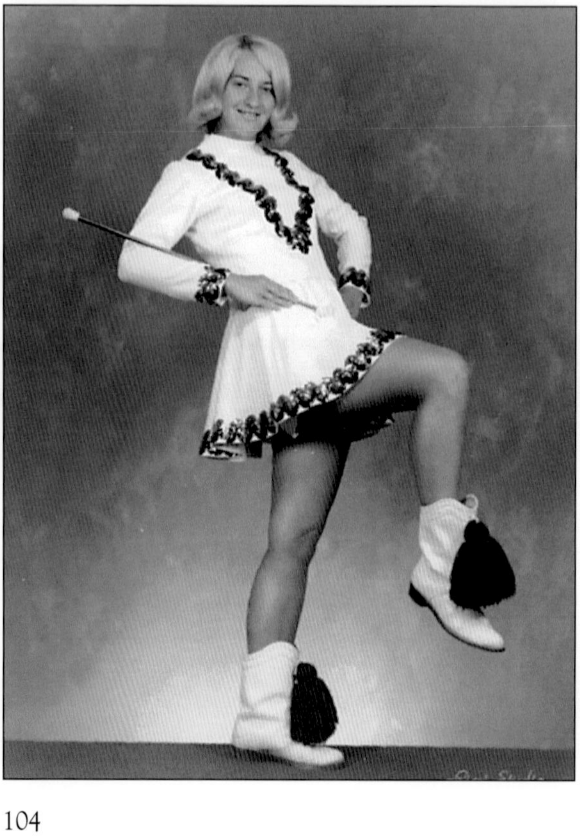

Carole Palumbo Williams was a Hubbard Majorette in this picture from 1968. When she joined the Majorettes, both the Majorettes and the band were going through changes. The first year the uniform was a modified band uniform. Later, the uniforms were customized and paid for by the Majorettes. (Photograph courtesy of Carole Palumbo Williams.)

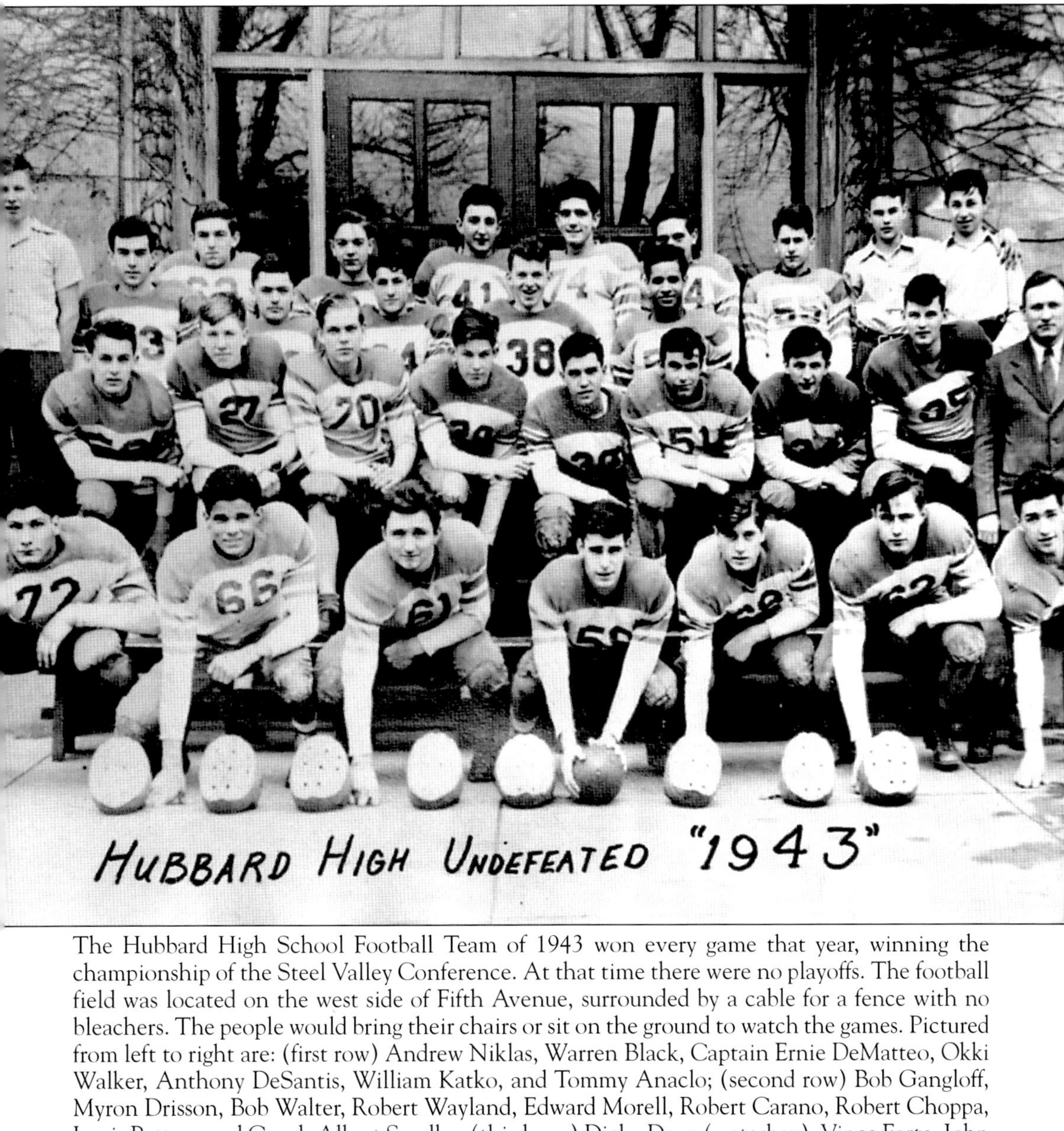

The Hubbard High School Football Team of 1943 won every game that year, winning the championship of the Steel Valley Conference. At that time there were no playoffs. The football field was located on the west side of Fifth Avenue, surrounded by a cable for a fence with no bleachers. The people would bring their chairs or sit on the ground to watch the games. Pictured from left to right are: (first row) Andrew Niklas, Warren Black, Captain Ernie DeMatteo, Okki Walker, Anthony DeSantis, William Katko, and Tommy Anaclo; (second row) Bob Gangloff, Myron Drisson, Bob Walter, Robert Wayland, Edward Morell, Robert Carano, Robert Choppa, Louis Patton, and Coach Albert Smelko; (third row) Dicky Dean (waterboy), Vince Forte, John "Dutch" Petten, Art Clement, unidentified, and Howard Faison; (fourth row) David Sauline, Robert Earhart, Al Carano, Louis Williams, Joe Mariotti, Ray Braykovich, Kenneth Vasey (waterboy) and Bill Sauline (waterboy). (Photograph courtesy of Vince Pompili, thanks to Ed Palestro for naming members of team.)

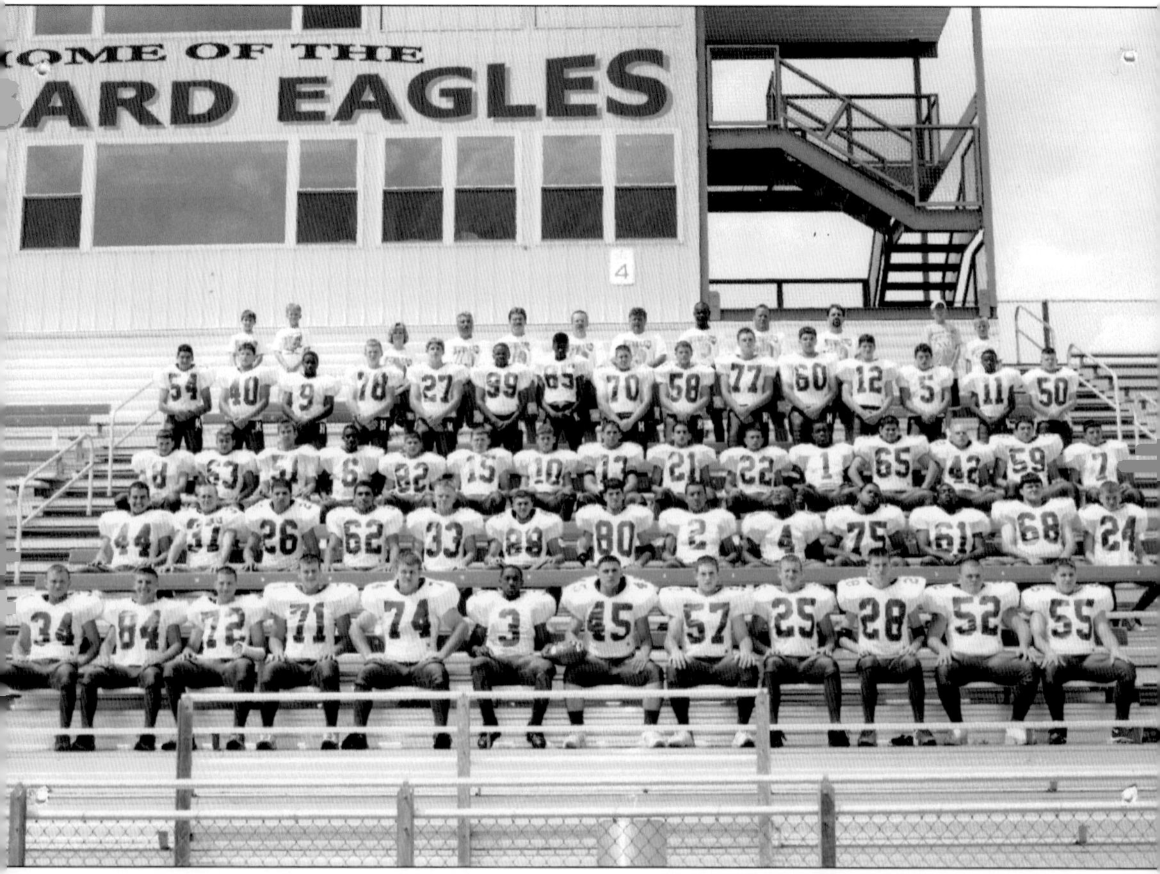

Jeff Bayuk coached the undefeated 2001 Hubbard Eagles Football Team with a record of 10-0. Pictured from left to right are: (first row) David DeSantis, David Ornelas, Dan Pushcar, Mike Flaugher, Michael Smida, Anthony Smith, Matt Clark, Mike Havalo, Sam Rakyta, Jon DeJulio, Ryan Fakner, and Joe Lewis; (second row) John Dominic, Jerad Jordan, Eric Lubonovich, Chris Sikora, Scott Watkins, Dean Marshall, Chris Horton, Matt Smith, Antonio Owens, Lidel Hilson, Donnie Smith, Brian Dell, and Nick Housman; (third row) Scott Ridel, Chris Duncan, Chris Helmick, Zack Willis, Anthony Alexander, Adam Jablonski, Dave DeJulio, Gabe McKee, William Boyce, Jeramy May, David Phillips, Tony Frazzini, Jon Fakner, Mark Mehalco, and Tony Ornelas; (fourth row) Brian Falhamer, Ryan Jankowski, Claude Fisher, Bill Baron, Paul Toth, Vince Carter, Jacoby Morris, Jordan DeMay, Tom Mahoney, Steve Mort, Nick Miller, Joe Horton, Chris Buccilli, Mike Biggs, and Andrew Tucciarone; (fifth row) John Bayuk, Frank Rosile, Mary Honard, Ron DeJulio, Rich Perline, Rod Greenamayer, Jeff Bayuk, Steve Hunt, Mickey Sikora, Brian Luther, Chase Rosile, and John Sikora. (Photograph courtesy of Maxmillan Studios, roster courtesy of Coach Jeff Bayuk.)

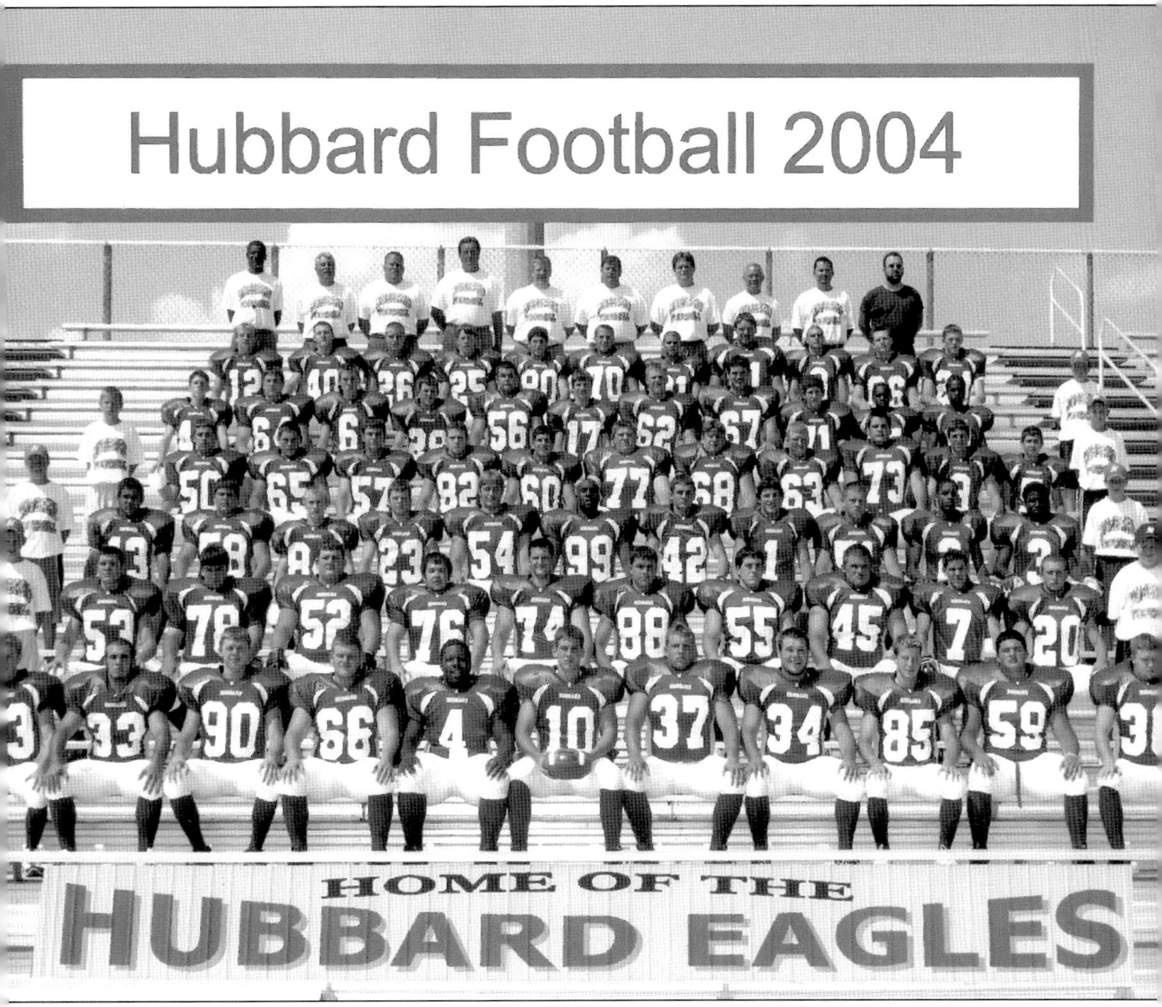

Jeff Bayuk coached the undefeated 2004 Hubbard Eagles Football Team with a record of 9-0. Pictured from left to right are: (first row) Christian Spear, Don Nadeja, Chad Pringle, Myron Drisson, Ben Lane, Bryan Boyce, Todd Coonce, Andrew Chick, Doug Gault, Larry Wolf, and David Antoniazzi; (second row) Ballboy Tyler Duez, Ken Sedlacko, James LaCivita, Frank Maietta, James Curran, Rob Zingale, Scott Patterson, Sam Gonder, Brandon Rydarowicz, Steve Petrinjak, Anthony Tarr, and Ballboy J.J. Palestro; (third row) Ballboy John Sikora, Rafael Lima, Josh Rydarowicz, Chris Staley, Mike Fry, Justin Rydarowicz, George Taylor, Tony Giancola, Eric Merrell, Cory Munnell, Russell Hawkins, Martel Fisher, and Ballboy Cory Hopkinson; (fourth row) Ballboy Mike Lopuchovsky, Josh Lucas, Matt Silvidi, Tom Senich, Mike O'Neill, Sam Pedaline, Chad Karabin, Jared Friend, Cory Donahue, Chris Rankin, Eddie Palestro, John Bayuk, and Ballboy Cory Groscost; (fifth row) Steve Kilar, Dan Havalo, Andrew DeJulio, Andy Ryser, Mark Dell, Taylor Torella, Clayton Ruminski, Anthony O'Hara, Tim Taafe, Jarvis Bills, Greg Givens, and Ballboy Justin Rosile; (sixth row) Tom Jones, Jacob Kerola, Joel Younkins, Billy Gibbs, Joe Marando, Ryan Mills, Chris LaCivita, Marcus O'Hara, Steve Cinicola, Cody Pitts, and Mike Maietta; (seventh row) Coach Hunt, Coach DeJulio, Coach Sikora, Coach Zetts, Coach Greenamyer, Head Coach Jeff Bayuk, Coach Perline, Coach Matthews, Trainer Mills, and Equipment Manager Luther. (Photograph courtesy of Ken Veisz, Memory Lane Photography, roster courtesy of Coach Jeff Bayuk.)

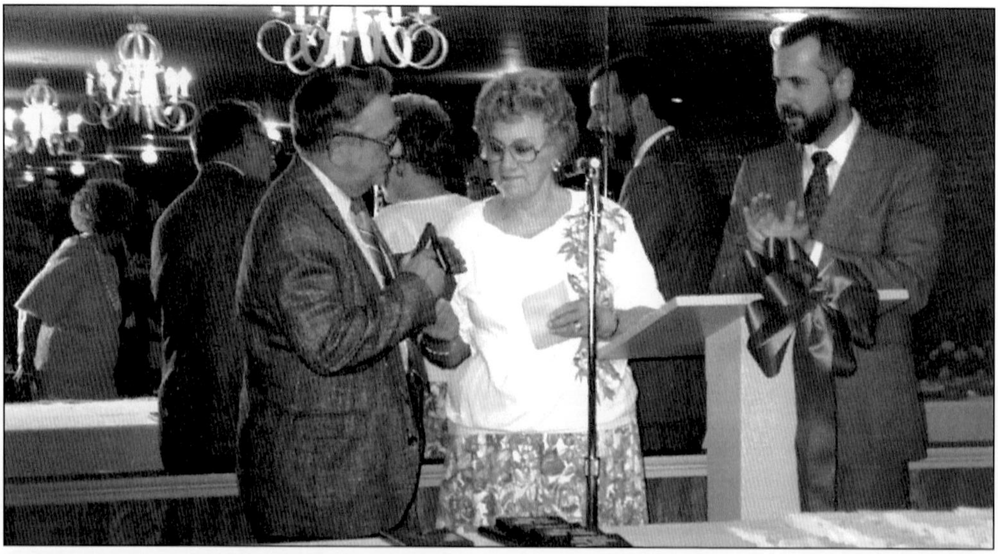

Hubbard High School Band Director Dominic Feorene is on the left in this picture taken at the Band Banquet at the Brentford House in 1983, the year he retired. Willa Ball, Band Sponsors president, and William Forrester, present band director, presented Mr. Feorene with an award for his many years of service. Mr. Feorene came to Hubbard High School from Niles in 1970 and increased the band from 90 to 200 students. (Photograph courtesy of William Forrester.)

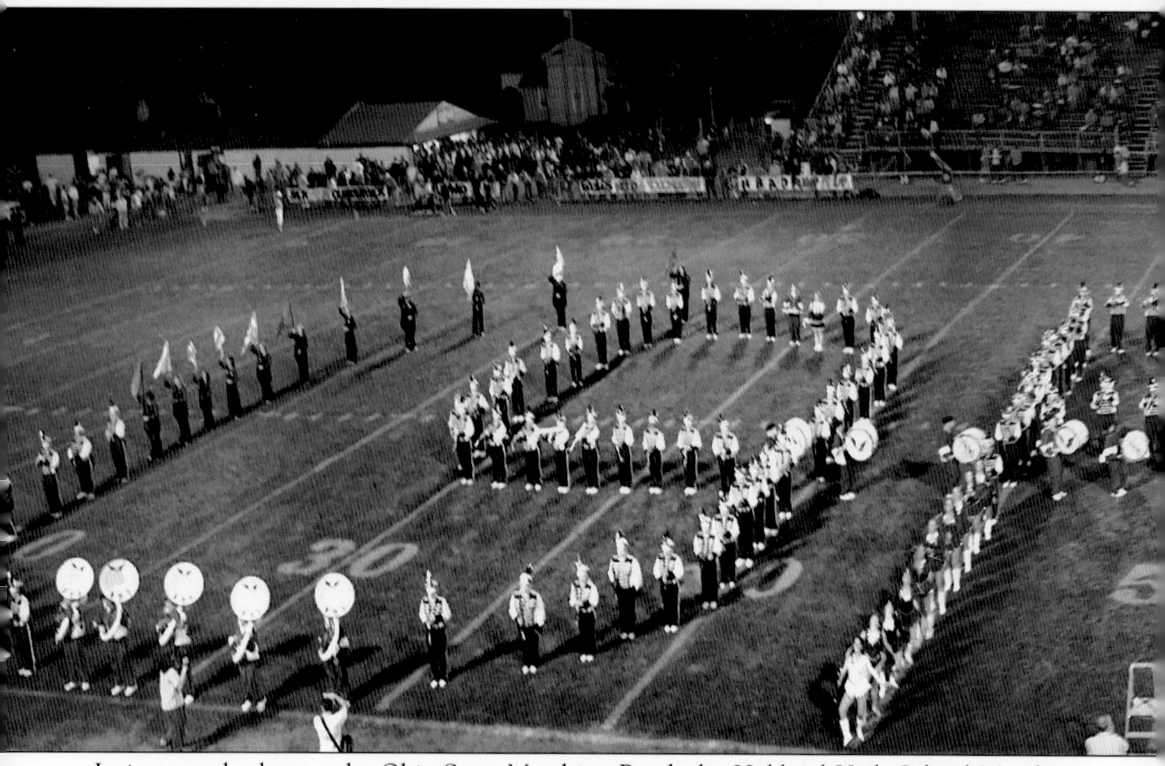

In its annual salute to the Ohio State Marching Band, the Hubbard High School Marching Band performed "Script Ohio" on October 1, 2004, at a home game with Lakeview.

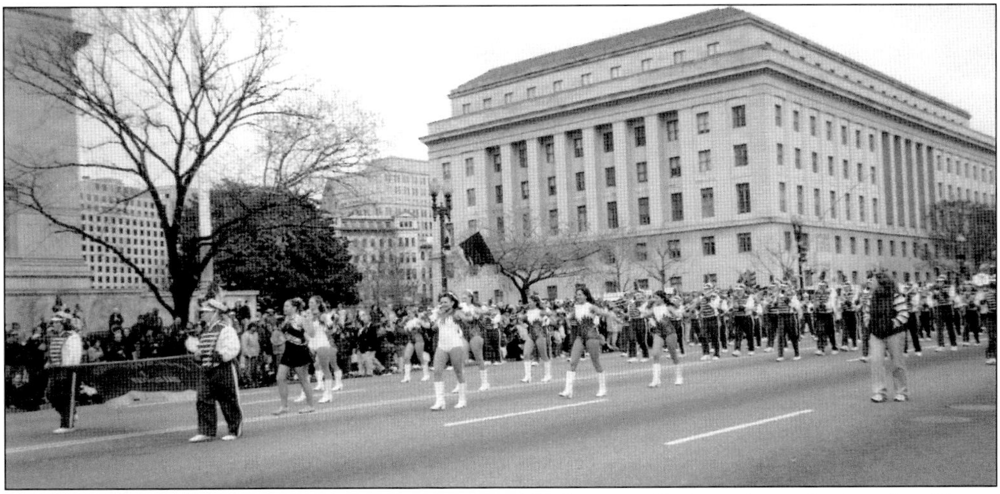

The 2003–2004 Hubbard Marching Band was in Washington D.C. and marched in the Cherry Blossom Parade on April 3, 2004 under current band director, William Forrester. Mr. Forrester was assistant band director in 1976 to Mr. Feorene, and became band director in 1983. The band has traveled to Disney World, Orlando, Florida, every four years since 1986. Their next trip is scheduled for April 17–22, 2006. Band members attend band camp every summer. While at camp, in addition to becoming a fine-tuned marching unit, band members bond to become a close-knit "family." (Photograph courtesy of William Forrester.)

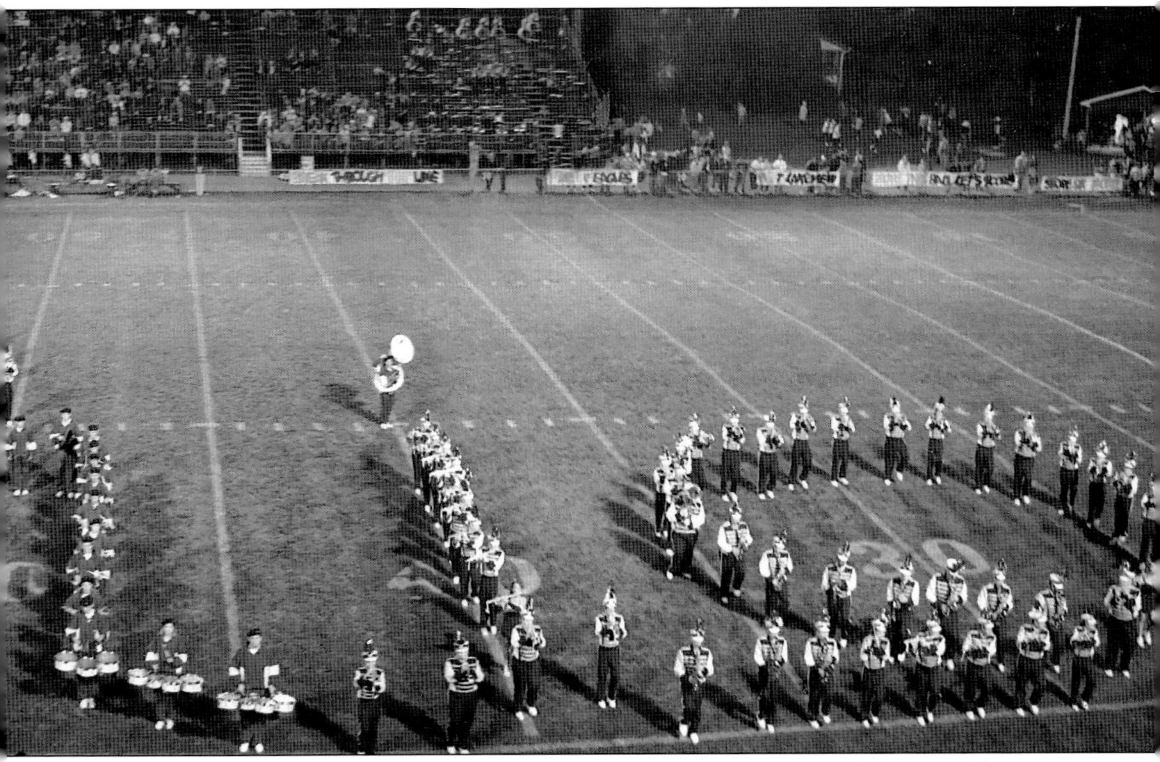

Christine Wilson, tuba player, capped off the performance by dotting the "i" in Ohio. Mr. Harold Gray in the Eagle's Nest announced the performance as he has done for many years.

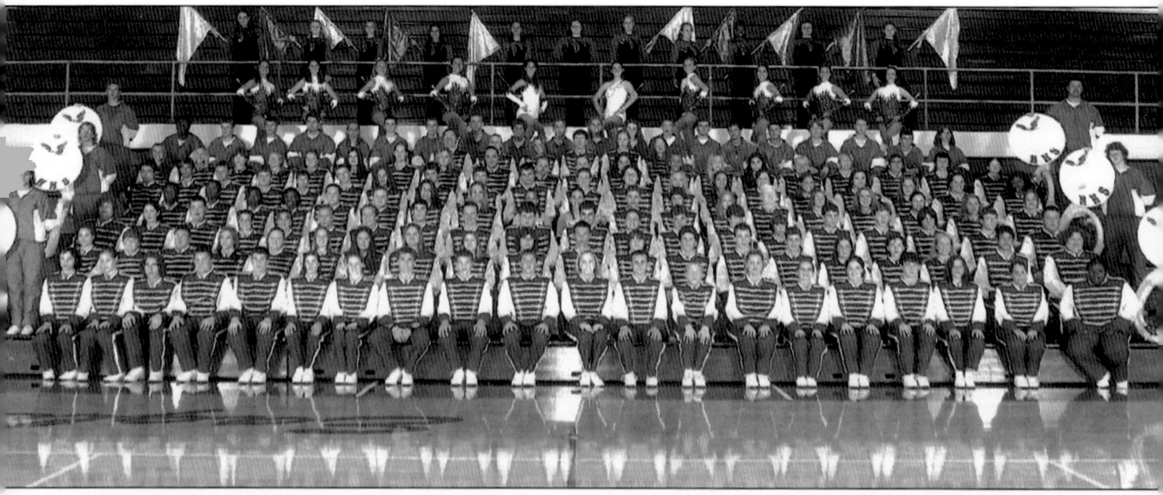

The Hubbard High School Band is shown in this photograph from the fall of 2004. The band had 180 members, and was the second largest band in Trumbull County. Members included: Trumpets—Trevor Balint, Kevin Fell, Scott Killian, John Reiter, Shane Carnahan, Stephanie Gilida, Shane Hughes, Andy Lockso, Adam Myers, Joe Schroeder, Garrett Silsbe, Dale Wardle, Ryan Antonucci, Joey Barr, John Buchenic, Heather Fannin, Leigh Ann Logan, Marie McCallen, Eric Offerdahl, Shane Pagnatta, Bryan Rosine, Brandon Wittenauer, Bill Adovasio, Jeremy Frazzini, Elliott Lanz, Emily Mogg, Shane O'Dell, Robert Vavrinak, Angela Verostko, and Megan Webb: Trombones—Michelle Forsythe, Joe Cummings, Justin Humenny, Cory Liston, Jason Tingler, Jordan Zamary, Dan Longo, Charlie Ryser, Jerri-Lynn Ashman, Tracey Campbell, Mike Carnahan, and Adam Mierzwa; Tubas—Daryl Babcock, Christine Wilson, Brendan Keiper, Ryan Nesbitt, Quintin Hughes, and Patrick O'Dea; Alto Sax—Janay Donaldson, Ryan Halicki, Markesha McRae, Lea Nesbitt, Elissa Rigby, BeAnn Julian, Tiffany Reid, Alex Balint, Bryan Darko, Joe Dohallow, Adam Howe, Corey Huff, Billy Leet, Brandon Moore, Steve Sisk, Josh Chaney, Kris Johnson, Forest Ryser, Rebecca Shamblin, Todd Tatarka, and Jessie Young; Tenor Sax—Darren Brush and Will Donahue; Frumpets—Ryan Rexroad, Elizabeth Weymer, Anne Grabaskas, and Becky Dixon; Baritones—Kyle Patrick, Kathy Stanford, and Shannon Dixon; Clarinets—Elizabeth Prelac, Elyse Ryhal, Stacie Bulmer, Ashley Gentile, Allison Luthern, Steph Mislevy, Jessica Shamblin, Amber Donahue, Derek Emch, Chad Gallo, Olivia Lane, Courtney McCullough, Ben Reiter, Kalie Riccitelli, Kim Rosile, Sarah Trumphour, Nicole Delsignore, Allysa Johnston, Courtney Kostka, Kyra May, Suzie Starheim, and Briauna Tyson; Percussion—Elliott Jordan, Joel Longo, Brandon Paul, Andy Howe, Mike Hudy, Joey Kostka, Rachel Owen, D.J. Dripps, Candace Hughes, Steve Logan, Tom Pysher, Brandon Valerio, Eric Zamary, Stephanie Reid, Robert Switzer, Robert Tigner, David Urey, John Williams, and Nicole Zipay; Flutes—Lucy Caruso, Melissa Gibbs, Chani Himes, Brittany Hughes, Kayla Marafiote, Trisha Mogg, Kelly Roth, Katie Schroeder, Terri Shaw, Jessica Urey, Amber Cunningham, Jamie Cunningham, Megan Hall, Amanda Kelley, Jill Mapes, Ashley Rovini, Samantha Shaffer, Marisol Blake, Annie Bruce, Karen Cover, Brittany Dripps, Jackie Hall, Malissa King, Marie Lingenfelter, Stephanie Meeds, Lisa McDowell, Kelsey Ryhal, LaVivian Bonner, Alisha Goldner, Rachel Kerr, Megan Luthern, Christina Nord, Elizabeth Robinson, Erin Senediak, Amanda Smith, and Michelle Stipetich; Bells—Jessica Mort, and Kadie Nesbitt; Majorettes—Nicole Hernandez, Amanda Fisher, Elice Hayek, Julie Boyce, Kelsey Demyen, Brooke Slemons, Lynn Yocum, Ashten Antonucci, and Kylee Sharisky; Feature Twirler—Katelyn Daniels; Flag Line—Julie Adams, Delores Leigh, Robin Leigh, Hannah Snider, Michelle Young, Ashley Prem, Charlotte Rogers, Holly Wehmeyer, Shante Wellington, Kelly Baun, and Amber Pulice. (Photograph courtesy of Memory Lanes Photography.)

Five

DISASTERS

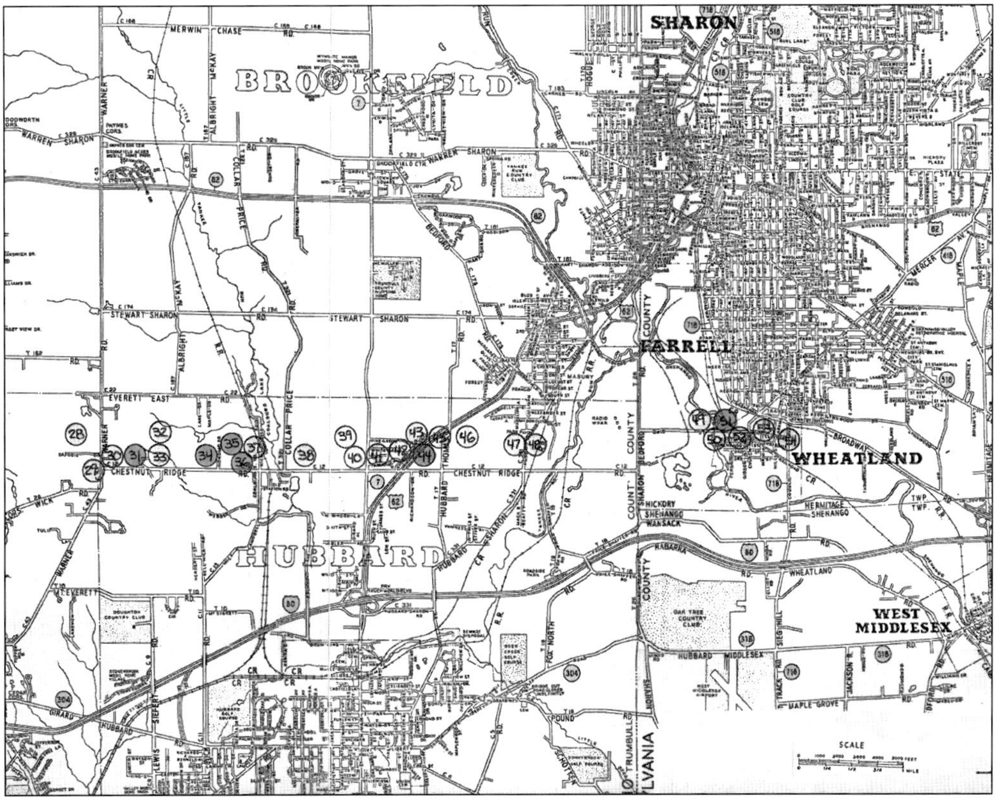

The tornado that passed through Hubbard Township on Friday, May 31, 1985, was one of many tornadoes that tore through Ohio, Pennsylvania, Michigan, and Canada. John Durkos of Chestnut Ridge Road took pictures of damage along the tornado's path. He pinpointed on a map the locations of all the pictures he took and also those that were taken by an aerial photographer from Niles. As can be seen on the map, most of the damage was to the north of Chestnut Ridge Road in Hubbard Township. (Photograph courtesy of John Durkos.)

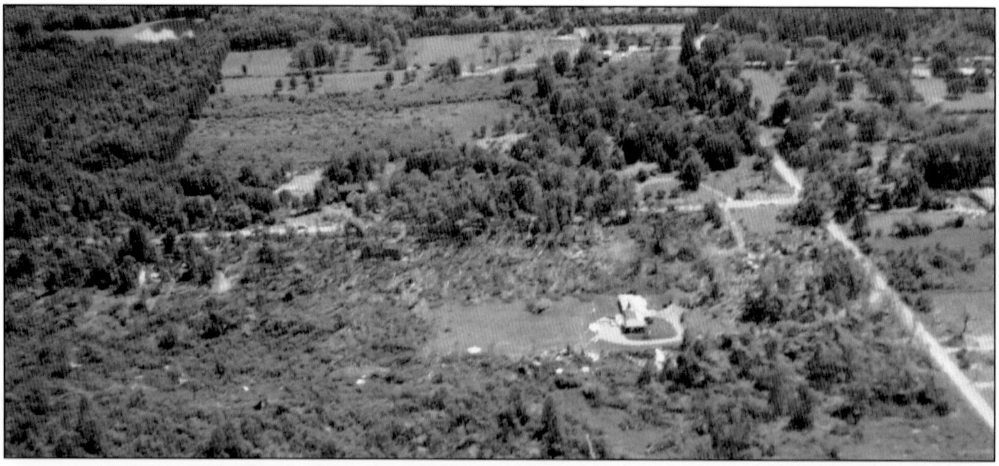

An aerial photograph taken after the tornado hit shows where it entered Hubbard Township. Warner Road is to the right or west and Chestnut Ridge Road is to the left. It was as though a giant weed whip mowed the trees down. The photographer was facing south when this photograph was taken and the tornado generally followed a west to east path just north of Chestnut Ridge Road. (Photograph courtesy of John Durkos.)

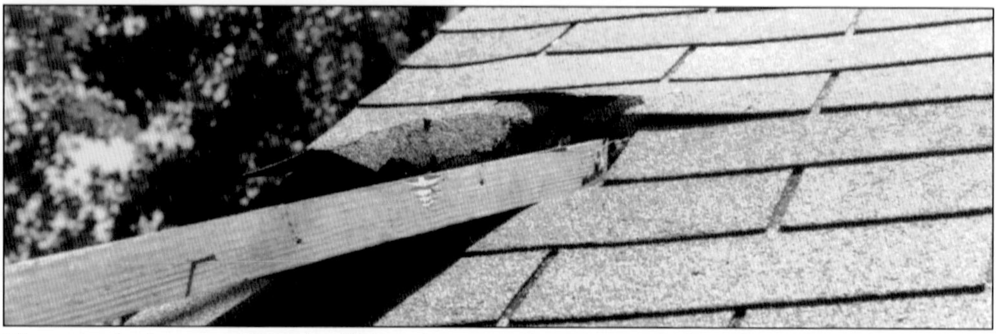

The tornado that struck Hubbard Township started in Newton Falls, Ohio, after a funnel cloud was sighted at 5:10 p.m. between Bloomfield and Orwell. It destroyed houses and businesses in Lordstown, Niles, and Liberty Township, and arrived in Hubbard Township around 6:50 p.m. In Hubbard Township, the tornado devastated houses on the north side of Chestnut Ridge Road, on Kokomo Drive, in the Kermont Heights area, and houses located on the southern portion of Thomas Road. The tornado would also touch down in Wheatland in Mercer County, Pennsylvania. The tornado drove a two by four through the roof of John Durkos' home, which is on the south side of Chestnut Ridge Road, east of Chestnut Ridge Campground. John remembers that Friday night on May 31, 1985, as though it happened yesterday. John, his girlfriend, and his sister Yvonne, were going to Phar-Mor in Niles and were traveling west on State Route 82. At that moment, the tornado was moving east along the north side of Chestnut Ridge Road. When he got to Phar-Mor, the power was out and they were told that a tornado had hit. He turned around and left to go back to Hubbard via State Route 82, but when they arrived at Chestnut Ridge Road they couldn't proceed because of all the downed trees. The tops of the trees were all over the road. By this time the police had arrived to secure the area. John went north on Warner Road and turned east onto Stewart-Sharon Road. He stopped at grandfather Luke Simeon's house. His mother, Rose Durkos, was there in tears thinking that her two children had been killed or injured in the tornado. Since their house was on the south side of the street, the only damage was downed trees and the two by four in their roof. (Photograph courtesy of John Durkos.)

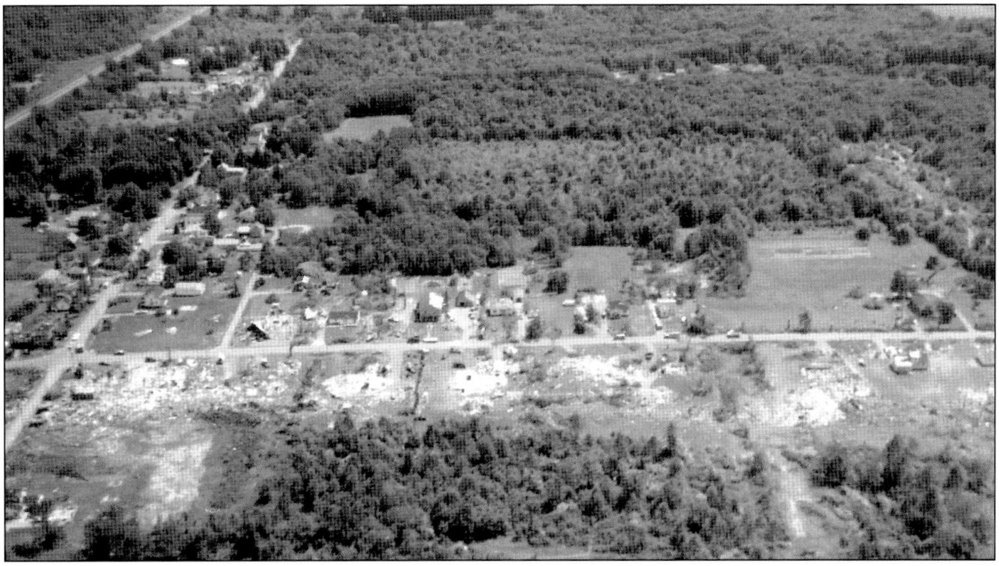

An aerial photograph facing south shows extensive damage to the north of Chestnut Ridge Road. Wick Campbell Road is on the left. The Knights of Pythias Hall, built in 1914, and the old store, built in 1882, were both completely demolished. Unbelievably, many people who lived just two miles south had no idea a tornado was occurring. It appeared to be a routine thunderstorm with occasional high winds and intervals of sunshine. There was no tornado warning, only a thunderstorm warning. (Photograph courtesy of John Durkos.)

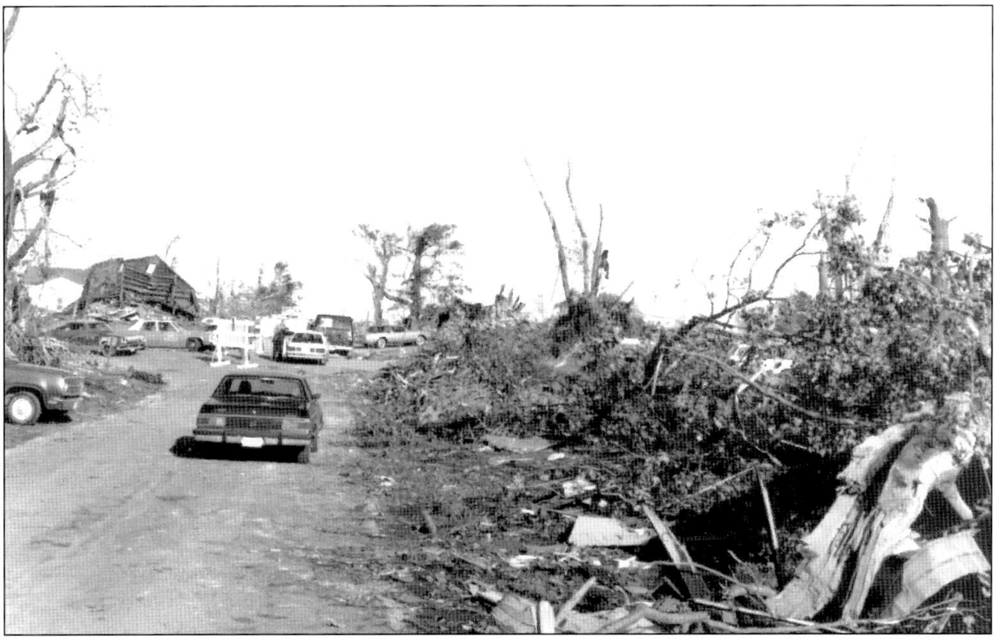

Looking west at the corner of Chestnut Ridge Road and Wick Campbell Road shows the utter devastation. Before the tornado, Chestnut Ridge Road was a beautiful road to travel on. The trees on either side of the road were so lush that they almost touched in the middle, as though you were driving under a green canopy. After the tornado, everyone said they missed the trees. (Photograph courtesy of John Durkos.)

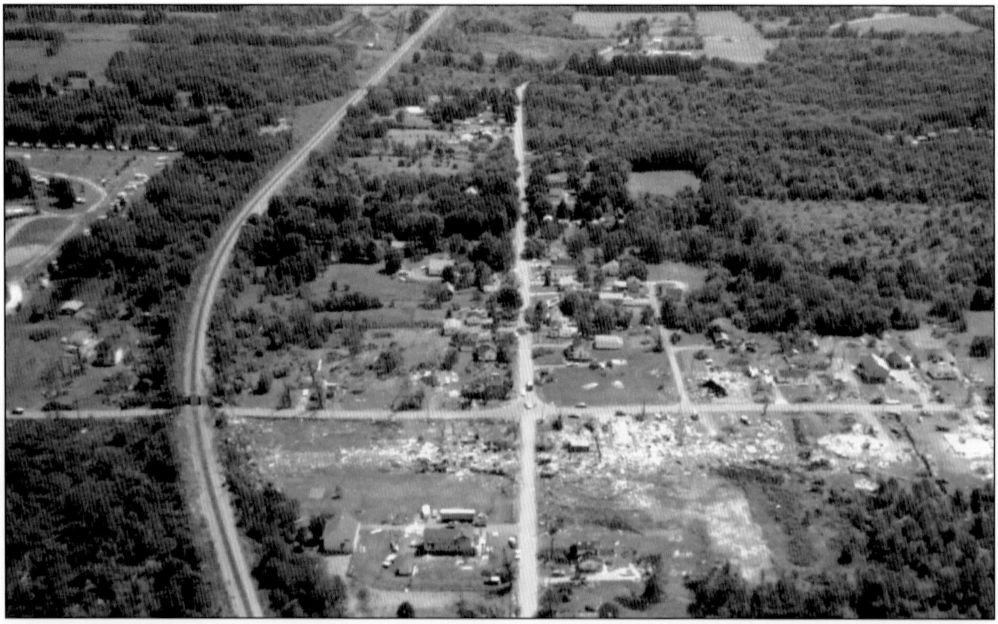

By the time the tornado reached the train trestle over Chestnut Ridge Road, it jumped over the tracks leaving them intact. The area around the intersection of Chestnut Ridge Road and Wick Campbell Road shows great devastation. The photographer was facing south when he took this picture. (Photograph courtesy of John Durkos.)

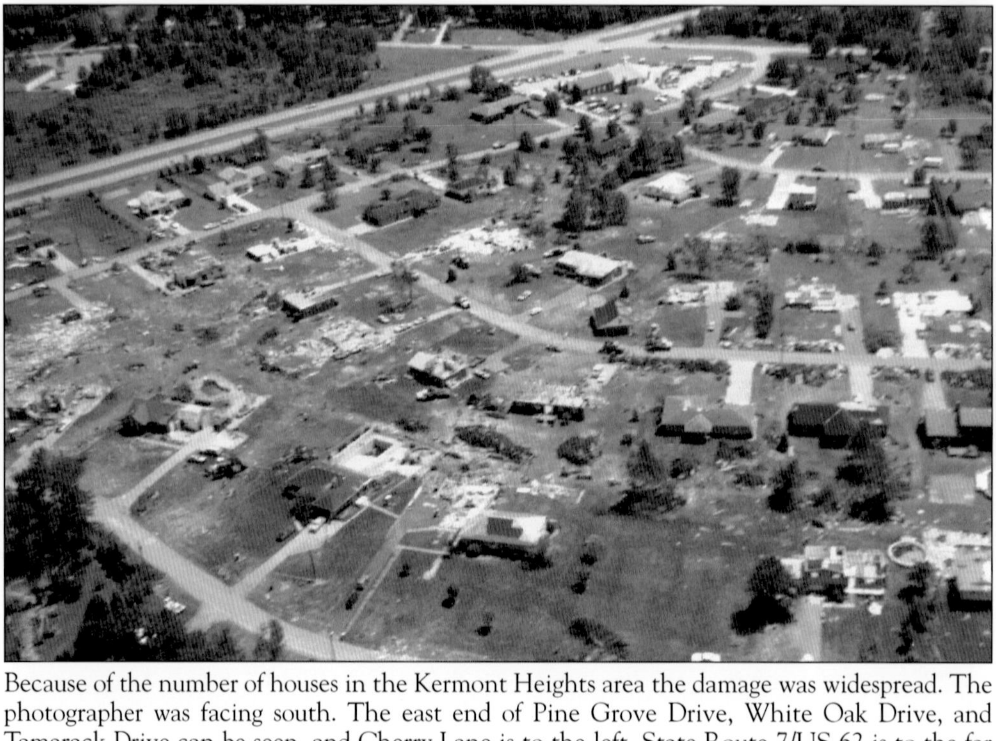

Because of the number of houses in the Kermont Heights area the damage was widespread. The photographer was facing south. The east end of Pine Grove Drive, White Oak Drive, and Tamarack Drive can be seen, and Cherry Lane is to the left. State Route 7/US 62 is to the far left. (Photograph courtesy of John Durkos.)

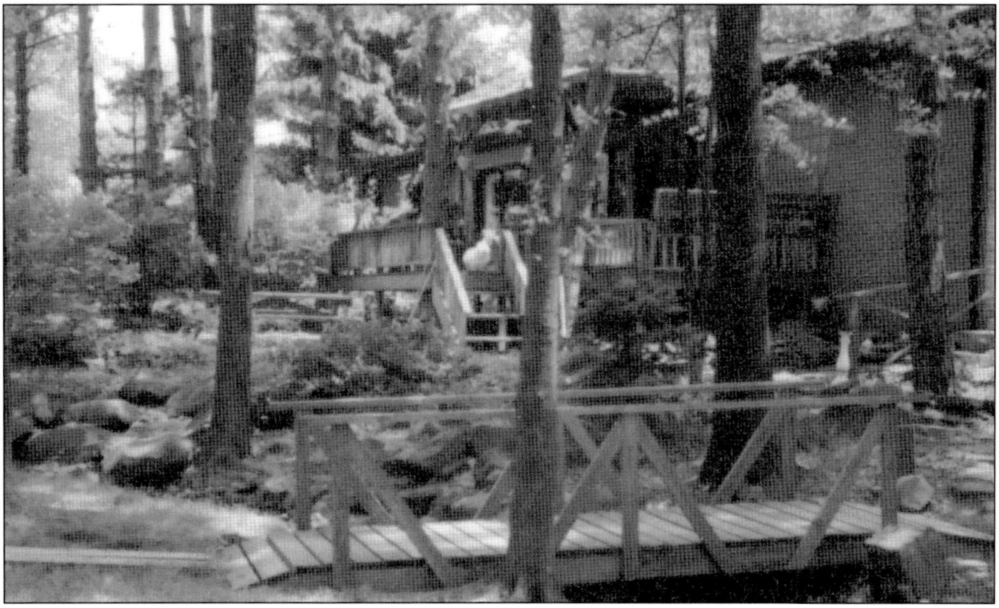

This is what Pat and Richard Hernandez' backyard looked like in 1979 before the 1985 tornado. The house was located at 7035 White Oak Drive in Kermont Heights. Pat and her son had beautifully landscaped the backyard by building a deck and a bridge, and planting fruit trees and dogwoods among the older trees that were already in existence. (Photograph courtesy of Pat Hernandez.)

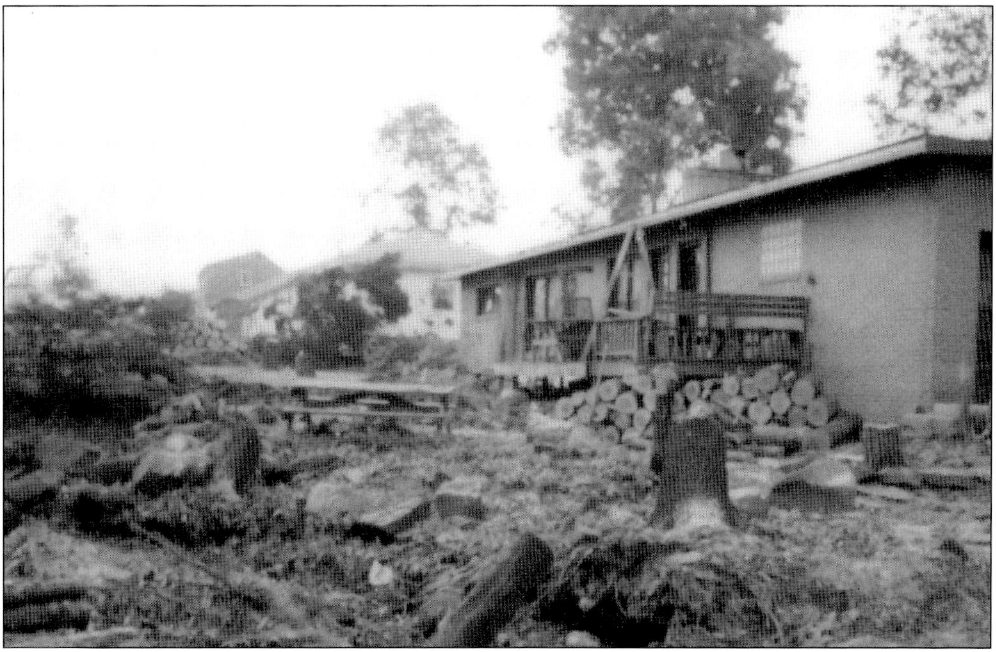

After the tornado passed through the Hernandez' property, this is all that was left of their backyard. Mennonites from the Hartville area came and helped clear the pine and oak trees approximately three weeks after the tornado. Richard wanted to pay them for their help, but they replied that the Lord would repay them. (Photograph courtesy of Pat Hernandez.)

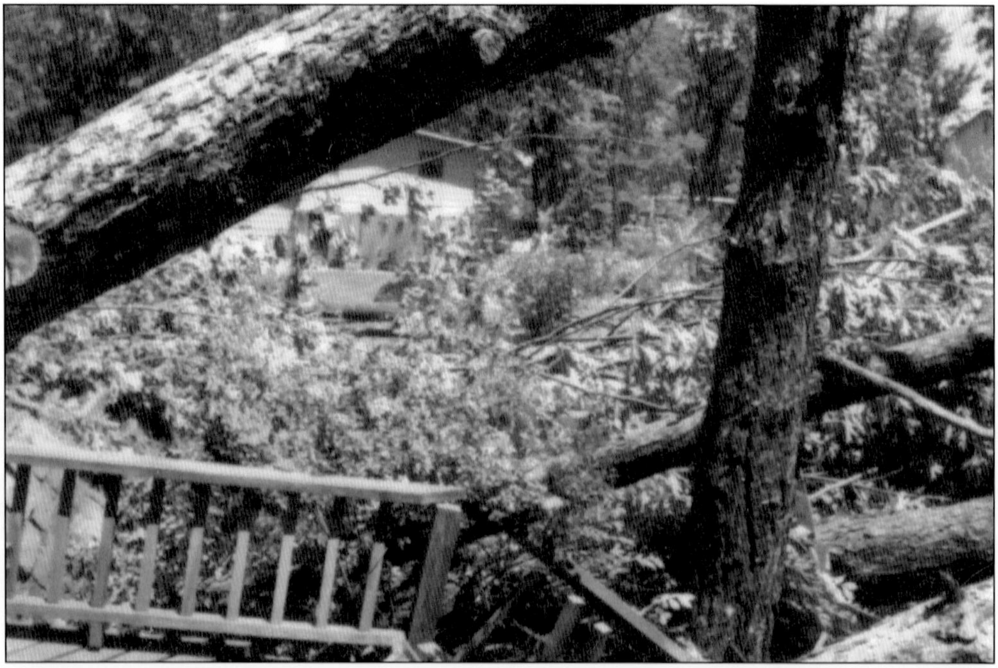

At 6:50 p.m. on the night of the tornado, Pat Hernandez looked outside, because it was so dark and windy. It became very quiet, and then the hail started. They heard a roar like a train coming. Richard cracked the windows open, gathered their dog and papers, while Pat grabbed the parakeets and they headed for the cellar. The lights went out and their ceiling was vibrating. Richard jumped down the stairs as they heard it going over them. Pat said "Lord save us," as it passed over. (Photograph courtesy of Pat Hernandez.)

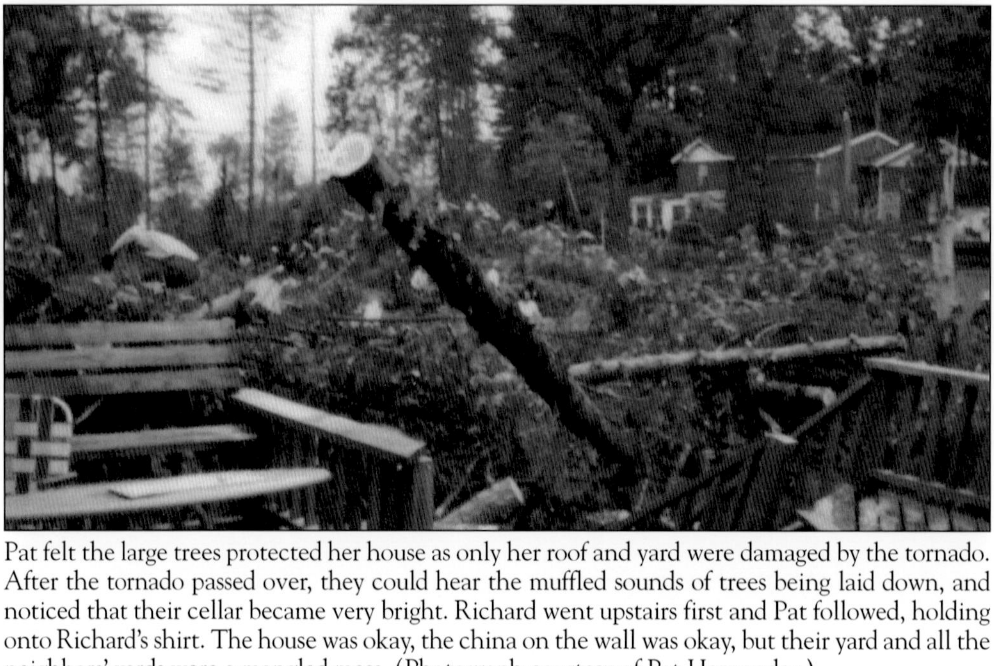

Pat felt the large trees protected her house as only her roof and yard were damaged by the tornado. After the tornado passed over, they could hear the muffled sounds of trees being laid down, and noticed that their cellar became very bright. Richard went upstairs first and Pat followed, holding onto Richard's shirt. The house was okay, the china on the wall was okay, but their yard and all the neighbors' yards were a mangled mess. (Photograph courtesy of Pat Hernandez.)

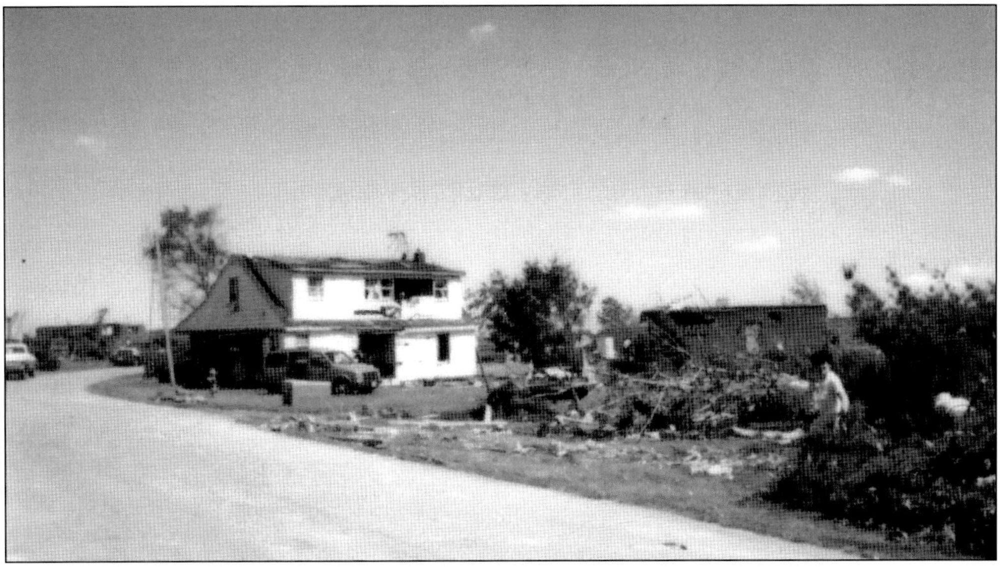

This photograph, taken Sunday June 2, 1985, on Cherry Lane shows the aftermath of the tornado. The worst damage was on Cherry Lane and White Oak Drive. The house on the left side of the picture, located east of the Hernandez's house, was lifted off its foundation and placed on White Oak Drive where the road joins Cherry Lane. A man who lived on Pine Grove was taking a shower, never heard a thing, and landed on his lawn, unhurt. (Photograph courtesy of Pat Hernandez.)

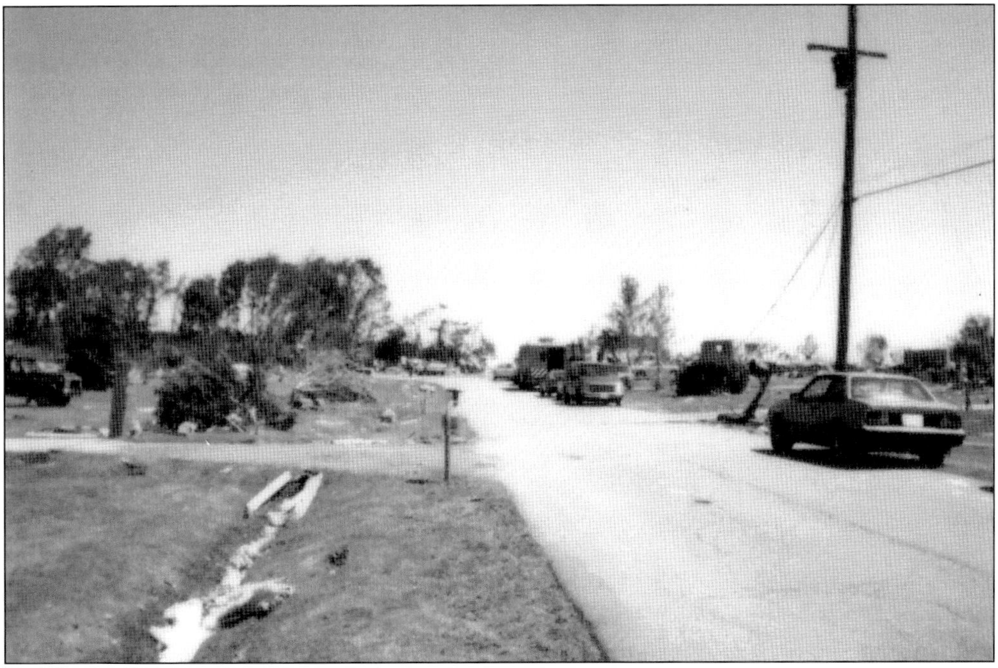

Another picture taken on Sunday June 2, 1985, shows the devastation on Cherry Lane in Kermont Heights. The homes that were damaged were either rebuilt or sold as is. Some lots where the tornado destroyed the houses were sold with only a basement remaining. (Photograph courtesy of Pat Hernandez.)

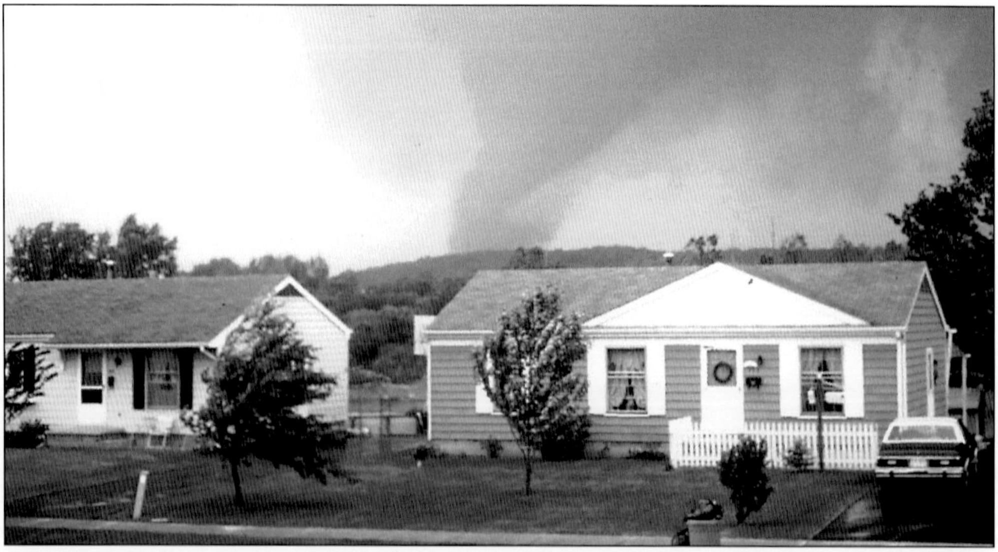

An unknown photographer took the following four photographs from Saul Drive of the tornado as it moved across Chestnut Ridge Road. Mala Smith was at Waugh Field coaching her son's baseball team. The sky had become golden colored, clouds were rolling, and there was a big gust of wind with hail. She sent everyone home, and went to Jones Field to pick up her oldest son. Mr. Ryser came by and told everyone that a tornado had taken Chestnut Ridge Road out. (Photograph courtesy of Mala Smith.)

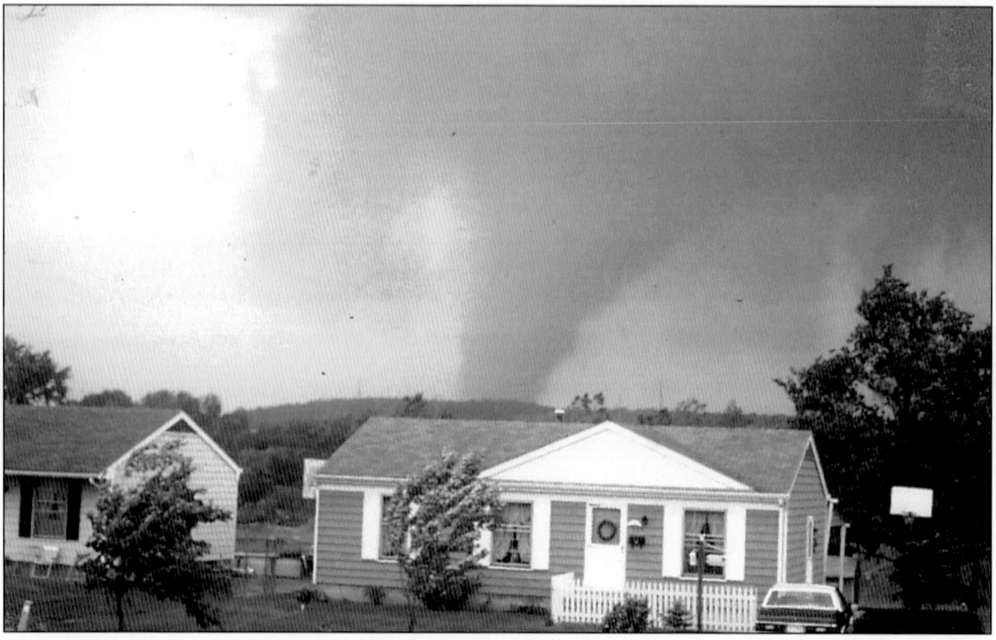

The tornado continues along Chestnut Ridge Road. Tom Foraker, and his wife, Candy, lived on North Main Street, across from the Flying J Truck Plaza. Candy looked out the window and said she saw a tornado. Tom said it didn't look the right color, as it was a light gray. Then he noticed trees and debris in the funnel so he knew what it was and headed for the basement with Candy and their three children. (Photograph courtesy of Mala Smith.)

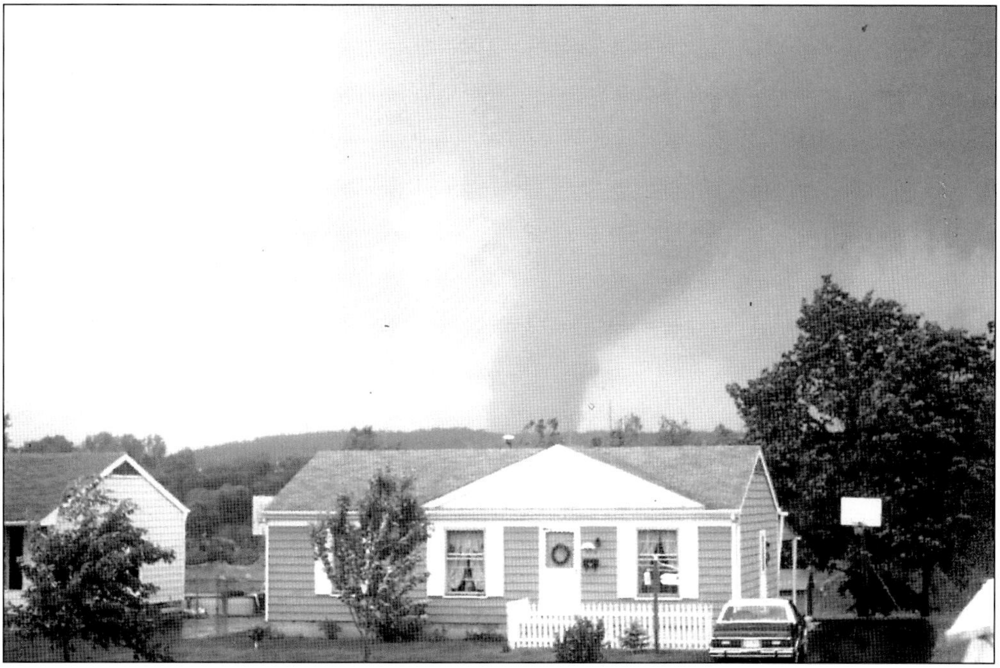

Tom Foraker could see people getting out of ditches where State Route 7 splits to the left of US 62 in the Kermont Heights area. He could see the tornado traveling into Wheatland, Pennsylvania. His brother-in-law, Elmer Takash, who lived in Masury, noticed two by fours stuck in the ground but his house was undamaged. (Photograph courtesy of Mala Smith.)

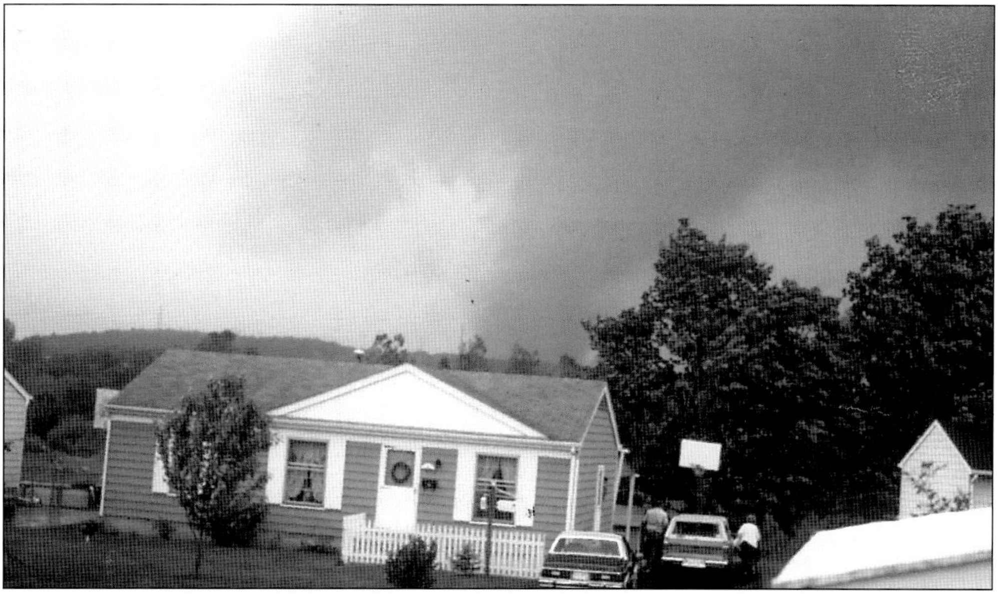

The tornado picked up quite a bit of debris as the color darkened considerably. It may have been traveling over Thomas Road where three houses were destroyed. The winds were estimated to be traveling at 260 miles per hour or more. It was listed as the most violent of the 21 tornadoes that occurred in Ohio and Pennsylvania on May 31, 1985. (Photograph courtesy of Mala Smith.)

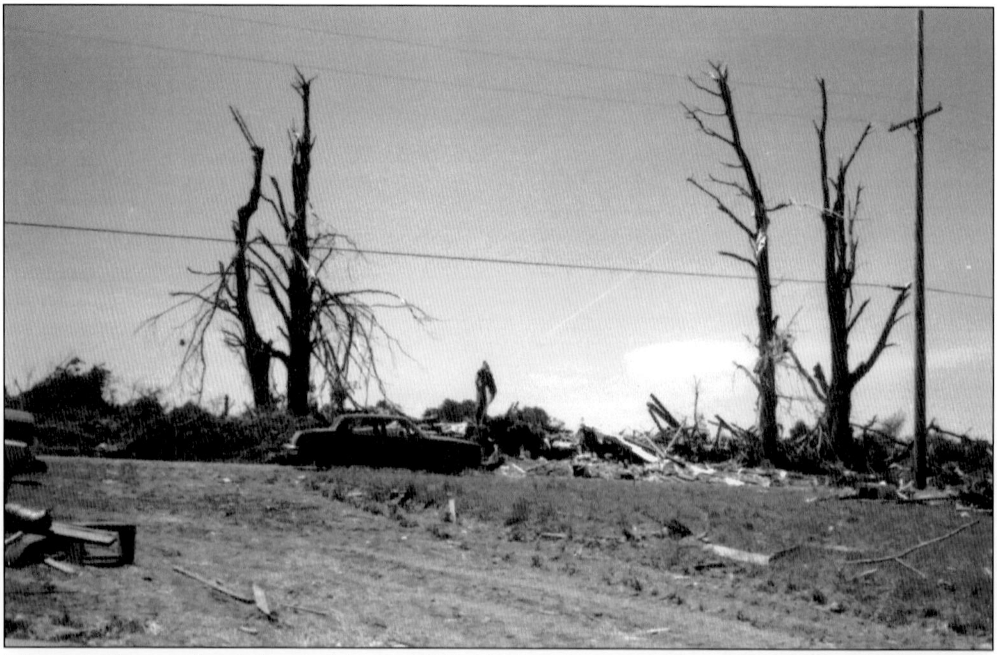

The tornado completely leveled the Corll family home at 328 Thomas Road owned by Bob and Nina Notman. Recently, the home had been divided into a duplex and thankfully both tenants were not home when the tornado struck. (Photograph courtesy of Bob and Nina Notman.)

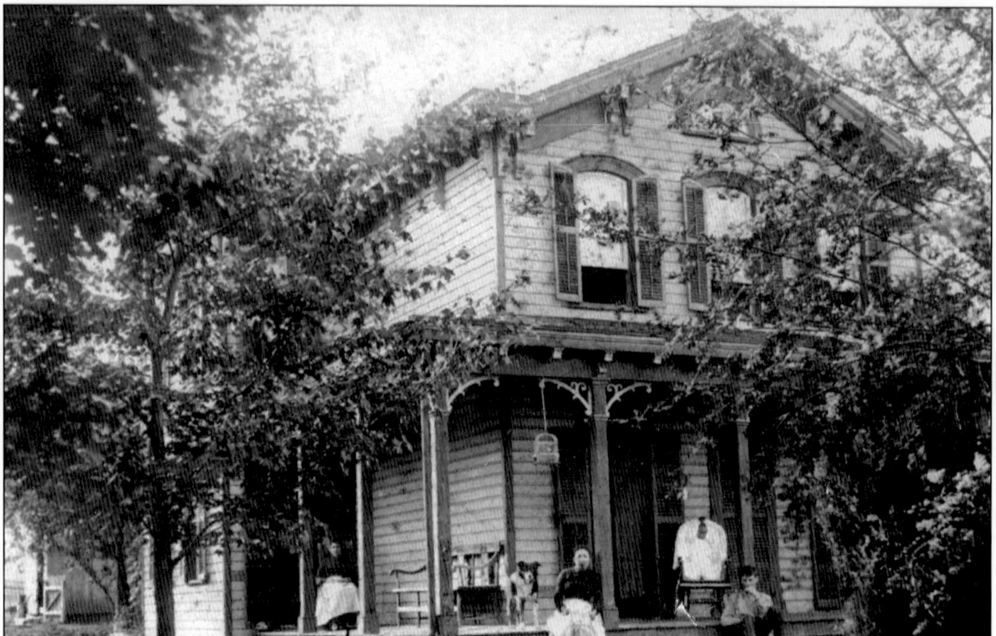

This is an early picture of the house at 328 Thomas Road, originally owned by James and Elizabeth Corll. Later, their son Paul and his wife, Mabel, lived in the house. Their daughter, Nina, and her husband, Bob Notman, owned the house at the time of the tornado. Bob was just getting ready to build a porch onto the house. (Photograph courtesy of Bob and Nina Notman.)

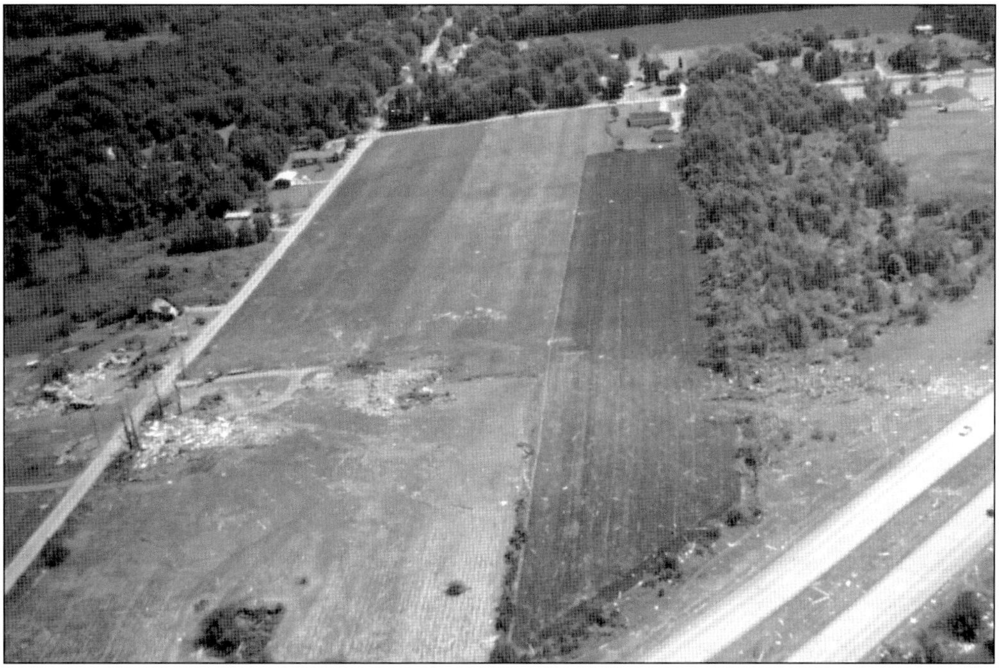

An aerial photograph facing south shows the damage to the three houses located on Thomas Road. Thomas Road is to the left, and State Route 7/US 62 is on the right and Chestnut Ridge Road is in the background. The Corll family home at 328 Thomas Road was hit first and is on the right or west side of Thomas Road. (Photograph courtesy of John Durkos.)

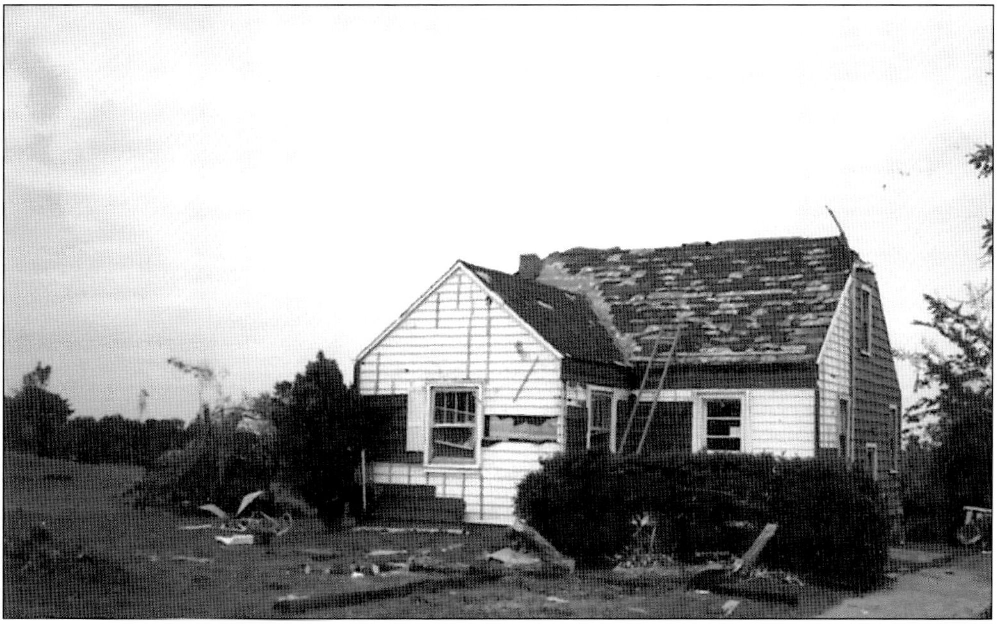

This house, located on the east side of Thomas Road, was picked up and set down by the tornado and even though it looked okay, was later torn down. Hubbard Township police officer Tom Forgas was living in the house but was not at home when the tornado hit. (Photograph courtesy of Bob and Nina Notman.)

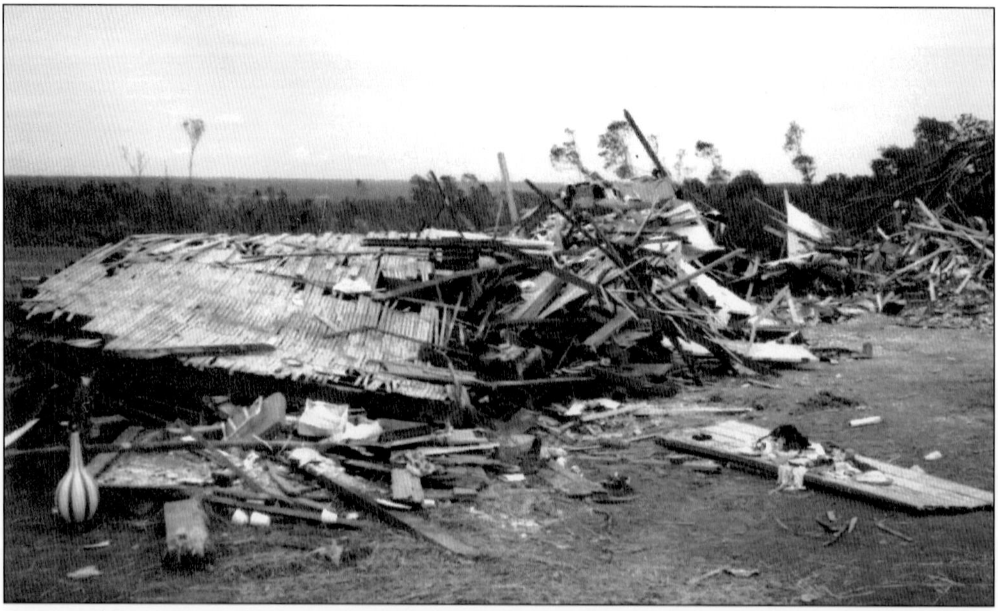

Doris and Evan Evans' home at 329 Thomas Road was lifted by the tornado and turned upside down onto their garage, which was next to the house. Doris did not hear the tornado but her son, John, yelled at her to get to the cellar. He was helping his dad, Evan, but the family only made it to the kitchen when the tornado struck. Evan was the only family member who did not survive. (Photograph courtesy of Bob and Nina Notman.)

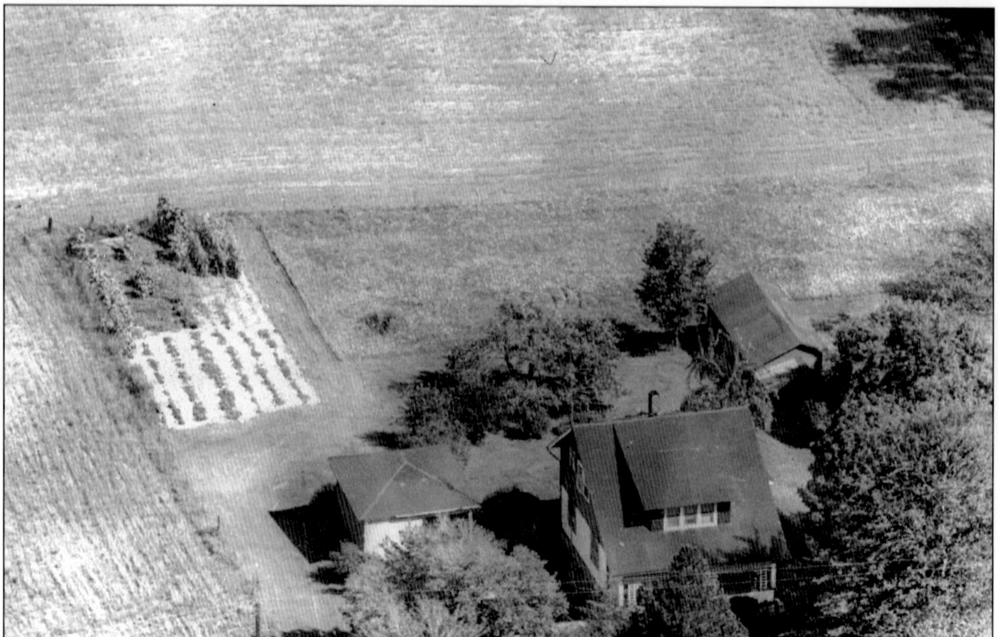

This aerial photograph, taken of Doris and Evan Evans' home at 329 Thomas Road, shows what it looked like before it was destroyed by the tornado. The home was on the east side of the road, to the north of the house that was picked up and set down by the tornado. (Photograph courtesy of Bob and Nina Notman.)

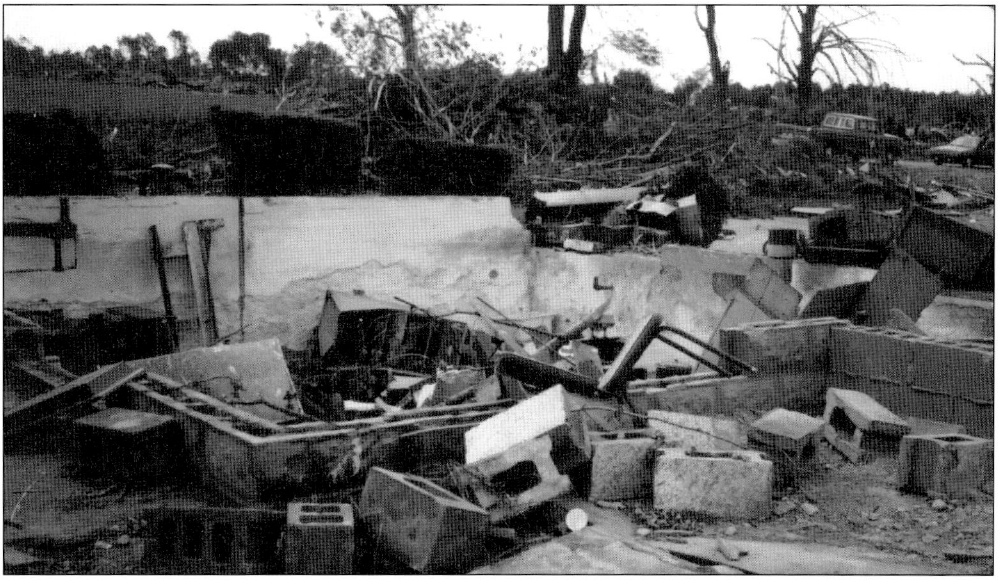

This is another view of the Evans' home that was lifted off its foundation. Doris remembers waking up in a pile of rubble, which was all that remained of her house. She had glass in her hair and abrasions and was taken by her nephew, Tom Notman, to Northside Hospital in Youngstown for treatment. Their dog was found two days later in the debris. (Photograph courtesy of Bob and Nina Notman.)

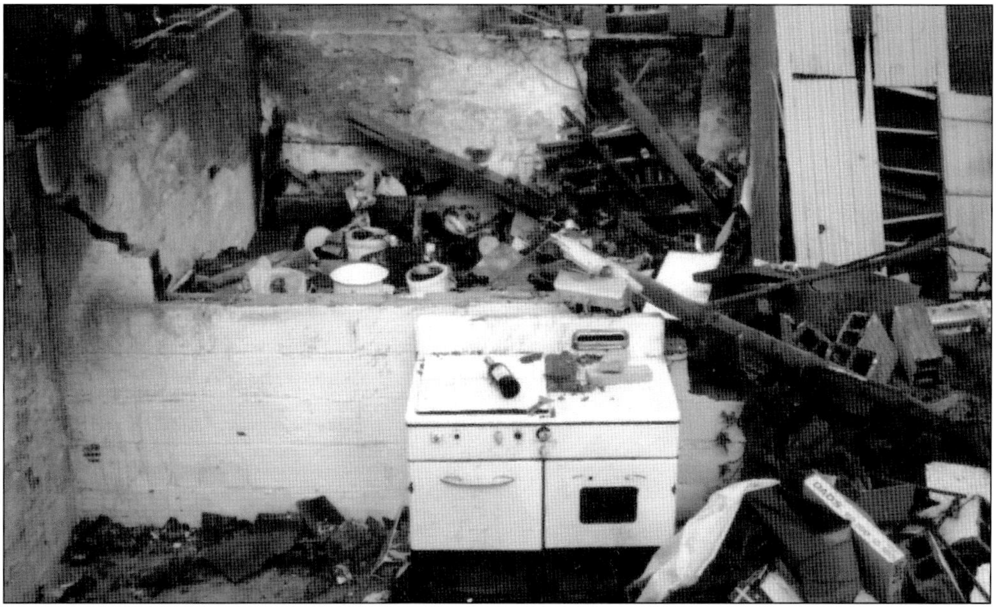

The Evans' basement is shown after the tornado destroyed their house. Doris' nephew, Tom and his wife, Liz, lived nearby and had gone to their cellar after seeing the neighbors pointing to the sky. When everything was quiet, Tom went upstairs, looked out the window, and realized his aunt's house was gone. They both ran to what was left of the house and it was a pile of rubble. Doris was taken to the hospital. Her husband, Evan, did not survive. (Photograph courtesy of Bob and Nina Notman.)

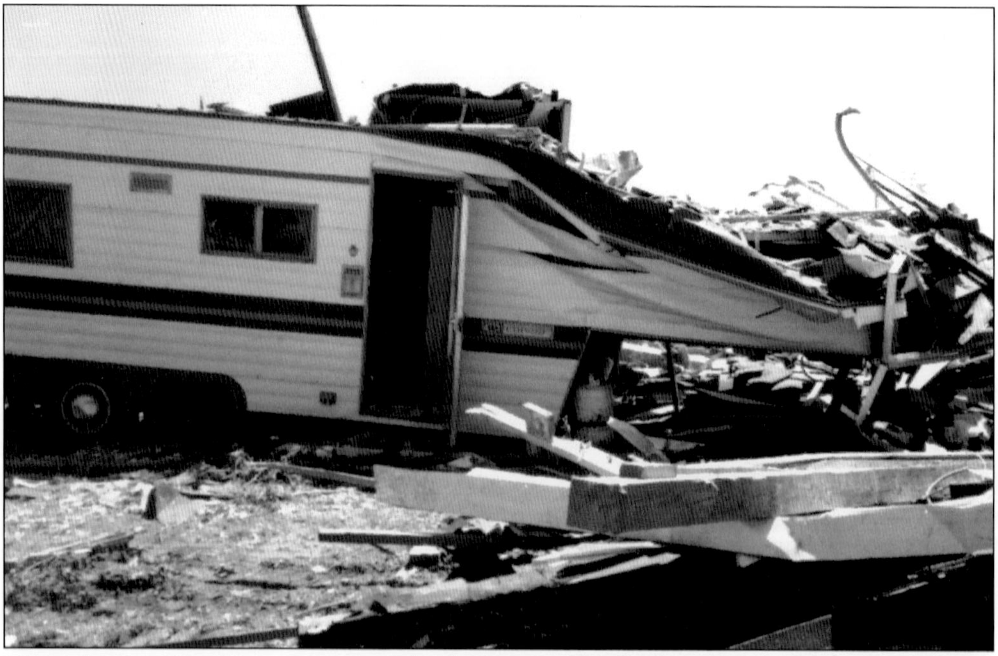

The only possession that was not completely destroyed by the tornado was the Evans' camping trailer. A few weeks later, Doris Evans' checkbook was found about 60 miles away in Emlenton, Pennsylvania, and was mailed back to her. (Photograph courtesy of Bob and Nina Notman.)

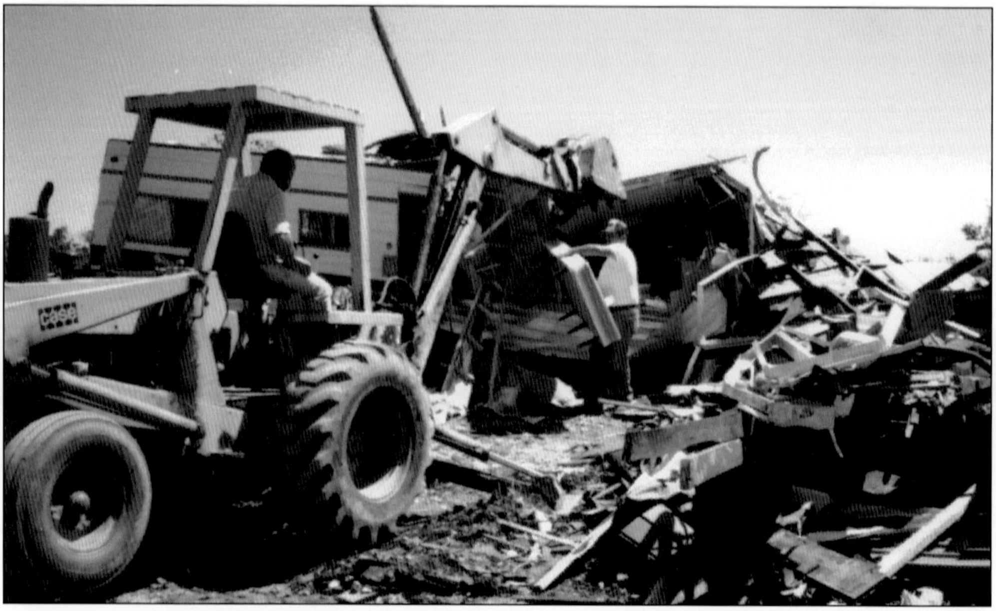

Norm Notman and Ed Maxwell are cleaning up the Evans' house after the tornado. In the week after the tornado, the Amish arrived with their saws and offered their help. Also, Carolyn Evans, a member of the Hubbard Christians in Action (HCIA), sent 15–20 young people from out of state to help with the clean up. They stayed at a camp on the east side of Hubbard overnight and later put on a talent show for the neighborhood. (Photograph courtesy of Bob and Nina Notma.)

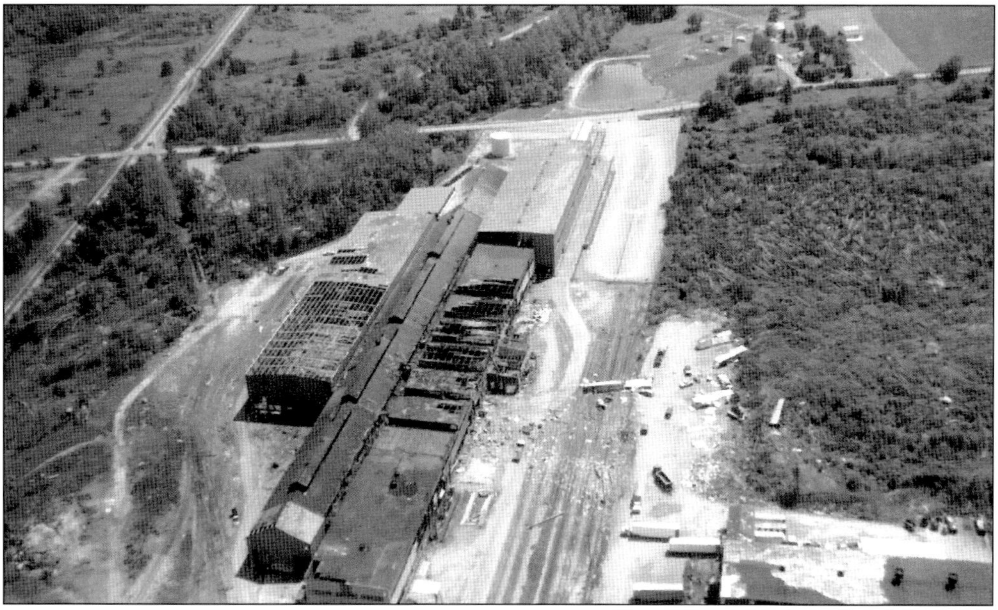

The General American Transportation Corporation (GATX) in Masury was damaged in the 1985 tornado as it had been in the tornado of 1947. The second person to die in Hubbard as a result of the tornado was Rose Leone, 75 years, who lived on Masury Road. She was pulled from the rubble of her home on Friday night. (Photograph courtesy of John Durkos.)

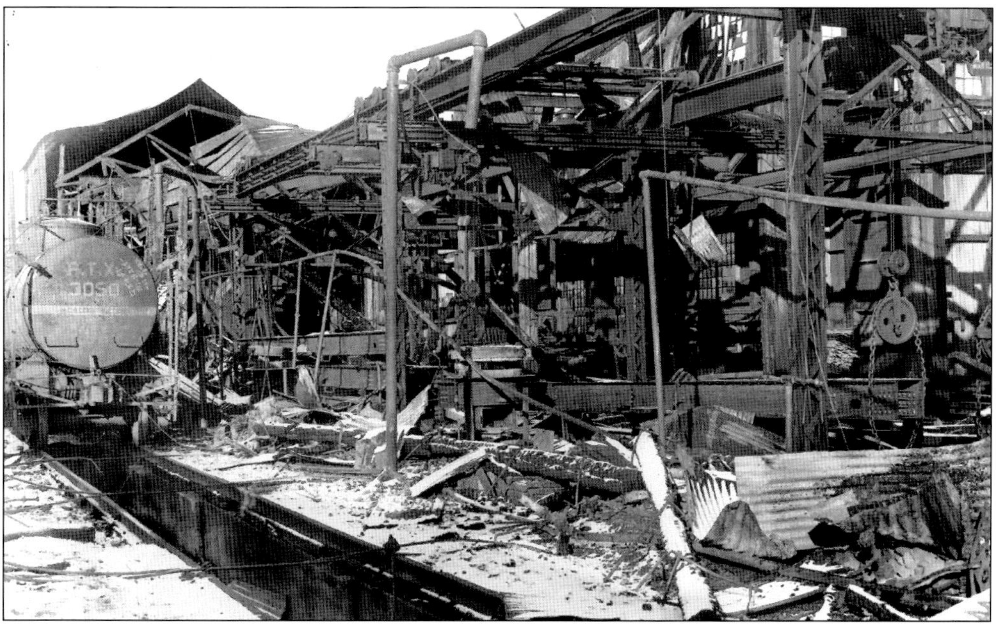

GATX was badly damaged after the June 7, 1947 tornado, which followed a more northern path. At that time, Jack Wilson was delivering a ham to a customer near old route 62 between Hubbard and Sharon for Budno Groceries in a 1938 Ford panel truck. He looked to the northeast and saw the tornado funnel approaching. He said that the old Ford made it back to Hubbard in record time. The tornado had gone over the hill and hit GATX in Masury and Flowers Lumber Yard in Sharon, Pennsylvania. (Photograph courtesy of Carole Palumbo Williams.)

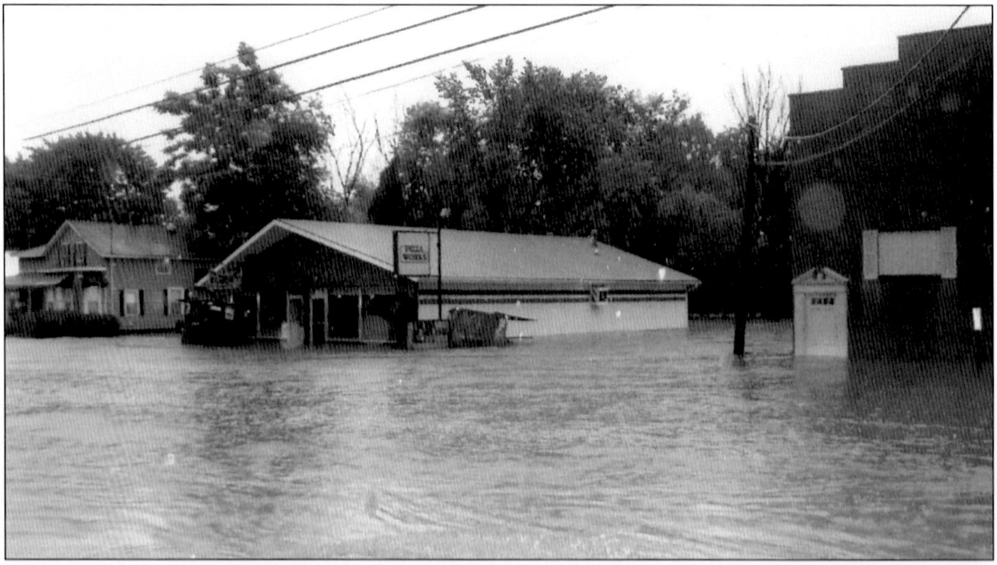

Dave Bailey co-owner of Pizza Works, 433 North Main Street, remembers looking across the street in horror from the Auto Zone parking lot on the evening of July 27, 2003, as floodwaters surrounded his store. He was in Cortland when the rain started but by the time he got to the store, there was nothing he could do, as the floodwaters had already reached two feet inside the store. Carryout service was available two days after the flood but it took until the spring of 2004 before all the remodeling and repair was completed. (Photograph courtesy of Dave Bailey.)

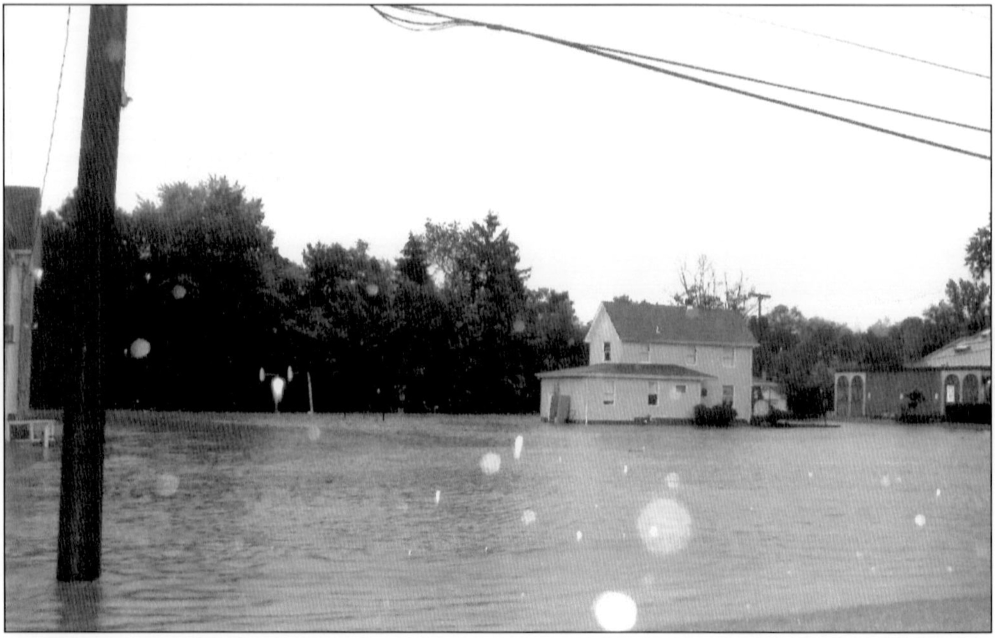

The Knights of Columbus Hall parking lot, St Vincent DePaul house on East Park Avenue, and St. Patrick's Church are all inundated with floodwaters in this photograph taken on the evening of July 27, 2003. North Main Street is nowhere to be seen. The rainfall, measured in Hubbard at 4.5 inches, was too much rain, in too short an amount of time. Official rainfall at the airport in Vienna only measured 1.3 inches. (Photograph courtesy of Dave Bailey.)

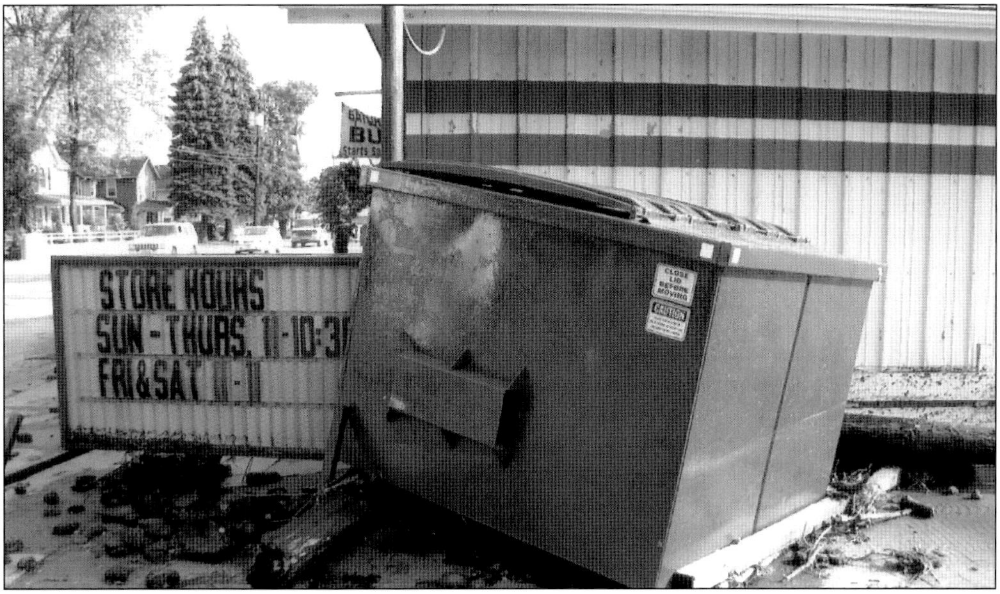

St Patrick's Church was preparing for their annual festival and had rented two dumpsters. The rising floodwaters picked up the dumpsters. One dumpster ended up floating next to Pizza Works and the other one, along with a pickup truck that was parked behind Williams Machine Co., became lodged under the bridge, which crosses over North Main Street. All of this added to the backing up of floodwaters. (Photograph courtesy of Dave Bailey.)

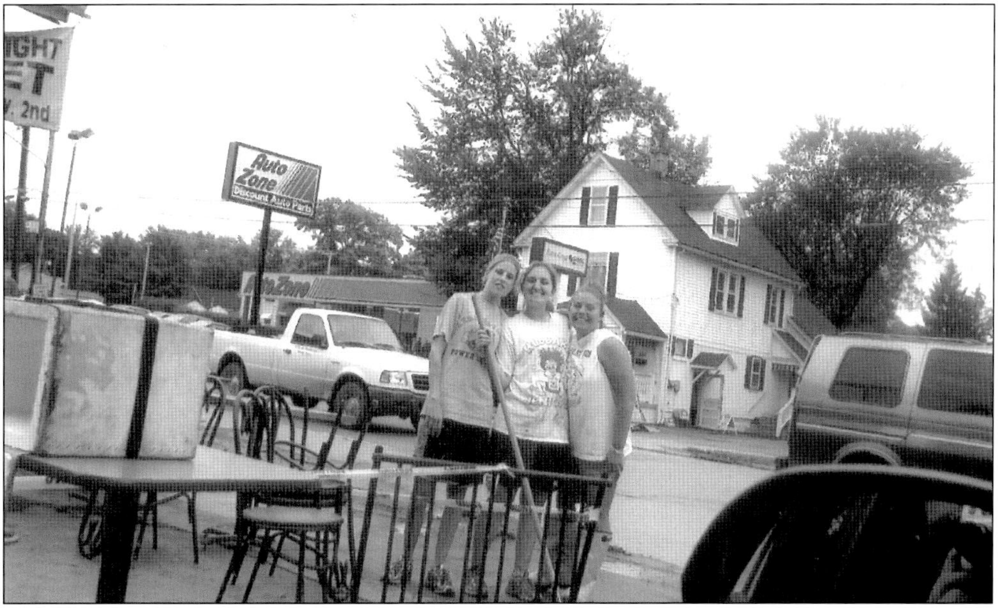

Employees Nicole Moffitt, Jenna Pagano, and Tiffany Ditman of Pizza Works clean up after the flood of July 27, 2003. Supervisor Anna Disilvio was working the day of the flood and noticed water was coming up over the sidewalk. It came in through the front door and the side of the building. She called Steve Bailey, closed the store, and told everyone to leave. When they left, there was one foot of water inside and three feet outside. Before she could reach her car, it was underwater. (Photograph courtesy of Dave Bailey.)

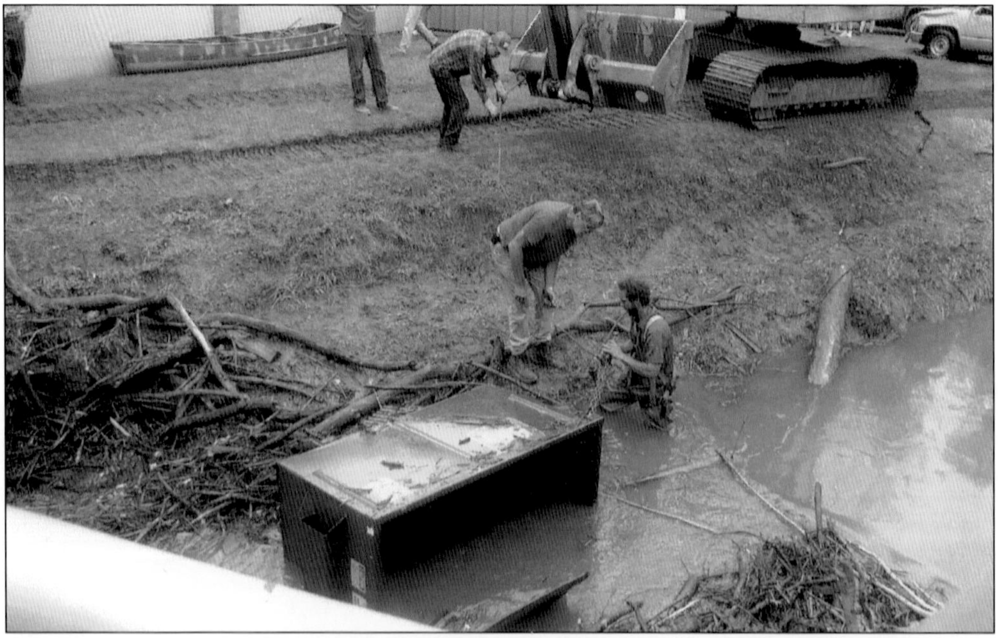

Here, workers tie a chain to a dumpster that had become lodged under the bridge that crosses over North Main Street near Williams Machine Co. A pickup truck had just been removed from under the bridge. The dumpster floated down Mud Run from St. Patrick's Church. Mud Run eventually meets Little Yankee Creek, and they join to form Little Yankee Run. They join Little Deer Creek and flow to the Shenango River. (Photograph courtesy of Dave Bailey.)

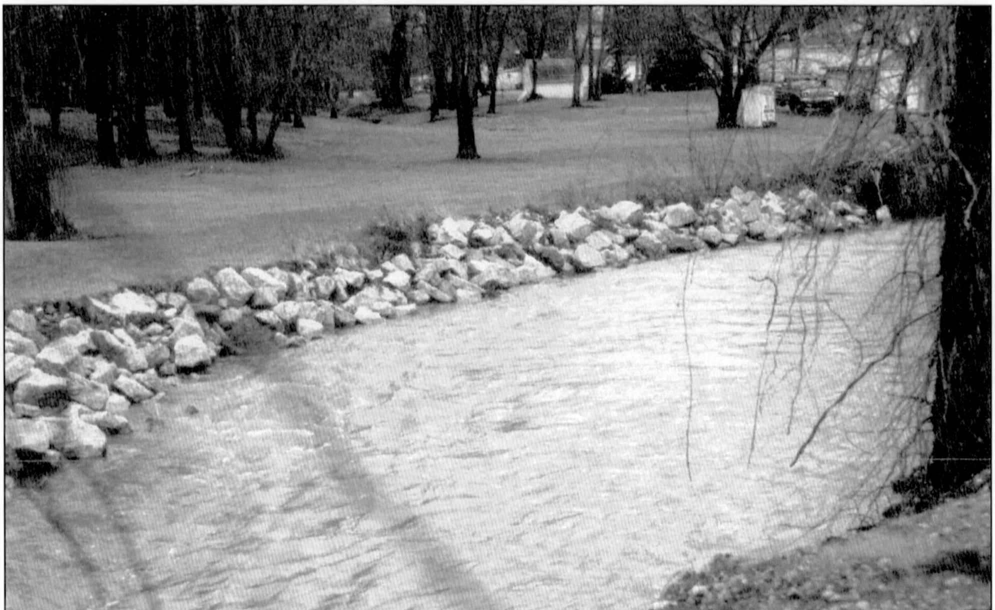

After the flood, Mud Run was dredged, debris was removed, and it was widened to prevent flooding in the future. It has helped somewhat, but in June of 2004, water covered the Pizza Works parking lot and in September of 2004, water reached the sill of the back door.